# Before *Brown*, Beyond Boundaries: Commemorating the 50th Anniversary of *Brown v. Board of Education*

## A Publication of The Association for the Study of African American Life and History

### Africa World Press, Inc.

P.O. Box 1892
Trenton, NJ 08607

P.O. Box 48
Asmara, ERITREA

## Africa World Press, Inc.

P.O. Box 1892
Trenton, NJ 08607

P.O. Box 48
Asmara, ERITREA

Copyright © 2004 ASALH

First Printing 2004

Cover Design: Roger Dormann

**Cataloging-in-Publication Data is available from the Library of Congress.**

ISBN: 1-59221-204-2 (hardcover)
ISBN: 1-59221-205-0 (paperback)

The Association for The Study of African American Life and History, Incorporated
Howard University
CB Powell Building
525 Bryant Street, Suite C142
Washington, DC 20059
www.asalh.org

# Permissions and Copyright Acknowledgements

# TABLE OF CONTENTS

## BEFORE *BROWN V. BOARD OF EDUCATION*

Legal Strategies and Strategists:

Segregated Education:

## *BROWN V. BOARD OF EDUCATION* CASES:

Delaware:

## LEARNING RESOURCES (LESSON PLANS AND CURRICULUM UNITS)

## BIBLIOGRAPHIES

## BLACK HISTORY MONTH RESOURCE PACKAGE
## 2004 CONTRIBUTING WRITERS

**Ophelia Gona** is a retired Associate Professor of Anatomy in the Department of Surgery at the University of Medicine and Dentistry of New Jersey-New Jersey Medical School. Dr. Gona is a photographer and is also working with the Briggs-De Laine-Pearson Foundation in Clarendon County, S.C., to teach and preserve the legacy of the *Briggs v. Elliott* case.

**Cheryl Brown Henderson** is President of the Brown Foundation for Educational Equality, Excellence, and Research in Topeka, Kansas.

**Samuel B. Hoff** is George Washington Distinguished Professor of History and Political Science and Law Studies Director at Delaware State University. He is a specialist on the American presidency and has served in three staff positions with the U. S. Congress. Dr. Hoff has published over 100 articles, chapters, and book reviews for edited books and professional journals.

**Irene Owens** is an information consultant, reviewer, and professional educator specializing in African American children's literature. Dr. Owens research interests are in the areas of communications, library studies, education, and African American literature. She is currently doing research on African American women who write children's books.

**Janet Sims-Wood** is the Assistant Chief Librarian for Reference/Reader Services at the Moorland-Spingarn Research Center at Howard University and a part-time Reference Librarian at Prince George's Community College. Dr. Sims-Wood is an oral historian specializing in African American women's history. She is founding editor of *Sage: A Scholarly Journal on Black Women* and a member of the Executive Council of ASALH.

**Bradley Skelcher** is a Professor of History and Director of the Graduate Program in Historic Preservation at Delaware State University. He is the author of several articles focusing on historic preservation and African American and African history. Additionally, he has published two books, *African American Education in Delaware* and *Delaware State University*. He was Associate Editor of the 2002 Black History Month Kit, *The Color Line Revisited*. Currently, Dr. Skelcher is working in partnership with Teleducation Film Company to produce an historical documentary, *With All Deliberate Speed*, which focuses on the desegregation of education in Delaware.

**Alonzo N. Smith** is a Research Historian at the Smithsonian Institution's National Museum of American History and an Adjunct Professor at Montgomery College.

**Robert T. Taggart** is Professor of Education History at the University of Delaware.

**Peter Wallenstein** teaches history at Virginia Polytechnic Institute and State University.

# FOREWORD

## "Revisiting Our Past: *Brown v. Board of Education*

The United States Constitution guarantees liberty and equal opportunity to the people of the United States. Historically, however, these fundamental rights have not always been provided as pledged. Our system of education is one such example.

From the earliest time in U. S. history, the educational system mandated separate schools for children based solely on race. In many instances, the schools for African American children were substandard facilities with out-of-date textbooks and insufficient supplies. Court cases against segregated schools have been documented as far back as 1849.

In 1861 a civil war was fought dividing the country and determining who should receive full rights and privileges under the U. S. Constitution. This conflict centered around the status of people of African descent who had been brought to these shores as slave labor. Those who would end the practice of slavery prevailed. Still, after the end of the Civil War in 1865, the inclusion of African Americans as full citizens required amending the U. S. Constitution.

As a result, the Civil War was followed by three crucial amendments to the Constitution. The enactment of the 13th Amendment, ratified in 1865, abolished slavery; the 14th Amendment, ratified in 1868, conferred citizenship to the formerly enslaved people of African descent and bestowed equal protection under the law. The last in this series was the 15th Amendment, ratified in 1870, that affirmed that the right of U. S. citizens to vote cannot be denied or abridged on account of race.

In spite of the mandates outlined in the newly amended U. S. Constitution, freedom and equal rights were not readily bestowed upon African Americans. Throughout this history, education was withheld from people of African descent. In some states it was against the law for this segment of the population to learn to read and write. Tremendous disappointment and disillusionment stirred African American people to continue to challenge this system of segregation.

In the first documented school case, *Roberts v. City of Boston*, in 1849, the courts denied Benjamin Roberts and other African American parents the right to enroll their children in certain Boston public schools. However, in 1855, the Massachusetts legislature banned racial segregation. Then in 1896, in the case of *Plessy v. Ferguson*, the United States Supreme Court declared it law that "separate" but "equal" facilities be provided for African Americans. This landmark case from Louisiana necessitated separate dining facilities, rest rooms, transportation, accommodations and more, including public education.

Equal rights remained virtually unattainable. Across the country, numerous cases were taken to court between 1849 and 1949. In the state of Kansas alone, there were 11 school integration cases filed between 1881 and 1949. In response to these unsuccessful attempts to ensure equal opportunities for all children, African American community leaders and organizations across the country stepped up efforts to change the educational system.

The National Association for the Advancement of Colored People (NAACP), founded in 1908, took a key role in the move toward equal educational opportunity. Members were involved at every level, providing legal counsel, and funding.

From the mid-1930s to the present, the NAACP provided strategy and legal expertise, using the courts as a proving ground to obtain full constitutional rights for African Americans. In the 1940s and 1950s, local NAACP leaders spearheaded plans to end the doctrine of "separate but equal." Public schools became the means to that end. Their local efforts would ultimately change the course of history.

The NAACP legal team devised a formula for success. As they built their cases, the first requirement was that they involve multiple plaintiffs. Among the final road to the U. S. Supreme Court, five excellent cases were developed from the states of Delaware, Kansas, Virginia, South Carolina and Washington, D. C. None of these cases succeeded in the district courts and all were appealed to the U. S. Supreme Court. At this juncture, they were combined and became known jointly as *Oliver L. Brown et. al vs. the Board of Education of Topeka (KS) et. al.*

The high courts decided to combine the cases because each sought the same relief from segregated schools for African Americans. In the end, the circumstances of the plaintiffs left no question that ending segregation as a historic practice would be the only viable outcome.

Charles Hamilton Houston argued most of the early NAACP cases. He had been the Dean of Howard Law School, a prestigious university for African Americans. He was teacher and mentor for many civil rights lawyers of that time including Thurgood Marshall. Houston died in 1950, leaving Thurgood Marshall as lead strategist and counsel for the school integration cases. Marshall took these cases all the way to the U. S. Supreme Court. On May 17, 1954, 105 years after the *Roberts* case, the U. S. Supreme Court issued a unanimous decision that segregation violated the 14th Amendment and was unconstitutional. Thurgood Marshall later became the first African American to serve on the U. S. Supreme Court.

The *Brown* decision initiated educational reform throughout the United States and was a catalyst in launching the modern Civil Rights Movement. Bringing about change in the years since *Brown* continues to be difficult. But the *Brown v. Board of Education* victory brought Americans one step closer to true freedom and equal rights. The combined cases were:

1. Delaware – *Belton v. Gebhart (Bulah v. Gebhart)*

   First petitioned in 1951, these cases involved two black schools: Howard High School in Wilmington and a one-room elementary school in Hockessin. Many African American students rode the bus nearly an hour to attend Howard High School. The school was over-crowded, located in the industrial area of town, and sorely lacking in educational areas. Children attending the elementary school in Hockessin wanted equal transportation to their one-room school. Relief for the initial requests for improvements was denied. The two cases were combined, both seeking integration because "the Negro schools were inferior with respect to teacher training, pupil-teacher ratio, curricular and extra-curricular activities, physical plant, and time and distance involved in travel." Their unsuccessful challenge in the U. S. District Court was appealed to the U. S. Supreme Court.

2. Kansas – *Brown v. Board of Education*

   In the fall of 1950 members of the Topeka, Kansas, chapter of the NAACP (National Association for the Advancement of Colored People) agreed to again challenge the "separate but equal" doctrine governing public education. Chapter president, McKinley Burnett, conceived the case strategy. He was assisted by attorneys Charles Scott, John Scott, Charles Bledsoe, Elisha Scott and the NAACP chapter secretary Lucinda Todd. For a period of two years prior to legal action Burnett had attempted to persuade Topeka school officials to integrate their schools. This lawsuit was a final attempt.

   Their plan involved enlisting the support of fellow NAACP members and personal friends as plaintiffs in what would be a class action suit filed against the Board of Education of the Topeka Public Schools. A group of thirteen parents agreed to participate on behalf of their children (20 children). Each plaintiff was to watch the paper for enrollment dates and take their child to the school that was nearest to their home. Once they attempted enrollment and were denied, they were to report back to the NAACP. This would provide the attorneys with the documentation needed to file a lawsuit against the Topeka School Board.

3. District of Columbia – *Bolling v. Sharpe*

   The petition in this case was on behalf of 11 African-American junior high youths who were refused admission to all-white schools. Their school was grossly unequal in terms of physical condition, located in a rundown part of the city, and lacking adequate educational materials. Led by local activist Gardner Bishop, a suit was filed on behalf of these students in 1951. Unsuccessful in the lower courts, their case was appealed to the U. S. Supreme Court.

4. South Carolina – *Briggs v. Elliott*

Twenty African-American parents from Clarendon County first filed a suit in 1951 on behalf of their children. With the help of the NAACP, they sought to secure better schools, equal to those provided for white children. The U. S. District Court found that the black schools were clearly inferior compared to white schools. Buildings were no more than wooden shacks, transportation and educational provisions did not meet basic needs, and teachers' salaries were less than those received in white schools. Further, the lower court "ordered the defendants to immediately equalize the facilities… [but the children were] denied admission to the white schools during the equalization program." Their case was appealed to the U. S. Supreme Court.

5. Virginia – *Davis v. County School Board of Prince Edward County*

One hundred and seventeen African-American high school students chose to strike rather than attend all-black Moton High, which was in need of physical repair. The students initially wanted a new building with indoor plumbing to replace the old school. Strike leader Barbara Johns enlisted the assistance of NAACP attorneys. A suit was filed in 1951 on behalf of the students. The U.S. District Court ordered equal facilities to be provided for the black students but "denied the plaintiffs admission to the white schools during the equalization program" Attorneys for the NAACP filed an appeal with the U. S. Supreme Court.

Reprinted with permission from *The* Brown *Quarterly*, Vol. 4, No. 2, Winter 2001.
http://brownvboard.org/brwnqurt/04-2-2a.htm

# Acknowledgements

The editorial staff of **Before *Brown*, Beyond Boundaries: Commemorating the 50th Anniversary of *Brown v. Board of Education*** wish to thank the many people who have made this learning resource manual possible. Thanks first to the plaintiffs and descendants, especially the Brown and De Laine families, who have been most helpful by providing time and materials for this manual. Thanks to the contributors for their articles and to the many agencies who gave permission to reprint articles. We also thank the ASALH officers, Executive Council members, and the hard-working staff at ASALH headquarters for keeping Carter G. Woodson's name before the world. Thanks to the staff of the Moorland-Spingarn Research Center, who helped with word processing, proofreading, scanning, etc. Thanks to the many libraries, humanities councils, research centers, and other institutions that provided information for this manual. Thanks to Kamili Anderson for copyediting assistance.

A special thanks goes to the members and staff of the *Brown v. Board of Education* 50th Anniversary Presidential Commission and to the staff of the *Brown v. Board of Education* National Historic Site for their support. A huge debt of gratitude is owed to Cheryl Brown Henderson and the Brown Foundation of Topeka, Kansas. Mrs. Henderson provided information, photographs, and moral support for this project.

Last but not least, we thank our families for their support and encouragement as we strive to collect, preserve, and disseminate information about *Brown v. Board of Education.*

**General Editor:**
Janet Sims-Wood, Ph.D.

**Associate Editors:**
Ida Jones, Ph.D.
Tamara Brown, Ph.D.
Bradley Skelcher, Ph.D.
Yohuru Williams, Ph.D.

# Dedication

This Learning Resource Manual is dedicated to the memory of all the plaintiffs in the five *Brown v. Board of Education* cases, who fought for equal education opportunities in their respective communities. This manual also honors the surviving plaintiffs and the many descendants who continue to fight for the rights of all people throughout the world. May this 50th anniversary commemoration lead us all on to future victories. The struggle continues!

# Introduction

May 17, 2004, will mark the 50<sup>th</sup> anniversary of the landmark *Brown v. Board of Education* desegregation case. This case is considered to be the most important legal case affecting African Americans in the twentieth century and one of the most important Supreme Court decisions in U. S. constitutional history.

*Brown* combined separate cases from Kansas, South Carolina, Delaware, Virginia, and the District of Columbia. The *Brown* companion cases presented segregation at its worst. Although supposedly guaranteeing African Americans "separate-but-equal" education, schools for African Americans were never equal, as many were often run-down buildings with overcrowded classrooms. Many schools had no indoor plumbing or heating, and there was little money for books and supplies. Bus service was rarely supplied for African American children, who often had to pass better-equipped white schools to attend segregated schools.

The NAACP (National Association for the Advancement of Colored People) decided to challenge segregation in schools and took the *Brown* case to the Supreme Court. After reviewing each case, the Supreme Court ruled that segregated schools were illegal. Speaking on behalf of the Supreme Court, Chief Justice Earl Warren found that, "in the field of public education the doctrine of 'separate but equal' has no place. Separate education facilities are inherently unequal." *Brown* signaled the end to the legality of segregation.

The Association for the Study of African American Life and History (ASALH) has chosen **Before *Brown*, Beyond Boundaries: Commemorating the 50<sup>th</sup> Anniversary of *Brown v. Board of Education*** as the Black History Month theme for 2004.

## *Brown v. Board of Education* Standards-Based Instruction

One of the primary focuses in education today is on meeting academic standards and on holding teachers and students alike accountable for their success in doing so. This has led to a desperate search by educators across the country for historical resources that will allow them to teach not just the facts but also the underlying principles of historical detection and analysis. This has often been a frustrating task, as individual states have adopted academic standards—especially in history and social studies—that vary widely in their approach to specific requirements. Traditional textbook publishers have struggled unsuccessfully to meet this demand, and most digital offerings have been game-oriented or poorly supported for classroom use.

*Foundations of Historical Inquiry*

Although it is patently impossible to design a teachers' resource manual around the fifty or more state history standards, the editors of this volume have employed the Mid-Continent Regional Education Laboratory's *Content Knowledge: A Compendium of Standards and Benchmarks for K-12 Education* (Second Edition) as well as consulted the state standards in California, Maryland, Illinois, and Virginia in creating this publication. The various state standards have several points in common:

Content:          There is general consensus that there are specific, historical content-names, events, trends, and phenomena with which literate and well-prepared American citizens should be familiar.

Chronology:          Students need to develop an awareness of the broad sequence of events, cause-and-effect relationships, change over time, and comparative time frames.

Analysis      Historians      utilize primary sources (contemporary documents, illustrations, artifacts, etc.) to develop a coherent picture of the past. Students need not just to read history but also to understand the relationship of the narrative to its source materials and the techniques historians used to examine those sources.

Interpretation:     Once the content has been established, the chronology determined, and the sources analyzed, historians create interpretations of the past. These interpretations reflect not only the original facts and surviving sources but also the questions asked of the material, the potential bias of the historian, and the context in which the narrative is presented. Students need to develop an appreciation for the distinction between interpretations, analysis, and historical fact.

Social Studies Themes

- Civilization, cultural diffusion, and innovation
- Patterns of social and political interaction
- Human interaction with the environment
- Conflict and cooperation
- Values, beliefs, political ideas, and institutions
- Comparative history of major developments

(Editor's note: Many of the lesson plans included in this manual list both national and state standards).

# Chapter 1
## Before *Brown v. Board of Education*

# Legal Strategies and Strategists

# Charles Hamilton Houston (1895-1950) and Social Engineering
### Genna Rae McNeil

On 17 May 1954, in *Brown v. Board of Education of Topeka* (347 U.S. 483, 1954) and *Bolling v. Sharpe* (347 U.S. 497, 1954), the United States Supreme Court declared racial segregation in public schools unconstitutional for the states and the District of Columbia, respectively. The *Brown* and *Bolling* rulings of 1954 became key precedents for a legal struggle against forced racial separation, i.e. segregation, as it affected virtually all aspects of life in the society. Added to the growing activism of civil rights advocates and the increased militancy of African Americans, the 1954 decisions set the stage for massive attacks on racial segregation in every phase of this nation's life.

Thurgood Marshall, then Director-Counsel of the National Association for the Advancement of Colored People (NAACP) Legal and Educational Defense Fund, Inc. (Inc. Fund), best understood how great had been the effort and the sacrifices. No victory could have been won without the Kansas, South Carolina, Virginia and the District of Columbia courts, where the school desegregation cases had been initiated, or without the support of countless individuals connected with the NAACP throughout the other states. Nor could the cases have been won without years of work by such attorneys as Harold Boulware, Robert Carter, James Nabrit, George E. C. Hayes, Oliver Hill, Louis Redding, Spottswood Robinson and Jack Greenberg on the cases that became the consolidated desegregation cases in *Brown* and the case of *Bolling*. Moreover, when Marshall called upon them, African-American and white scholars such as Kenneth Clark, John Hope Franklin, and Alfred Kelly worked tirelessly doing research to provide historical and social scientific date for the NAACP and the Inc. Fund. Finally, the NAACP's and the Inc. Fund's work had been designed, informed, planned, implemented and guided from 1934 to 1950 by one who died fighting racial injustice before the U. S. Supreme Court handed down its historic ruling. Reflecting on this fallen soldier, Marshall declared in 1954: "It was Charlie who taught us the law..." He wanted neither the press nor history to forget his teacher and friend, Charles Hamilton Houston, affectionately known to his friends, family, and fellow civil rights advocates as "Charlie." Charles Hamilton Houston played a principal role in defining and pacing the legal phase of the struggle of African Americans for freedom, justice, and recognition of equality. The 1954 decisions were the culmination of a deliberately planned and prosecuted legal campaign against racially segregated public education designed to bring about the Court's rejection of the established nineteenth century doctrine of "separate but equal." Marshall knew better than any other that Charles Hamilton Houston had been the man with the vision and the long-range strategic plan for a collaborative struggle against racial segregation. After he had become the first African-American justice on the U. S. Supreme Court, Marshall commented: "You have a large number of people who never heard of Charlie Houston. But...[w]hen *Brown* against the Board of Education was being argued in the Supreme court... [t]here were some two dozen lawyers on the side of the Negroes fighting for their schools... [O]f those...only two hadn't been touched by Charlie Houston... That man was the engineer of it all..." Beyond civil rights in education Houston played a central role in U. S. Supreme Court cases pertaining to racial justice in employment (*Steele v.*

*Louisville & Nashville*, 1944), and housing (*Hurd v. Hodge*, 1948). Before the title was passed down to his student, Thurgood Marshall, Charles Hamilton Houston was "Mr. Civil Rights."

Charles Hamilton Houston, the descendant of free and enslaved African Americans, was born in Washington, D.C., on 3 September 1895 to William LePre Houston (1870-1953), a lawyer, and Mary Ethel Hamilton Houston, a former teacher and hairdresser (1867-1947). He attended the racially segregated public schools of Washington, D.C., receiving his diploma from M Street College-Preparatory High School. In 1915, he earned his Bachelor of Arts degree with honors at Amherst College, and in1922 and 1923, respectively, Houston earned the Bachelor of Laws and Doctor of Juridical Science degrees at Harvard Law School. Although his higher education was briefly interrupted by his service during World War I from 1917 to 1919, Houston excelled at Harvard, becoming the first African-American editor of the *Harvard Law Review*. Following an additional year of studies in civil law at the University of Madrid in Spain and travel to northern Africa, Houston returned in 1924 to Washington, D. C. He passed the District of Columbia bar, entered law practice establishing Houston and Houston (with his father), and accepted a teaching position at Howard University Law School. Charles Houston's practice of law at Houston and Houston consisted of some criminal cases but included mainly civil cases, many of which were civil rights claims. Charles remained with the firm until his death in 1950.

After three years as an attorney-at-law and professor, Charles Houston conducted a national survey on the status and activities of African-American lawyers during 1927-1928. His findings revealed a striking shortage of African-American attorneys. He addressed this in two ways. First he prepared a challenge to African-American law students and attorneys, which later appeared in the *Journal of Negro Education* under the title "The Need for Negro Lawyers" (See *Journal of Negro Education*, 4 [January 1935]: 49-53). Second, when Houston served as Vice Dean (and Chief Administrative Officer) of Howard's Law School from 1929 to 1935, he not only transformed the Howard University Law School from an evening school serving part-time students to a fully accredited school for full-time students, but also established a new mission for the school. He believed that he and other faculty at Howard had a duty to both "equip its students with direct professional skills…" and to train students for "social engineering."

During his years at Howard in the late 1920s and the early 1930s, Charles Houston developed, expounded and then began to teach his "social engineering," an element of Houstonian Jurisprudence. Houston formulated this philosophy – which scholars have called "Houstonian Jurisprudence" since J. Clay Smith, Jr.'s first use of the term in 1963 – over a number of years during which he seriously examined and analyzed his situation and the plight of other African Americans in the United States. He engaged in what a scholar-teacher-activist Paulo Freire would describe as the development of "critical consciousness." Houston believed human beings were equally entitled to "life, liberty and the pursuit of happiness," regardless of race. He believed, as well, that a society could not be a morally and legally *good* society unless it "guarantee[d] justice and freedom for everyone." He compared this with dominant white ideology and explanations for the discriminatory treatment of African Americans in the United States. As a consequence, Houston rejected the oppressors' ideology and explanations, and then identified both flaws in the thinking and some causes of continuing racist oppression. Having done this he used the advantages of his education, opportunities, and position to develop and communicate ideas that could become weapons in the struggle of African Americans against injustice. Houston maintained a life-long commitment to the freedom struggle of African Americans and was particularly concerned that through "social engineering" he and other lawyers test the limitations of law – despite continuing racial oppression and the inevitability of the white ruling class's repression – in order to fight for the greatest freedom and justice possible. He insisted, according to former students Oliver Hill and Thurgood Marshall, that "a lawyer's either a social engineer or..a parasite of society."

A lawyer who worked as a "social engineer" had several functions beyond traditional practice, according to Houston: (1) serving as "the mouthpiece of the weak and the sentinel guarding against wrong," (2) "guid[ing] antagonistic and group forces into channels where they will not clash," (3) ensuring that the "course of change is..orderly with a minimum of human loss and suffering," (4) recogniz[ing] that the written Constitution and inertia against its amendments give lawyers wide room for social experimentation," and (5) "engag[ing] in a carefully planned [program of litigation] to ensure decisions, rulings and public opinion on..principle[s] while "arousing and strengthening the local will to struggle." Because they were members of an oppressed minority in the USA, the African-American lawyers' additional duties of "social engineering" included: (6) being "prepared to anticipate, guide and interpret group advancement," and finally (7) "us[ing] the law as an instrument [for the] minority..to..achieve its place in the community and nation." About this Houston was uncompromising.

When approached in 1934 by the bi-racial NAACP and The American Fund for Public Service, an interesting funding agency, about addressing the legal status of African Americans nationally and recommending an approach for change, Houston applied "social engineering" to the task. First, he carefully studied both the data that had been collected and the proposal for taking cases to court (i.e., litigation) that had been included in a report prepared earlier by Nathan Margold. After critical analysis of written materials and other critical factors, Houston presented to the NAACP and representatives of The American Fund for Public Service a long-range plan of protracted struggle to establish gradually new precedents through litigation and community involvement. The plan called for gradual invalidation of the principle underlying legal segregation of the races, the doctrine of "separate but equal" articulated by the Supreme Court in the 1896 case of *Plessy v. Ferguson* (163 U.S. 537, 1896). Houston's plan reflected his understanding of history, white racism, and the operation of the judicial system, particularly its reliance on precedent, i.e., *stare decisis*. On Houston's plan, with modification, attorneys of the NAACP and its Legal Defense Fund would rely through the early 1950s as they sought to have racial segregation declared unconstitutional. In

1934 Houston was hired to direct a campaign of litigation. He served as part-time NAACP Special Counsel from October 1934 to June 1935 and full-time Special Counsel from July 1935 to 1940, working in Washington, D.C., and New York City. After 1936, he was ably assisted by his former student, Thurgood Marshall, who in 1940 succeeded Houston as Special Counsel.

The first African American selected by the biracial NAACP to join its staff as a salaried attorney to direct its legal affairs nationally, Houston had responsibility for handling a variety of legal matters that individuals and branches directed to the NAACP. Beyond education cases, the most notable were unconstitutional denials of due process of law and jury discrimination, such as *Hollins v. Oklahoma* (295 U.S. 394, 1935) and *Hale v. Kentucky* (303 U.S. 613, 1938). Primarily, however, Houston designed and gave leadership to a strategically-planned campaign of litigation, education and community activism, the ultimate goal of which was "[the] complete elimination of segregation" in public education. For the goal, Houston offered this rationale in 1935: "No segregation operates fairly on a minority group unless it is a d[o]minant minority"; "..these apparent senseless discrimination in education against Negroes have a very definite objective on the part of the ruling whites to curb the young and prepare them to accept an inferior position in American life without protest or struggle." There was no doubt in Houston's mind that in the 1930s the majority in the United States still viewed "white supremacy" as appropriate and that the place reserved for Africa Americans in this society was still "the bottom." Although Houston advocated efforts to have working-class whites and African Americans recognize their common problem in the United States, he would not delay or dilute the demands of African Americans while waiting for such bi-racial attacks on an oppressive economic-political system. His role, he commented later, was to "prob[e] in the courts...how far the existing system will permit the exercise of freedom before it clamps down" since "we are fighting a system." Throughout the legal campaign, Houston emphasized the need for "intelligent leadership plus intelligent mass action." In fact, when he began the NAACP's legal campaign he offered the words of the nineteenth century anti-slavery crusader Frederick Douglass for the consideration of oppressed African Americans: "To make a contented slave you must make a thoughtless one,..darken his moral and mental vision, and..annihilate his power of reason."

Throughout his life, Houston would work with non-African Americans who were committed to civil rights and racial equality as well as African Americans, but he insisted the NAACP begin to challenge the assumptions of racist America and honor the principle of Black Self-determination by looking to and calling upon African Americans for leadership in this protracted struggle. Houston never equivocated: "Essentially, leadership must develop from the aspirations, determinations, sacrifices and needs of the group itself." First, he persuaded Walter White, the Executive Director of the NAACP, to support the use of African American attorneys to argue the cases pursued in the course of the campaign to challenge racial discrimination in public education. Second, Houston communicated through reports, documents, and articles that appeared in the NAACP's *Crisis*, principles of justice and equality as well as important objectives of the campaign against racial discrimination in public education. The objectives were "(1) to arouse and strengthen the will of the local communities to demand and fight for their rights; [and] to work out model procedures th rough actual tests in court which can be used by local communitie s..". Im plementing Houston's plan, African American attorneys and local leaders utilized a three-pronged strategy: (1) selecting cases that presented clear legal issues and building strong records in those cases, (2) overturning negative legal decisions by invalidating gradually or att acking directly controlling precedents, and (3) developing a sustaining community or mass interest in each case. Over the years the plan's modification cam e about through the process of struggle, ev aluation or progress and consultation with Houston.

Between 1935 and 1938, Special Counsel Houston publicized the cam paign against discrimination in education, toured the South to film the inequ alities in Af rican American and white public schools, encour aged community initia tive and continuous involvem ent among African Am ericans of all ages, developed m odel procedures, regularly provided advice or collaborated with other African Am erican attorneys throughout the states, argued cases f or equality of education and equalization of teacher' salaries and led the developm ent of many cases in the state and federal courts. Special Counsel Charles Houston ar gued several cases attackin g discrimination in public education before state and fe deral courts. Cases in wh ich African Am ericans sought admission to state-supported law schools in Maryland and Missouri were especially significant as first and sec ond steps in the assault upon *Plessy v. Ferguson*, namely *Pearson (University of Maryland) v. Murray* (169 Md. 478; 182 A. 590, 1936) and *Missouri ex rel. Gaines v. Canada* (305 U.S. 337, 1938). In the University of Maryland case, which was handled by Houston and Marsha ll, Maryland's highest court affirmed the Baltimore City Court's ruling that Donald Gaines Murray's equal protection rights had been violated and ordered Murray's admission to the tax-supported law school. During 1938, Charles Houston, with St. Louis atto rney Sidney Redmond, won the NAACP's first major U. S. Supreme Court victory, *Gaines*, in the legal campaign. In *Gaines*, the Supreme Court ruled that Missouri neither could meet its Fourteen th Amendment obligation of "equal protection" through provisi on of out-of-state scholarships to African Americans seeking adm ission to law school, nor could the state constitutionally exclude an African American from the white state un iversity law school unle ss it made provisions for separate and equal law school educa tion of African Am ericans in Missouri.

Beyond *Missouri ex rel. Gaines v. Canada*, Houston's m ajor victories included establishing new preced ents in em ployment and housing. In 1944 the court respon ded favorably to Charles Houston's arguments in *Steele v. Louisville and Nashville* (323 U.S. 192, 1944) and *Tunstall v. Brotherhood of Locomotive Fireman and Enginemen* (323 U.S. 210, 1944) and ruled that a white labo r union authorized under the federal law to serve as the collec tive bargaining representative m ust fairly represent all wor kers regardless of race, including African Americans ex cluded from white unions' memberships. *Steele*, a landmark decision, established th e duty of fair representation. Addressing housing discrim ination and the inability of Afri can Americans to purchase home in some neighborhoods beca use of clauses in contract s that prohibited sale to African Americans, i.e., racia lly restrictive covenants, Hous ton assisted the NAACP with a law suite from Missouri (*Shelly v. Kraemer* [334 U.S. 1, 1948]) and prepared a strong, comprehensive written le gal argument, i.e., brief, against restrictive coven ants for a case in the District of Columbia (*Hurd v. Hodge* [334 U.S. 24,1948]). Houston made the newspaper headlines w hen, in his oral argum ent to the justices on racially restrictive covenants in W ashington, D.C., he told them bluntly, "Racism must go!" In 1948 the U. S Supreme Court ruled that restrictive covenants for the states ( *Shelley*) and the District of Columbia (*Hurd*) could not legally be upheld by courts of the United States.

In his private practice during the late 1940s, Houston focused his attention on not only several aspects of raci al discrimination in the nation' s capital such as the Consolidated Parents Groups' cases concerning the segregated public schools and the segregation of public facilities, but also the NAACP/Inc. Fund' s legal campaign. Meanwhile, he tried to balance civil rights advocacy with his ob ligations to his wife Henrietta and his son, Charles, Jr. (who had be en born in March of 1944). In the end, Houston had little tim e with his family and wa s unable to maintain good health. A heart condition caused Houston to be hospitaliz ed for a time in 1949. On 22 April 1950 Houston suffered acute coronary throm bosis and died, a relapse fr om his earlier heart attack.

Houston' s significance has both theoretical and practical dimensions. He trained scores of African Am erican law students at Ho ward and advised or served as m entor for many attorneys affiliated with the NAACP and its Inc. Fund. He developed Houstonian Jurisprudence and articulated as part of it "social engineering." Teaching and communicating "social engineering," he in fluenced the thinking and actions of generations of lawyers in rega rd to the use of the law for s ocial change. This concept regarding the use of the law for social progr ess and for the improvem ent of conditions of the oppressed continues to influence lawyers today. Houston conceived and im plemented a long-range, strategically planned attack on a specific, concrete expression of injustice, and such delibera te planning for litigation of cases continue s to be a model of procedure for lawyers of legal defense organizations. He argued m ajor cases in the Supreme Court that expanded civil rights for African Am ericans in education, e mployment, and housing. As succinctly summ arized in the Spingarn Me dal citation, which Charles, Jr. accepted for his father in June 1950: "It is doubtful that there has been a single im portant case involving civil rights during the past fifteen years [ 1935-1950] in which Charles Houston has not either participated directly or by consultation and advice..". Re membering Charles Houston, Supreme Court Justice William O. Douglas declared: "I sincerely believe he was one of the top te n advocates to appear before this court in my 35 years." Houston' s high competence and effectiv eness in work as an educator, legal strategist, advisor, litigator and constitu tional lawyer had immediate im pact on opportunities for African Americans and far-reaching consequenc es. He left a legacy of groundwork for the continuing freedom struggle.

## SUGGESTED LEARNING ACTIVITIES

1.    Charles Houston quoted from Frederick Douglass when introducing the NAACP's legal campaign against racial discrimination in public education: "To make a contented slave you m ust make a thoughtless one,..darken his m oral and mental vision, and...annihilate his power of reason." How might you interpret his statement in the era of slavery? How might you interpret this statem ent differently in 1935, the year in which Charles H ouston used it?

2.    Using a standard dictionary and a legal dictionary, or a dictionary with Latin phases, find the definitio ns of "precedent" and *stare decisis.*

      Why would *stare decisis* as an operating principle of the United States S upreme Court, in combination with white r acism in the United States, dictate a gradual approach to elim inating legal r acial segregation in public schools?

3.    Interview an African Am erican who experienced racial se gregation in public education or public acco mmodations. Compar e his or her experien ces of racial segregation with your own experiences.

4.    Identify Charles Houston's preparation for the NAACP legal cam paign. Discuss the importance of education, history, res earch or study and strategic planning when trying to accom plish a goal in a hostile environm ent

5.    Invite a speaker to your group who was either a plaintiff/participant or attorney in a civil rights case. Discuss the relati onship between court cases and comm unity activism.

6.    If time permits, plan and present over a period of two or thre e weeks in February a moot court (simulated hearing of a case) on one of Houston's Supreme Court cases: *Missouri ex rel. Gaines v. Canada* (305 U.S.337, 1938); *Steele v. Louisville & Nashville* (232 U.S. 192, 1944); or *Hurd v. Hodge* (334 U.S.24, 1948): (a) With the assistance of a teacher, law student, la w librarian or lawyer, visit a law library to locate and copy the opinions of the U. S. Supreme Court and briefs filed by attorneys before argum ent of one of Houston's cases argued in the U.S. Supreme Court; (b) Invite two attorneys to prepare arguments as opposing counsel for a moot court presentation and one attorney to serve as chief justice of the m oot court; (c) Select eight other students to serve as associate justices who will as k questions of the attorneys; divide into eight small groups; and study the opinions and the legal briefs. E ach group should prepare questions to be asked of each attorney concerning racial discri mination in either education ( *Gaines*), employment (*Steele*), or housing ( *Hurd*).

## REFERENCES

Elwood, William and Mykola Kulish. *The Road to Brown* (a video). San Francisco: California Newsreel.

Harper, Conrad. "Charles Hamilton Houston," in Rayford Logan and Michael Winston, eds., *Dictionary of American Negro Biography*. New York: W. W. Norton, 1982, pp. 328-30.

Hastie, William. "Charles Hamilton Houston," *Negro History Bulletin*, 13 (June 1950): 207-8.

Houston, Charles H. "The Need for Negro Lawyers," *Journal of Negro Education*, 4 (January 1935): 49-52.

_____. "Foul Employment Practices on the Rails," *Crisis*, 56 (October 1949): 269-71.

"College Honors Charles Houston ' 15." *Amherst Magazine*, (Spring 1978): 12-14.

Kluger, Richard. *Simple Justice*. New York: Alfred Knopf, 1976.

McNeil, Genna Rae. *Groundwork: Charles Hamilton Houston and the Struggle for Civil Rights*. Philadelphia: University of Pennsylvania Press, 1983.

_____. "'To Meet the Group Needs': The Transformation of Howard University School of Law," in James Anderson and V. P. Franklin, *New Perspectives on Black Educational History*. Boston: G. K. Hall, 1978, pp. 149-71.

McNeil, Jesse Jai, Jr. "A Critical Analysis of Planning for Social Change." (Ed.D. dissertation), University of Massachusetts, 1975.

Robinson, Spottswood. "No Tea for the Feeble." *Howard Law Journal*, 20 (1977): 1-9.

Segal, Geraldine. *In Any Fight, Some Fall*. Rockville, MD: Mercury, 1975.

Smith, J. Clay, Jr. *Emancipation*. Philadelphia: University of Pennsylvania, 1993.

Reprinted from the ASALH Black History Month Learning Resource Package for 1997 ("African Americans and Civil Rights: A Reappraisal").

## Thurgood Marshall: Legal Strategist for the Civil Rights Movement
F. Michael Higginbothan and Jose Felipe Anderson

When considering the great lawyers in American history, the work of Daniel Webster, Clarence Darrow, and John W. Davis are often cited as examples of courtroom skill and eloquence. Yet among those who might be added to the list of the top legal advocates of all-time, no American lawyer would be more deserving or has had a greater impact on the quality of life in the United States than Thurgood Marshall. Born July 2, 1908 in Baltimore, Maryland, Marshall will be remembered as the first African American to serve on the Supreme Court of the United States. He was appointed to that position by President Lyndon Johnson on August 20, 1967, after a period of service on the United States Court of Appeals for the Second Circuit and as Solicitor General of the United States, the federal government's highest ranking lawyer. Equally impressive, however, is his record as a catalyst for complex civil rights litigation. Marshall won 28 of 31 cases he argued in the nation's highest Court[1] and was responsible for guiding many other cases in lower federal and state courts. Together these cases helped to bring down legal impediments to and open up political, social, and economic opportunities for those who had previously been excluded solely because of their color.

Marshall has left his imprint on American jurisprudence through his work of nearly three decades as the premier civil rights lawyer for the NAACP.[2] The litigation strategies that he formulated and implemented led to the dismantling of the shameful legacy of the "separate but equal doctrine"[3] and the crippling impact of "Jim Crow"[4] laws designed to keep African American people as second-class citizens under the law.

What makes the work of Marshall more remarkable were the additional challenges he faced as only a few African American attorneys during the prime of his legal career.[5] For example, in his home state of Maryland there were only 32 African American lawyers in 1935, up from about 20 at the turn of the 20ᵗʰ century,[6] and there were less than 1,500 in the entire country during the early 1950's.[7] With so few lawyers it was difficult for Marshall to manage the complicated civil rights cases against better-financed and larger opposing legal staffs. The small staff of the NAACP was comprised of six lawyers, seven secretaries, seven paralegals, and two bookkeepers. At one time the office would handle six Supreme Court appeals, and Marshall personally would handle as many as 50 cases in lower courts during the same year. Marshall "logged on average six thousand miles a year traveling from courthouse to courthouse across the country. The volume of his responsibility was three to four times that normally demanded of a lawyer."[8]

Funding for supplies and expenses was also meager. There were no computers and the NAACP offices had no modern equipment. Marshall worked from an old typewriter and carbon paper that had been used over and over again. He and his staff often went for weeks without pay when money was needed for filing papers or paying train fare for attorneys handling cases in the field. One story related by a former NAACP lawyer who was working in Virginia during the early 1950's describes how he often had to request Marshall bring money with him to pay for legal work that had been done months, even years earlier. The grave financia l conditions were a result of the fact that the civil rights organization relied on donati ons and modest membership fees to finance its efforts.

Moreover, Marshall' s courage was inspirational. The work was often dangerous and death threats were common. "In making trips to southe rn courthouses, there were many close calls. Threats of lynching, assault and murder were routine."[9] There were often rumors of contracts to take Marshall' s life when he entered a hostile state to arg ue a case. Yet the mere whisper that Marshall was on his way would oftentim es breathe life into a cause without hope.

The work of Marshall came at enormous personal sacrifice to his fam ily and his health. He was often away from home for months at a time working on cases throughout the United States. He was often very ill, "simply ground into misery by dozens of trips from one corner of Am erica to another to fight the myriad manifestations of racism."[10] Yet when tired or sick, he seemed to gain strength from the famous words of his form er law teacher and mentor, Charles Hamilton Houston: "I would rather die on my feet than live on my knees."

Through the adversity, there were m any cases that were lost that should have been won. Because of hostile judges, fear by lo cal African Americans of becom ing involved in civil rights battles, and th reats against those people filing suits to enforce their rights, Marshall could never be sure whether a seem ingly strong case would m ake it to court. It became necessary to learn how to m anage risky litigation an d reduce disappointm ents by cultivating a num ber of plainti ffs ready to file suit. It was expected that intim idation, harassment, and legal chicanery would follo w, causing many cases to be discontinued.

In one South Carolina case a very cour ageous local farmer named Levi Pearson filed suit against the Clarendon County Board of Education to obtai n a single school bus so that African Am erican children would not have to walk several m iles to the county' s only school for non-whites. W hite students had several buses and several schools. While the suit was pending, the white-owned bank a nd feed store refused Pearson credit to purchase seed and fertilizer for his farm, and local merchants refused to buy his products.[11] When the case finally cam e to court it was dismissed because of a technicality regarding Pearson' s farm and where he paid his property taxes.[12]

When Marshall entered the case, the sk illed litigator recognized that such problems should be avoided in the future. In beginning the case a second tim e Marshall would seek a "firm, unified group of twenty plaintiffs..."[13] Since the legal resources w ere scarce and civil rights litigation dif ficult to win, Marshall was prepared to m ake a difficult choice in the South Carolina case. He informed the African Am ericans in Clarendon County who were inte rested in proceeding with a new case that, "if [they] could assemble twenty sturdy plaintiffs w ho would stay the cour se...the NAACP would bring a major test case there. If not, it would take the fight elsewhere." [14]

Marshall's quick decision-making ability helped him focus needed attention to the cases that would have the greatest impact on the largest number of people. His careful planning was characteristic of the strategies and training given to him by Charles Hamilton Houston. Following the philosophy that good civil rights litigation was neither accident nor luck, Houston attempted to implement the "Margold Strategy"[15] in the school desegregation cases. The essence of the strategy was to focus on the "equal" part of separate but equal. Since it was well known that far less money was spent on public schools and other facilities for non-whites than for whites, Houston believed in the "idea of making it too expensive for the South to maintain segregated schools." [16] Houston began his early cases with the Margold research as part of his approach. Houston shared the Margold Strategy with Marshall as he carefully guided Marshall's early career.

In fact, Houston helped Marshall achieve his first major civil rights victory during 1935 in the case that desegregated the University of Maryland's law school.[17] Marshall was particularly pleased with the victory against the University of Maryland since he could not attend its law school in 1930 because of its whites-only admissions policy. "Houston's close supervision of Marshall's work in *Murray* was Marshall's real introduction to the careful practice of law. Marshall quickly appreciated the importance of attention to detail..." [18] It was this attention to detail that helped him adjust to the shifting sands of desegregation litigation. It is important to remember that Marshall managed hundreds of cases in many states at the same time. Some of these cases involved the same legal issues, but each had important differences.

As with Houston before him, Marshall recognized the need to take charge of the increasing load of civil rights litigation. When he took charge of the NAACP's legal efforts, he treated the matter like the war it was. He recognized that an army requires a commanding general to lead it, a clear authoritarian chain of command, and loyal troops to carry out the mission. Someone had to take ultimate responsibility for all major decisions. Clearly, Marshall was the man who took charge. One litigation colleague described Marshall as a "you-go-your-way guy as long as your way was his way...making it clear that he was the architect, the coach and everything had to be built his way." [19]

Under Marshall's guidance victory after victory was achieved. Not only had Marshall been successful desegregating professional schools, [20] but also in rulings which prohibited discrimination in the sale of housing, [21] and his efforts to desegregate the United States Army during the Korean War.[22]

Of all the innovations Marshall brought to complex civil rights cases was the use of social science research to support his legal claims. That strategy, which is still considered controversial, [23] helped to shape the role of the courts as a protector of individual rights through the examination of the measurable consequences of certain types of government action. In the famous *Shelley v. Kraemer* case,[24] Marshall persuaded the Supreme Court to strike down agreements in real estate deeds, which prohibited the private sale of property to African Americans. Some researchers had established the harmful economic effects of segregated housing. Although Marshall focused on the legal aspects of the case, he was also conducting a symphony of sociologists, economists and fifteen amicus curiae organizations designed to influence the court's decision. These efforts were "designed to impress the Supreme Court with the board coalition that opposed racial covenants."[25]

In his most famous case, *Brown v. Board of Education*,[26] Marshall continued his use of social science research combined with careful legal planning to persuade the Supreme Court to rule unanimously that separate public schools are inherently unequal. The *Brown* litigation in the Supreme Court occurred over four years and resulted in three opinions. Marshall was known as an emotional, sometimes angry warrior while preparing his cases, however, in the court he was a model of composure and control. In his memoirs, former Chief Justice Earl Warren praised Marshall's composure and skill. Warren recalled that "Marshall made no emotional appeal, and argued the legal issues in a rational manner as cold as steel."[27]

Marshall's reputation as a careful and persuasive writer was also well known. Former Supreme Court Justice Hugo Black also described Marshall, the lawyer, as a man of character and ability. During the early 1960's when Justice Black was asked by historian Irving Brant who should be the next man appointed to the Supreme Court, Black suggested it should be Marshall. Showing Brant one of Marshall's briefs Black said, "any man who writes that brief deserves to be on this court."[28] Hugo Black administered the oath of office to Marshall when he joined the Supreme Court.[29]

Marshall's scholarly work as a jurist was also exceptional. As a member of the Federal Court of Appeals for the Second Circuit he authored 118 majority opinions, not one of which was overturned by the Supreme Court. After being elevated to the high court, he delivered 769 opinions in his 24 terms on the court.[30]

During his work on the court he never forgot the struggles suffered by the poor and disenfranchised that he had represented when working for the NAACP. He tempered his respect for the law with the need to be ever mindful that one of the primary roles for the Constitution was to protect the powerless. In his final opinion issued the day of his retirement, he cautioned that the court should not use its power to "squander" its "authority and legitimacy...as protector of the powerless."[31]

Marshall always understood that it was only through lawyers and the courts that the rights of unpopular people and their unpopular causes could be protected. Often referred to by his supporters as the "conscious of the Court," those who may have disagreed with his views on particular cases recognized that he alone could bring decades of personal observation and litigation experience in the area of civil rights into the Supreme Court's decision making. As his colleague Justice Sandra Day O'Connor observed: "[h]is was the eye of a lawyer who had seen the deepest wounds in the social fabric and used law to help heal them."[32]

Whether as a lawyer or jurist, Marshall maintained a principled view that civil rights were entitled to v igorous protection.  His interest in enforcing the Constitutio n in general and its equal protection principals in  particular were rooted in his personal experience with racial discrim ination and his unwavering respect for constitutional governm ent and the rule of law.  Pe rhaps the va lues that Marshall held so dear are best captured in his own comments about the value  of equal rights under the law.  In a 1979 speech, he said: "the goal of a true democracy such as ours...is that any baby born in the United States, even if born to the blackest,  most illiterate, most underprivileged Negro in Mississippi, is, merely by being born and draw ing its first breath in this democracy, endowed with the exact sam e rights as a child born to a Rockefeller." [33] It was Marshall' s lifelong struggle for true equality under the la w for black and white, rich and poor, m ale and female, that sets him apart from all others that went before and all those who will come after.  While many disagreed with  his goal, none can dispute his record of accomplishment.  His contribution s shaped America and moved the nation closer to a society where all people m ay be judged by the  content of their character rather th an the color of their skin.

## Suggested Student Learning Activities

1. Visit the Civil Rights Museum  in Birmingha m, Alabama.
2. Visit the United States S upreme Court in Washington, District of Colum bia.
3. Read any of the cases mentioned in this essay and the acco mpanying briefs filed on behalf of the litig ants.
4. Read any of the biographies of T hurgood Marshall cited in this essay.

## Endnotes

1. Drew S. Days, *Resolution in Tribute of the Late Justice Thurgood Marshall,* Vol. 114, S. Ct. CXIX, CXXXIV (November 15, 1993).

2. Marshall was appointed to the NAACP' s top legal job in 1938 upon the recommendation of his former law professor and m entor, the great Charles Hamilton Houston.  Houston left the post to return to Howard University Law School as Dean.  Marshall wa s paid an annual salary of $8,500.  Carl T. Rowan, *Dream Makers, Dream Breakers* (New York: Little, Brown, 1993), pp. 81-83.

3. The doctrine of separat e but equal emer ged from the Supreme Court' s controversial decision in *Plessy v. Ferguson,* 163 U. S. 537 (1896). *Plessy* rejected the position tha t the Constitut ion prohibite d state imposed racial segregation in  public faciliti es.  The decision resulted in the passage of law s requiring separation of the race s in all aspects of public life from  schools and neighb orhoods to hotels and trains, especially in states located in the South.

4. The phrase "Jim Crow," which originated  from a popular minstrel show act and song, became asso ciated with the many laws throughout America designe d to separate the races.  The practical effect was to render African Americans second-class citizens.  See

C. Van Woodard. *The Strange Career of Jim Crow* (New York: Oxford University Press, 1977, 1982, 3rd ed.), p. 7.

5.　　The first African American lawyer admitted into practice in the United States was Macon Bolling Allen in 1844. He was a member of the Bar of the State of Maine. See J. Clay Smith, Jr., *Emancipation, The Making of the Black Lawyer, 1844-1944* (Philadelphia: University of Pennsylvania Press, 1993) pp. 8-9.

6.　　Joseph C. Reid, "The African American Lawyer: Historical Sketches," *Maryland Bar Journal*, Vol. 28, (1995), pp. 37, 39.

7.　　Gilbert Ware, *From the Black Bar, Voices for Equal Justice* (New York: G. P. Putnam's Sons, 1967), p. xxix. Only about 232 of the Black lawyers admitted in the early 1950's were in the South, where most of the early civil rights litigation took place.

8.　　Michael D. Davis, and Hunter R. Clark. *Thurgood Marshall, Warrior at the Bar, Rebel on the Bench* (New York: Birch Lane Press, 1992), p. 21. In 1951, the NAACP Legal Defense Fund lawyers traveled 72,000 miles litigating civil rights cases. See Jack Greenberg, *Crusaders in the Courts* (New York: Basic Books, 1994), p. 81.

9.　　Days, *Supra*, at p. CXXV.

10.　　Carl T. Rowan, *Dream Makers, Dream Breakers*, p. 7.

11.　　Richard Kluger, *Simple Justice* (New York: Knopf, 1976), pp. 3-17.

12.　　*Ibid*.

13.　　*Ibid*, p. 18.

14.　　*Ibid*, p. 18.

15.　　The "Margold Strategy" was developed by Nathan Margold, a Rumanian-born lawyer of Jewish heritage. He drafted a 218-page report outlining an attack on public school segregation. His work was financed by an organization of lawyers and activists who comprised a group known as the "Garland Fund." The report focused on the lack of equal school funding throughout the South. Although much of what Margold suggested was never used, many of his conclusions about unequal funding and the suggestion to use the courts to shape the law were the key to the early civil rights movement. See Kluger, *Simple Justice*, pp. 134-139.

16.　　Mark V. Tushnet, *Making Civil Rights Law: Thurgood Marshall and the Supreme Court, 1936-1961* (New York: Oxford University Press, 1994), pp. 2-13.

17.　　*Murray v. Maryland*, 182 A. 590, 169 Md. 478 (1936).

18.　　Tushnet, *Making Civil Rights Law*, p. 15.

19.    Rowan, *supra*, p. 6. Quoting former civil rights colleague and federal Judge Spottswood Robinson, III, who Marshall had hired to file civil rights litigation in Virginia and who assisted in key litigation in South Carolina.

20.    See *Sweat v. Painter*, 339 U.S. 629 (1950); *McLauren v. Oklahoma State Regents*, 399 U.S. 637 (1950). These Supreme Court cases ordered the desegregation of stat e graduate schools.

21.    *Shelley v. Kraemer*, 334 U. S. 1 (1948).

22.    Davis and Clark, *supra*, pp. 120-133 (describing Marshall's efforts to desegregate the military using a combination of investigative, negotiation and litigation skills and strategies).

23.    See Harold Cruse, *Plural but Equal* (New York: Morrow, 1987), pp. 68-69. Cruse questions the validity of using social sciences data to quantify racial harm.

24.    Note 21, *supra*.

25.    Peter Irons, *The Courage of Their Convictions* (New York: The Free Pres s, 1988), pp. 68-70 (describing the *Shelley* litigation planning process) .

26.    347 U.S. 483 (1954).

27.    Earl Warren, *The Memoirs of Chief Justice Earl Warren* (New York: Doubleday, 1977, 1994), p. 287.

28.    Roger K. Newman, *Hugo Black: A Biography* (New York: Pantheon, 1994), p. 591.

29.    *Ibid.*

30.    Days, 114 S. Ct., at CXXX.

31.    *Payne v. Tennessee*, 111 S. Ct. 2597, 2619 (Marshall, Dissenting) (1991).

32.    Sandra Day O'Connor, "A Tribute to Justice Thurgood Marshall: The Influence of a Raconteur," 44 *Stanford Law Review,* 1217 (1992).

33.    115 F.D.R. 349, 354 (1979); Transcript, WUSA-TV's "Searching for Justice, Three American Stories," September 13, 1987.

Reprinted from the ASALH Black History Month Learning Resource Package for 1997 ("African Americans and Civil Rights; A Reappraisal")

## Taking Segregation to Court:
## The NAACP's Legal Defense and Education Fund
### Bruce Watson

Battles for civil rights were fought in the streets and at the ballot box. Most, however, were won in the courts. Using words as their weapons, a dedicated team of attorneys gradually chipped away at the walls of segregation. These lawyers were part of the NAACP.

In 1939, the NAACP's board of directors authorized the creation of a Legal Defense and Education Fund (LDF, as it came to be known). This team of attorneys would continue the associati on's legal battles against segregation. At its head was a brilliant lawyer, Thurgood Marshall.

By the time Marshall graduated from high school, he could recite nearly all of the U.S. Constitution from memory. After earning a law degree at Howard University in Washington, D.C., Marshall began challenging se gregation laws such as the ones that had kept him out of the University of Ma ryland. Hired by the NAACP in 1936, Marshall became the first director of its LDF.

Marshall created a plan of action for br eaking down segregation using the careful, rational arguments he had learned from his law school teacher, Charles Hamilton Houston. Houston often was called "the Mo ses of the civil rights movement." Passionately believing in law as a means to achieve justice, he crafted the legal strategy that gradually defeated segreg ation. "A lawyer's either a social engineer, or he's a parasite." Houston often told his law student s. Together, Houston and Marshall headed the NAACP's legal department and went up against the mountain of discrimination that the U.S. Supreme Court had declared legal.

In 1896, the Supreme Court had ruled th at segregation was legal. Schools, streetcars, and other public pl aces could be labeled "white s only" and "blacks only," as long as they were "separate but equal." For decades, the Court's decision allowed segregation to continue, implying that Afri can Americans were second-class citizens. Marshall and the NAACP could end segregation only by skillfully proving that "separate" was never "equal." To do so, they would use the law to help black people instead of exclude them.

Did black teachers deserve the same pay as white teachers? The LDF argued that they did, winning that case in 1940. Could bus es traveling from the integrated North to the segregated South keep the races separated? The NAACP's legal team said "No"— another case won. Could homeown ers sign agreements to keep African Americans out of their neighborhoods? In 1948, th e Supreme Court agreed with the NAACP's attorneys' stand that this was unconstitutional.

Marshall argued and won an incredible twenty-nine out of thirty-two cases before the Supreme Court. He and the NAACP's LDF won lawsuits that allowed African

Americans to vote in primary elections and serve on juries. While Rosa Parks and Dr. Martin Luther King, Jr., boycotted segregated buses in Alabama, the NAACP fought in court. When protesters staged sit-ins to integrate eating establishments, the association defended them. But the NAACP's most important case came when it fought school segregation throughout the South.

In 1951, a group of black students in Virginia were fed up with their rundown school and its tarpaper building. It was greatly inferior to the local white high school. They took their case to the NAACP, as did students in Kansas, South Carolina, Virginia, and Delaware. The NAACP represented them before the nation's highest court in what became known as *Brown v. Board of Education of Topeka, Kansas.*

Marshall and other NAACP lawyers presented the Supreme Court with three arguments why segregation was unconstitutional. It was imposed without any good reason. It violated the Fourteenth Amendment of the U.S. Constitution, which outlaws discrimination based on race or color. And, it had a negative effect on black children by giving them a sense of inferiority.

Finally, on May 17, 1954, the U.S. Supreme Court agreed. Segregation gave African American children

"a feeling of inferiority as to their status in the community that may affect their hearts and minds in a way unlikely to ever be undone."

Segregated schools, which had been the law for more than fifty years, would have to be integrated. It was a tremendous victory. But, the South would not give up segregation without a fight.

Segregated restaurants, segregated bus stops, segregated hospitals—one by one, the NAACP's attorneys challenged them in court. The cases went from lower courts in cities and counties across the South up to the highest court in the land. Each time, the NAACP won. The group became so successful that the U.S. Treasury Department began to investigate the LDF at the urging of southern segregationists. The Treasury questioned the Fund's tax-exempt status. Anxious to preserve the LDF and its ability to fund legal programs, the NAACP authorized the separation of the LDF from its parent organization.

Thurgood Marshall went on to become the first African American U.S. Supreme Court justice, where he served from 1967 to 1991. And today, though two separate legal entities, the NAACP and the LDF share a commitment to equal rights and continue to work together for civil liberties.

---

Reprinted with permission from *Cobblestone*, February 2002, pp. 26-29.

### "Nobody Really Dared to Believe It Would Happen"
(An Interview with Mrs. Althea Simmons)

LUMUMBA: I would like to ask you a little more about, well, since you also attended Howard University, and were presen t at the school—the se gregation case, I was concerned with the uniqueness of the approach used in that case in terms of introducing a large scope of social scientis t evidence in order to help resolve the ca se. Can you tell us something about whether or not it was the pr ecedent in the courts and whether or not there has been any follow up in this type?

SIMMONS: I think this was very signifi cant, Malaika, because you see, we had to overcome the *Plessy v. Ferguson* decision. Which really said in effect that the black man had no rights, that a white man was bound to respect. Because we h ad certain rights accorded to all peop le under our United States Constitution, and the Constitution had not been interpreted in favor of the Negro. It was thought by the legal st aff of NAACP that a new dimension would have to be brought to the attention of the Court and that now we ought to deal with not just the legal aspect s but how does this a ffect a young person, in his social adjustment. Dr. Kenneth Clark wa s one of the persons who was contacted to give his expert opinion with regard to how segregation affect ed young people. This argument, when it was presented to the Court, interested the Court very much. And the Court used the argument to boost up the opinion that segregation was harmful to the black child. Now we' ll go a little further and we say segregation is harmful to the white children too, because if you have to live a nd work in a multi-racial society the sooner you get to know each other, in a multi-racial society, the sooner you can get rid of misconceptions. And then you don' t have one gr oup of persons feeling they are superior to another group, and the next group feeling th at it' s inferior. This argument was won— it was a calculated risk. Of course, the attorneys did not kno w how the Court would react to it, but the decision of the national board was, to throw everything into the hopper and we knew it was som ething that should be done , and we felt that enlightened m en who were trying to do the best they could for our country, would alm ost have to say that this was a consideration before they m ade their decision. They did, and it was a shocking kind of thing. I' d like to, if I can, just to give you m y feeling at the time, we heard the decision being read.

We had been waiting. Every Monday is d ecision-reading day. And of course, som ebody would always go down to the Suprem e Court, then call back to say, "No, the decision would not be read today." And then that morning came May 17, and the guy was speaking very incoherently, "Man, they fixing to read the decisions." So we hopped into taxis and went down to the Supreme Court a nd sat there with bated breath and listened because we didn' t know what Chief Justice W arren was going to say. And when he read that phrase—it was a phrase that I would neve r forget: "..that seg regation in p ublic education is unconstitutional"—we sat there in stunned silence. W e knew it should have been that way, but nobody really dared to believe it would happen. One of the nice things about that day was the fact that one of our law professors took us back to the chambers of one of the judges and we were able to talk with him . And we came back out and went back on campus and the only thing we could say to each other was, "Did you hear what he said? Did he really mean it? Did you hear him?" Because it took time for it to sink in that here the rights of black people were going to be recognized as being equal rights. And I recall very vividly standing in line that morning trying to get into the Supreme Court and hearing and talking rather a man from *Time* magazine who found out I was from Louisiana and Texas and he asked me this question: "Do you think that going to segregated schools has hurt you?" And my answer was "No." He started scribbling very fast. I said, "I know they hurt me." I had to think about it, and went on to tell him that my undergraduate and my high school work, rather, I didn't have chemistry, I didn't have biology, I didn't have shorthand, I didn't have typing because in Louisiana they felt that blacks didn't need that. And since my father was a high school principal, if there had been anyway possible to get those things in school he would have. When I went to college I found it kind of rough because I didn't have that kind of background. Graduate school the same thing, but I knew I had to do and so I did. And it seems to me a little bit unfair to ask a youngster to go under those same conditions in a world that is so wide awake that we can put men on the moon. So, I got a strong feeling and in the Supreme Court that day, that the judges had taken into consideration all the evidence presented before them and that the sociological data that was presented to them made sense. And I'd like to further state that this became the turning point, in the law it became a turning point even further than that, in the entire, let's say, scope of the black man's activities in this country. Because since 1954 the pendulum has been swinging steadily forward and that one decision has helped to cause the court to rule that segregation housing is unconstitutional. We have been able further to get an Equal Employment Opportunity Commission, all these things would have not been possible but for that key decision. We have now gotten an extension and we hope another extension of Voting Rights Act all of these things hinged upon what we call that last great decision. And I think that blacks in this country feel now that they've got the law to stand on, they can push into all areas to bring about true equality of opportunity under the law. That was a long-winded answer, but I kind of felt I had to say all of that.

LUMUMBA:         A great number of the major decisions—legal decisions in civil rights—have come as a result of the work of lawyers that have graduated from Howard Law School. Do you feel that there is a particular heritage of black lawyers from Howard University? And how would you describe this heritage?

SIMMONS:         I certainly do Malaika. The late Charles Houston, who was formerly the dean of Howard University [Law School], felt very strongly about black lawyers and civil rights. And so he brought this kind of atmosphere into the law school at Howard University and every Supreme Court case that has been handled by the NAACP has gone through a dry run at Howard University. Let me explain what a dry run at Howard is, because I think this will help you to see the kind of influence Howard has had on its law students. With a dry run, lawyers from across the country come into Howard and they sit as justices and I recall when I was at Howard, from '53 through '56, that you had a fellow was the law clerk to Justice Frankfurter, his name was Bill Coleman out of

Philadelphia. He would always sit as Mr. Frankfurter. The late Loren Miller used to come from Los Angeles he would sit as anot her justice. Robert Ming out of Chicago would come and sit as a justice and lawyers across the country would do this. The lawyers who were going to present the case before the Suprem e Court would argue before this panel of "justices," and the members of the Howard University L aw School would sit in there and listen. Now one of the things that I thought was unique about Howard was the fact that these noted lawyers would let first-, second- , and third-year law students ask questions, propose methods of presentation, and in general tear the cases down if they thought they could do that. Then they [would] put the cases back together again as they saw it. And by the time they went before the Suprem e Court practically every angle had been considered. A nd being a student at Howard, having the opportunity to do this, made you feel that there was something very wort hwhile about th is type of involvem ent. I know I had typing s kills and I felt very pro ud to be pulling down books and looking up law for the lawyers like T hurgood Marshall who is now on the Supreme Court. And to say, "But look, I think this means so and so"—now this is the kind of opportunity you don' t get very often as a student. So those of us who attended Howard, we knew we would get a good education in ci vil rights and constitutional law. And therefore, when we wen t back to our home communities to practice, we had the kind of background that a lawyer who had graduated fr om another law school just did not have. Another thing they instilled in us, was that, being black, we owed a certain am ount of our time to working [with the] NAACP to help brin g about change. And I think this is a kind of commitment you will not find in other schools, but because of the heritage at Howard and how this program was developed you' ll find it in all Howardites.

Reprinted with perm ission from the Ralph Bunche Oral History Collection, Mrs. A lthea Simmons: Moorland-Spingarn Research Cent er, Howard University, June 18, 1970. Interviewer: Malaika Lumumba.

**Significant Race-Based Legal Cases in the Civil Rights Movement:**
**An Historical Perspective**
Taunya Lovell Banks

There are three United States Supreme Court cases of unquestioned significance to efforts by persons of African descent to obtain equality under law: *Dred Scott v. Sanford* (1857), *Plessy v. Ferguson* (1896), and *Brown v. Board of Education* (1954). In the first case, Dred Scott had been taken as a slave by his owner from Missouri, a slave-holding state, into Illinois, a free state. Upon his return to Missouri, Mr. Scott sued in federal court claiming that under Illinois and federal laws, he was free and a citizen of the United States with all the rights granted citizens under the United States Constitution. The United States Supreme Court, in *Dred Scott v. Sanford*, rejected his claim saying that under the law slaves were treated as property, not as persons and that neither slaves nor their descendants were citizens of the United States. Therefore, they had no individual rights under the Constitution.[1]

Following the Civil War, the *Dred Scott* case was repudiated by the adoption of the Thirteenth and Fourteenth Amendments. The Thirteenth Amendment, adopted in 1865, conferred citizenship on persons of African descent residing in the United States. The Fourteenth Amendment, adopted in 1868, guaranteed all persons within the country equal protection and due process of the laws. In 1896 the *Plessy* case tested the meaning of the Fourteenth Amendment's guarantee of equal protection of the laws.

**Legalization of Racial Segregation**

It is not surprising that in 1890 a bill was introduced in the Louisiana legislature requiring racial segregation on railroad cars. An excerpt from a New Orleans newspaper article written the same year provides insight into the racial climate that resulted in segregated trains in Louisiana: "A man that would be horrified at the idea of his wife or daughter seated by the side of a burly negro in the parlor of a hotel or at a restaurant cannot see her occupy a crowded seat in a car next to a negro without the same feeling of disgust."[2] Seventeen prominent New Orleans citizens of African descent representing the American Citizens Equal Rights Association of Louisiana Against Class Legislation petitioned the state legislature calling the bill unjust, discriminatory, and a denial of equality. Subsequently, the bill was passed and the citizen group decided to test the constitutionality of this new law.

On June 7, 1892, Homer Adolph Plessy took part in a pre-arranged effort to test racial segregation laws in Louisiana. Mr. Plessy purchased a first-class train ticket from New Orleans to Covington, Louisiana and took a seat in the train car reserved for white first-class passengers. The train conductor demanded that Mr. Plessy leave the coach and go to the coach reserved for "colored" passengers. When Mr. Plessy refused, he was arrested and charged with violating state law requiring racially segregated train cars. He appealed his arrest to the United States Supreme Court.

Homer Plessy never indicated his race to the state authorities, and his race was never listed in the state criminal proceedings. He was simply charged with "going into a coach used by the race to which he did not belong." Only on appeal to the Supreme Court did Mr. Plessy's lawyer describe him as "near-white" with seven-eighths Caucasian and one-eighth African blood, and no discernible Afro-American features. Based only on this statement, the United States Supreme Court concluded that Homer Plessy was a member of the "colored race."

On May 18, 1896, seven of the nine members on the United States Supreme Court upheld the Louisiana statute saying that laws mandating racial separation in public settings "do not necessarily imply the inferiority of either race to the other."[3] On appeal Mr. Plessy had argued that under the federal constitution, he was entitled to the same privileges and immunities as white people. The Supreme Court responded that the Louisiana statute did not violate the equal protection clause of the Fourteenth Amendment to the Constitution, and did not imply that one race was superior to the other. Astonishingly, the Court continued saying that any suggestion that enforced racial segregation suggests racial inferiority "is not by reason of anything found in the act but solely because the colored race chooses to put that construction upon it."

Justice Henry Billings Brown, author of the majority opinion, wrote that legal or political equality is different from social equality. To that majority of the Supreme Court, riding integrated train coaches was an expression of social equality, and the Fourteenth Amendment guarantees legal or political equality, not social equality. The Massachusetts native pointed out that Jim Crow practices existed prior to the adoption of the Fourteenth Amendment. He cited *Roberts v. City of Boston*, an 1850 Massachusetts Supreme Court case in which African Americans unsuccessfully challenged racially segregated public schools in Boston. According to Justice Brown, the *Roberts* case, decided before adoption of the Fourteenth Amendment, was proof that the Amendment permitted racial segregation. The majority opinion also contained approving references to other examples of Jim Crow practices in states like Indiana, New York, Kentucky, California, Ohio, and by congressional legislation aimed at the District of Columbia. As Justice Brown clearly knew, by 1896 Jim Crow practices were commonplace throughout the United States.

Assumptions of white superiority are woven throughout the majority opinion in *Plessy*. On the one hand, Justice Brown denies that legalizing racial segregation connotes racial inferiority, yet later in the same paragraph he states, "[i]f one race be inferior to the other socially the Constitution of the United States cannot put them on the same plane." Justice Brown also concedes that there might be a property interest in "belonging to the dominant race"—the "white" race— by acknowledging that a white person could sue for damages if wrongfully assigned to a colored coach, but implying that an African American could not sue if mistaken for a white person.

Justice John Marshall Harlan, a former slaveholder from Kentucky, was the lone dissenting vote on the Court. Justice Brewer, the ninth Supreme Court justice, missed the hearing and did not participate in this decision. Although now considered the great liberal of the *Plessy*-era Court, Justice Harlan chided the majority for refusing to acknowledge that the Louisiana statute did not treat African Americans and whites equally, but was designed to exclude African Americans from coaches occupied by whites. Unlike the majority, Justice Harlan was not concerned that integrated trains would connote social equality between the races because, as he wrote, "[t]he white race deems itself to be the dominant race in this country...So, I doubt not, that it will continue to be for all time." In essence, Justice Harlan agreed with the majority that African Americans were not and probably never would be the social equals of whites.

A mere two sentences later, Justice Harlan wrote those famous words, "There is no caste here. Our Constitution is color-blind." These words currently are interpreted to mean that all races are equal before the law. However, when read in context, it is apparent that in 1896 Whites already believed that African Americans were their social inferiors. Thus, Justice Harlan reasoned, more harm than good came from segregated-train laws. He warned that these laws "certainly create and perpetuate a feeling of distrust between these races" and "proceed on the ground that colored citizens are so inferior and degraded that they cannot be allowed to sit in public coaches occupied by white citizens." Besides, Justice Harlan reasoned, whites faced no real danger from sitting in integrated train coaches since they greatly outnumbered African Americans. Pointing out that "the destinies of the two races, in this country, are indissolubly linked together," Justice Harlan questioned the fairness of a law that treated non-citizens better than African American citizens.

In 1896 federal laws prohibited Chinese immigrants from becoming citizens. Yet, according the Justice Harlan, under the Louisiana statute Chinese immigrants could ride in the white coach. In using this analogy Justice Harlan might have been a bit disingenuous since the Supreme Court a year earlier had ruled that people of Chinese ancestry were not white. Thus, it is open to question whether a person of Chinese ancestry could ride in the white coach in Louisiana.

**Public Reaction to *Plessy***

The *Plessy* decision was met with mild surprise by the white press. For example, there was a brief mention on the front page of the *Baltimore* (Maryland) *Morning Sun*, but no blaring headlines to mark the legal sanctioning of Jim Crow. An editorial that day entitled "Separate Coaches for Colored Passengers" appeared on page four. Indeed, the whole nation, as historian C. Vann Woodward said, "received the news of [the Court's] momentous decision upholding the 'separate but equal' doctrine in relative silence and apparent indifference." Ironically, the *New York Times*, which between 1866 and 1896 prominently published approximately 150 articles on public accommodation cases, buried the case on page three in its regular Tuesday column on railway news. Even prominent legal publications like the *Harvard Law Review* and the *Yale Law Journal* did not mention the case.

The only alarm came from the African American press. The *Baltimore Afro-American*, in a front page article entitled "Negrophobia," began: "History seems to teach that no people ever yet secured a recognition of their rights in their fullness and entirety who were not willing, if need be to fight for them. Justice sometimes waits on slaughter, and liberty on victory." An editorial in the African American-owned *Washington Bee* called on the country to adopt "some constitutional amendment, that will stand the test of the United States Supreme Court, or let the white man suffer the consequences and the dangers that confront and threaten this Nation."

In truth, the *Plessy* decision was the culmination of a whole series of court cases of that era undermining attempts to secure racial equality for African Americans. For example, the history of Jim Crow practices in Baltimore is clear. In 1876 a federal district court in *Cully v. Baltimore* permitted Jim Crow cars on Baltimore streetcars. The federal judge mentioned two earlier cases involving race-based discrimination on the street, suggesting that Jim Crow in intrastate transportation was practiced in Baltimore by the mid-1870's, twenty years before *Plessy*. But as Woodward notes, Jim Crow practices "often anticipated and sometimes exceeded the laws."

By the mid-1880's Jim Crow cars also existed on steamboats operating between Maryland and Virginia. In 1885 a Maryland federal district court upheld the practice of assigning racially separate accommodations on these steamboats, but allowed the black women passengers to recover damages because the sleeping facilities provided them were not equal to those provide white women traveling first-class. But in 1889, the court refused to find unlawful discrimination where a black plaintiff was forced to sit at a separate table on the steamboat. The absence of many reported cases challenging Jim Crow practices may be deceiving. At least one historian suggests that few of the many cases challenging racial segregation in public accommodations ended up in legal reports because their outcomes were so obvious. These cases were more likely to be reported in newspapers. Further, most of these cases occurred in the North, suggesting that African Americans in the South knew better than to challenge customary segregation practices.

The *Plessy* decision ushered in an era of pernicious psychological racial oppression from which the country is still trying to recover. The *Baltimore Sun* editorial acknowledged that southern states had "agitated for several years" for separate coaches but feared that the courts would strike them down. It concluded, "[n]ow that the Supreme Court has declared the Louisiana statute constitutional, it is probable that the legislatures of other Southern States will enact similar laws." As the *Sun* editorial predicted, following *Plessy*, states enacted an incredible number of detailed laws and ordinances mandating racial segregation. Maryland was no different, formally adopting Jim Crow laws for streetcars in 1904. In 1910 Baltimore adopted a residential segregation law mandating that, in areas where both blacks and whites resided, blocks be segregated by race. Some Maryland Jim Crow laws remained in effect for more than fifty years and some practices continued into the 1960's.

The "separate but equal doctrine," growing out of the *Plessy* decision, remained the law of the land until 1954 when a unanimous Supreme Court in *Brown v. Board of Education* said that African American children were harmed by legally enforced racial segregation in public schools "even though th e physical facilities and other tangible factors may be equal."[4] The Court concluded that segregated public schools are "inherently unequal," overruling in part the *Plessy* case. However, it took more than a decade, several more Supreme Court decisions, and federal civil rights laws before the full legal impact of *Plessy* was overturned.

## SUGGESTED LEARNING ACTIVITIES FOR STUDENTS

1. Members of the Supreme Court are appointed by the President with the advice and consent of the Senate. The Justices se rve for life. Is it undemocratic for nine people who are not elected by citizens of th is country to have so much power? Discuss the lessons learned from the Supreme Court's decision in *Dred Scott, Plessy,* and *Brown.* Do these decisions, the constitutional amendments, and federal laws suggest that the government ultimately will correct significan t injustices to groups of people treated unfairly?

2. What constitutes equality under the law? Discuss the role of law in bringing about equality among different racial and ethnic groups in the United States. Should the law guarantee social as well as political and legal equality? Is it sometimes difficult to determine what activity involves social as opposed to legal equality?

3. The federal government is required by the Constitution to take a census of the inhabitants of the United States ever y ten years. Included in the census information is a listing of the number of people by race. The government defines what constitutes a race or ethnic group for the purposes of the census, but individuals can chose the racial or ethnic category that applies to them. Is this process really different from what happened to Homer Plessy? Should government have this power?

## ADDITIONAL READINGS AND RESOURCES

Richard Kluger. 1975. *Simple Justice.* [Gives a full discussion of the social, political, and legal history of *Brown v. Board of Education*]

Charles A. Lofgren. 1987. *The* Plessy *Case: A Legal-Historical Interpretation.*

Otto H. Olsen. 1967. *The Thin Disguise: Turning Point in Negro History*—Plessy v. Ferguson, *A Documentary Presentation, 1864-1896.*

C. Vann Woodward. 1955. *The Strange Career of Jim Crow*. [Discusses the history of both the *Plessy and Brown* cases.]

## VIDEORECORDINGS

*Simple Justice*. 1993. [PBS visual history of the history of *Brown v. Board of Education*.]

*The Road to* Brown*: The Untold Story of "The Man Who Killed Jim Crow."* 1990. University of Virginia. [Story of African American lawyer Charles Hamilton Houston, considered the legal strategist behind the legal attack on Jim Crow; includes teaching guide.]

## ENDNOTES

[1] *Dred Scott v. Sanford*, 60 U.S. 393 (1985).

[2] *African Americans: Voices of Triumph* (Time-Life, 1993-94).

[3] *Plessy v. Ferguson*, 163 U.S. 537 (1896).

---

Reprinted from the ASALH Black History Month Learning Resource Package for 1997 ("African Americans and Civil Rights: A Reappraisal").

# Segregated Education

***Roberts*, *Plessy* and *Brown*: The Long, Hard Struggle Against Segregation**
James Oliver Horton and Michelle Gates Moresi

It was no coincidence that Homer A. Plessy, a thirty-four-year-old middle-class "colored man," purchased a ticket on the train from New Orleans to Covington, Louisiana, on June 7, 1892. Nor was it unexpected that he would be arrested when he attempted to board the "whites- only" rail car. The purchase and the arrest were part of a well orchestrated, ongoing attack on Louisiana's Separate Car Act of 1890 by New Orleans blacks, with the sympathetic cooperation of the East Louisiana Railway Company, which enforced the state's new discriminatory law with reluctance. Homer Plessy was a perfect candidate for this legal test. He was totally acceptable in manners, demeanor and attire so that the denial of accommodations pointed to the absurdity of the law, and because he was extremely light in complexion, "the mixture of colored blood [hardly] discernible," it also emphasized the arbitrariness of the law's enforcement. For four years the case of *Plessy v. Ferguson* worked its way through the court system so that by 1896 it reached the Supreme Court of the United States. After five weeks of argument, the Court handed down its decision, which upheld the Louisiana law and declared separate accommodations based on race constitutional. The separation of the races by law, the Court argued, did not compromise equality before the law.

The *Plessy* decision was a milestone in American legal history and a turning point in American constitutional law. The highest court in the land set the constitutional foundation for the "separate but equal," racially discriminatory, Jim Crow legislation that became the hallmark of southern law and northern custom for the next half-century. But this decision neither initiated the "separate but equal" principle in law nor settled the question of legal racial segregation. It was based on pre-Civil War legal precedent and became the foil for the most far reaching court decision of the 20th century. In his statement of the court's majority opinion in *Plessy*, Justice Henry Billings Brown cited an 1849 decision rendered in his home state of Massachusetts by state Chief Justice Lemuel Shaw in the case of *Roberts v. The City of Boston*. That case resulted from a black printer's determination to enroll his daughter at her neighborhood school. Benjamin Roberts violated no law when he took five-year-old Sarah to be enrolled. In fact, a state law instructed that students should attend the school nearest their home. The statute further allowed any student unlawfully excluded from public school to recover damages, and when Sarah was refused admittance, Roberts sued the city of Boston under this provision. School authorities argued that special provisions had been made for "colored" students. Since Boston maintained racially segregated schools, the fact that Sarah passed five white schools on her way to the black school, the school board contended, was of no consequence.

In his cause, Roberts retained the talented attorney, abolitionist and later United States senator, Charles Sumner. Sumner was assisted by the young black abolitionist and activist lawyer from Boston, Robert Morris. This formidable legal team broke new ground in their argument before the court. Invoking "the great principle" embodied in the Constitution of Massachusetts, they asserted that all persons, regardless or race or color, stand as equals before the law. More specifically, they argued that racially segregated schools and equality of education are mutually exclusive, that segregation is unconstitutional because it infringes on the civil rights of individuals, and that it is socially and emotionally damaging to both black and white students. "The school is the little world where the child is trained for the larger world of life...and therefore it must cherish and develop the virtues and the sympathies needed in the larger world." The inculcation of caste distinction among citizens, they argued, precluded "those relations of Equality which the Constitution and Laws promise to all."

Chief Justice Shaw, unmoved by impassioned oratory about freedom and equality, decided the case on narrow legal grounds, ruling in favor of the right of the school committee to set education policy as it saw fit. The Boston School Committee strongly asserted that right, and the court decision went against Roberts, establishing the principle of segregated education in law in Massachusetts.

Thus the foundation for the Supreme Court decision in the *Plessy* case was laid. Even more specifically, Sumner and Morris provided the argument which, augmented by modern social science, became that of Thurgood Marshall and the National Association for the Advancement of Colored People (NAACP) legal team in the *Brown* decision in the 1950s. Like the *Brown* case, *Roberts* had been a school desegregation case and, like both *Brown* and *Plessy*, the arguments in *Roberts* had implications far beyond the specifics of the case. Together these three landmark decisions tell the history of the struggle for racial justice in America. Each was the result of planning, organization, direct action and support from the African-American community. Each was also the undertaking of a strong progressive interracial alliance that facilitated the legal effort. It was no accident that Roberts was represented by Sumner, an abolitionist who had provided his legal services to fugitive slaves and the antislavery movement on numerous occasions, and that Robert Morris was a black abolitionist lawyer. These crusaders against slavery had worked together before and would continue as allies for freedom throughout the Civil War period.

Although these efforts were almost always a product of joint community action, they did not necessarily imply a single African-American opinion. Boston blacks had struggled for decades to provide their children with quality education, which in the late 18ᵗʰ century meant withdrawing them from the city schools. The Boston School Committee was correct when, during the Roberts trial, it argued that early in the city's history, African Americans had petitioned the city to provide for a separate school. Blacks had done so because teachers and white students in the integrated schools frequently mistreated black students and subjected them to public ridicule. The private African School had been established in 1798, and a generous trust bequeathed to the city in 1815 by a white philanthropist provided adequate funds for the continued support of a separate black school, renamed the Smith School. Some black Bostonians felt strongly that separate schools were necessary to educate their children without the degrading experiences of racial prejudice and did not support the efforts to desegregate Boston schools.

Yet, as the physical facilities badly dete riorated at the all-black Sm ith School, it became clear to many that separated education in the Boston schools was not likely to be quality education for black students. A centu ry before sociologist Kenneth Clark helped NAACP lawyers make the case before th e Supreme Court in the *Brown* case, many black Bostonians understood that sepa ration of the races had harm ful long-term consequences for the psychological well-being of their children. William Cooper Nell, a community leader active in the campaign to integr ate Boston schools, related the personal experiences that m otivated him to become an activist. In 1829, he and two other students were judged as the three brightest students of the Negro school. However, they were not awarded the Benjam in Franklin medal that was given to white students by the city school board and were not invited to the dinner give n in honor of the winners. To satisfy his curiosity, Nell managed to attend the dinner as a waiter. During dinner, Massachusetts Lieutenant Governor Arm strong privately told him that he deserved to be at the dinner alongside the white students. Nell was the child of an econom ically successful fam ily and the son of a prom inent comm unity leader in Boston. Nonetheless, the feeling that he could "never be anything but a nigger an yhow" plagued his sense of self-worth. Segregated education, he believed, was im plicated in his dim inished self-im age.

Although debate over the benefits of inte grated education versus black-controlled education continued among Boston blacks, Nell and other parents organized an effective boycott of Boston' s black schools. Black activists and white abol itionists challenged segregation policies through peti tions, nonviolent protest, and th e introduction of bills to outlaw Jim Crow regulations. Repeated petitions to the Boston School Committee throughout the 1840s decried the injustice of exclusive schools "solely on account of color," which deprived blacks of the equal privileges and adv antages to which they were entitled as citizens. Thus, when Benjam in Roberts brought suit against the city, he did so as part of a series of efforts and strategi es by the community to desegregate Boston schools. The interracial lega l team of Sumner and Morris was merely presenting before the court arguments and valid g rievances black residents had expresse d before. The most eloquent desegregation argum ent revealed the detriments of segregation policies in the lives of Nell and m any other African Am erican children in Bosto n and elsewhere: "Nursed in the sentiments of Caste, receiv ing it with the earliest food of knowledge, [whites] are unable to eradi cate it from their natures..A de spised class, blasted by prejudice and shut out from various opportunities, [blacks] feel this proscription from the Common Sc hools as a peculiar brand..It adds to their discouragem ents." No matter that the Massachusetts court was not sym pathetic, black people understood only too well, from personal experience.

Justice Shaw, ignoring the m oral issues involved, narrowly focused on the question of whether separation by race in public schools violated R oberts' right to political, social and civil equa lity. When he reasoned that separation of the races does not perpetuate class distinctio n since existing prejudice in society "is not created by law, and probably cannot be changed by law," he foreshadowed the racial philosophy basic to 20th-century segregationist law. Echoing this philosophy, the 1896 *Plessy* decision reflected a dominant perception among whites that the races were somehow fundamentally different, a difference immutable by law. "Legislation is powerless to eradicate racial instincts or to abolish distinctions based upon physical differences," said the Court. "If one race be inferior to the other socially, the Constitution of the United States cannot put them upon the same plane." Further, the Court flatly rejected Plessy's claim, as the Massachusetts court had rejected Roberts' contention, that separation marked blacks with "a badge of inferiority." "If this be so," wrote Justice Brown, it is only "because the colored race chooses to put that construction upon it."

These were the assumptions of popular culture of the 19th century that remained strong even by the mid-20th century. It would not be until social attitudes, fostered and supported by social scientific evidence, began to reconsider the wisdom of racial hierarchy that the "separate but equal" doctrine would be reevaluated by the U.S. Supreme Court in 1954 with the *Brown v. Board of Education* case. By mid-century the harmful effects of racial segregation were scientifically documented and could no longer be easily dismissed. During the 1920s, mainstream social scientific thought had moved from the assumption that mental inferiority and anti-social behavior are racially inherited, to the understanding that environment and social process are the primary determinants of intellect. Gunnar Myrdal's *An American Dilemma* (1944), a widely acclaimed critique of American racism, which detailed the cycle of social prejudice and economic deprivation, was one source used by Marshall to urge the Court to reconsider *Plessy*. Further strengthening the argument against segregation was President Truman's report in 1947 from the Committee on Civil Rights, which also cited social scientific evidence and called for an end to legally-enforced segregation. The time was right for the Supreme Court to declare decisively that "in the field of public education the doctrine of ' separate but equal' has no place. Separate educational facilities are inherently unequal."

Yet, this declaration was a long time in the making and it was the result of more than a century of determined struggle. Like the overnight sensation who has worked a lifetime for that distinction, the Civil Rights Movement, which many Americans assume to have begun in 1954, was a long time coming with the sacrifice and support of thousands, black and white, committed to racial equality and justice long before *Brown* and even before *Plessy*. The *Plessy* decision, the *Brown* decision and all those who struggle for racial justice stand on the shoulders of a man who simply wanted a good education for his daughter at her neighborhood school: Benjamin Roberts.

FURTHER READING

Bordman, Marcia Beth. 1994. "Dear Old Golden Rule Days: A Study in the Rhetoric of Separate-but-Equal in *Roberts v. City of Boston* (1849), *Plessy v. Ferguson* (1896), and *Brown v. Board of Education* (1954)." Doctoral dissertation, University of Maryland, College Park, MD.

Finkelman, Paul, ed. 1992. _The Struggle for Equal Education_ (Volume 7). New York: Garland.

Horton, James O. 1993. _Free People of Color: Inside the African American Community_. Washington, DC: Smithsonian Institution Press.

Horton, James O., and Horton, Lois E. 1979. _Black Bostonians: Family Life and Community Struggle in the Antebellum North_. New York: Holmes & Meier.

Kluger, Richard. 1975. _Simple Justice: The History of_ Brown v. Board of Education _and Black America's Struggle for Equality_. New York: Vintage B ooks.

Levy, Leonard Williams. 1972. _Judgments: Essays on American Constitutional History_. Chicago, IL: Quadrangle Books.

Levy, Leonard Williams, and Jones, Douglas L. 1974. _Jim Crow in Boston: The Origin of the Separate but Equal Doctrine_. New York: Da Capo Press.

Lofgren, Charles A. 1988. _The_ Plessy _Case: A Legal-Historical Interpretation_. New York: Oxford University Press.

Mabee, Carleton. 1970. _Black Freedom: The Nonviolent Abolitionists from 1830 through the Civil War_. New York: Macmillan.

Whitman, Mark. 1993. _Removing a Badge of Slavery: The Record of_ Brown v. Board of Education. Princeton, NJ: Markus Wiener.

Reprinted with permission from _Cultural Resources Management_ (_CRM_), Vol. 19, No. 2, 1996. http://_brownvboard_.org/brwnquart/03-1/03-1h.htm and www.oah.org/pubs/magazine/deseg/horton.htm l).

## Du Pont Philanthropy and Black Schools of Delaware: 1918-1930
Robert J. Taggart

Like the Old South, Delaware had been a slave state. However, the Delaware experience differed from the rest of the South in the extent of philanthropic aid to Black schools because the state never seceded from the Union and needed no "Reconstruction." Therefore, Delaware never gained significant assistance from northern foundations. The result was a widespread, though badly supported Black public school system.[i] Yet, the 1920s saw the school laws revamped, state centralization in administration and finance accomplished, and almost every Black school building in Delaware built anew. This was done by a combination of state legislation and the guidance of one Delaware philanthropist, Pierre S. du Pont (1870-1954). He gave some $6,000,000 to public education in Delaware within twelve years, 1918-1930, in a more direct manner in a shorter period than was done by foundations in other southern states.[ii] The question is, did du Pont's philanthropy improve educational opportunity for the state's Black youth while decreasing the Blacks' dependence upon the whims of white Delawareans in order to gain that opportunity?

Any progressive reformer could find much to improve upon in the Delaware public school system of 1918. As a Southern border state, Delaware had never had a strong tradition of free, tax-supported education. Reliance upon local control produced a decentralized conglomeration of 450 school districts in a state of barely 200,000 people.[iii] Students and teachers paid the price for this freedom from centralized interference. A Delaware elementary school of 1918 was typically a one-room affair with a young teacher without normal school or college education. Most buildings were more than forty years old, some from the eighteenth century. Salaries and teacher standards were below the national average. Attendance for both races was dismal. Outside of Wilmington, white pupils averaged about 90 days daily attendance a year and Black pupils, 70 days. In 1918, Leonard Ayres placed Delaware 38th in the nation in his famous index of public school quality.[iv]

The state also lacked educational opportunity beyond grammar school before 1920. There were only two four-year high schools in Delaware, one for each race, both in Wilmington. Local school taxes could not assist Blacks toward equal facilities because local taxes were totally segregated by race in Delaware. There were 69 Black schools by 1910 in the state, but they were almost all one-room shacks of inadequate construction and poor sanitation. Even with tax rates two to three times that for whites, so many Blacks were tenant farmers and migrants without significant real property to tax that Blacks lacked the resources to bond themselves for school construction. The state helped little. Despite small state grants each legislative session for school operations, there was still no regular state support for Black school construction in 1918.[v]

The 1910s was a time of reform in Delaware, however, as in other states. In 1917, the governor appointed an educational commission to review needed school laws, and it hired Abraham Flexner of New York, who wrote a devastating survey of the Delaware schools. [vi] During the next four years, there was a monumental battle over reform of the school code, some provisions of which originated in the 1790s. The result was one of the most modern state school systems in the nation by 1921. In the midst of this upheaval was the super capitalist, Pierre S. du Pont. He and the two organizations he founded served as the financial and organizational backbone of the reform effort.

In order to coordinate the social reform efforts that seemed to be faltering at the end of the World War, du Pont met with friends and business associates in July, 1918, to form the Service Citizens of Delaware, Inc. He pledged $1,500,000 for a trust fund that would yield $90,000 for seven years. [vii] Through his hand-picked agents, du Pont used the Service Citizens to promote specific reforms. As the savior of the Du Pont Company and of General Motors, Pierre du Pont had the organizational experience necessary to bring about desired ends. During the next nine years, the Service Citizens employed constant propaganda and lobbying to secure an entirely reformed school code, a centralized state school system, improved school attendance, and the adoption of new school construction standards. In destroying the county system, the 1921 school code gave the state complete responsibility for the 368 Black and white schools outside the 14 special (town) districts. With newly-gained centralization, educational reform could be guided from the top.

The most far-reaching change in the school law of 1921 was the provision for a statewide revenue and budget system. This law was not a reform but a revolution in school support. [viii] As of 1921, the vast majority of school funds raised in Delaware became state rather than local appropriations, an extreme reversal from 1919 when the state provided only 20 percent of total school funds. For Black education, the rewards were enormous. Even though the 1921 law reiterated legal separation of schools by race, state funds were meant to be color-blind. [ix]

Though there were far more funds available for education after the new school codes had been passed, Delawareans were unclear as to the best use of that money. From 1918 through 1921, Pierre du Pont sought to fill the information gap. He funded five surveys about Delaware schools, which were completed by nationally-known experts and were rapidly published and distributed throughout the state and nation by the Service Citizens.

The message of the reports was clear: Delaware's schools were a disgrace to its citizens. Using a 1,000 point "scientific measuring system," the Columbia University team visited all Delaware schools during July 1919. The results were shocking. Only eight of the almost 400 schoolhouses of both races outside Wilmington attained the 500 point minimum which educational surveyors deemed worthy of renovation. Rarely had the buildings been constructed by those familiar with rudimentary principles of sanitation, safety, and comfort. Outdoor toilets were often located near wells, and sometimes within ten feet of a schoolhouse window, blackboards were often missing, as were lamps, globes and even textbooks, sites were often on swampy lands, 40 to 50 pupils were sometimes packed into shacks designed for 20, and m aintenance funds sometimes did not exist. It was no wonder that most of Delaware' s children outside Wilmington attended school only three to four months annually. [x]

The surveys levied the most devastating i ndictment against the Black schools. All should be abandoned. The legacy of state neglect of school construction and maintenance had caught up with Delaware. [xi] Pierre du Pont, belie ver in modern school buildings as the key to a skilled, m oral, and responsible citizenry, rebuilt all but four non-Wilmington Black schools between 1920 and 1924 without public funds. Du Pont incorporated the Delaware School A uxiliary Association (D SAA) in June, 1919, with a $2,000,000 construction fund which eventu ally totaled $3,819,000 after five supplemental donations. [xii] Unlike the trust fund for the Service Citizen s, the principal was to be spent along wi th the interest.

Pierre du Pont intended to assist Black s as well as whites in p roportion to Delaware' s population. Therefore, he earmarked twenty percen t of the original fund, or $400,000, for the Black schools. The Colum bia University reports dem onstrated the need for more assistance at once, however, so du P ont wrote the Auxiliar y trustees that the Black schoo ls were in the "greatest need of reconstruction" and could not await a slow building process. He believe d that Delaware' s Black population had already waited too long for good school buildings, and stated that we should have "called attention to our defects" so that "we would not now be c onfronted with a condition that should bring shame to all of us who have had in our power to secure better things for our State." Therefore, he announced an additio nal $500,000 gift for the sole use of Black school construction, and appointed a board of m anagers to oversee a survey of t he Black school population and to review and se lect school plans and sites. [xiii]

Mr. du Pont hired another team from Rockefeller' s General Education Board to report how best to us e his School Auxiliary co nstruction funds. The team made several suggestions. First, the s mall schools s hould be consolidated "wherever possible," although these consolidations should be "near enough to the children for them to walk to and from school." Such a conclusion preclud ed many consolidations. Schools m ust be neither too cheaply built nor t oo elaborate, for the long-term maintenance cost m ight be so burdensom e as to lessen public funds availa ble for instruction. Schools were to serve other than the basic three R' s function, with adequate acreage for playgrounds and a building suitable for use as a social center for comm unity meetings. There should be a Black high school for each county to perm it equal access to secondary educatio n by Black students. As for immediate action, the report stated that "a complete survey be made of the child ren in the dis trict to be served" so that the location of each new sch ool could be determ ined. [xiv]

During early 1920, the County Superintende nts paid surveyors to locate Black homes, so as to place new school s near enough children so that they could walk to them. The Auxilia ry then worked quick ly to gain the best possible locations wh ile safeguarding public control of decisions. The procedur e for constructing Black rural schools included a relatively smooth cooperative agreement between the DSAA and the County and State school authorities. First, the County Board of Education requested that the DSAA help them construct a particular school. The Auxiliary then sent an engineer to locate a suitable site. The engineer submitted the proposed site and topographical survey to the State Board of Education. After the State Board approved the site, the Auxiliary secured site options. Then the Auxiliary architect James Betelle of Newark, New Jersey, made the plans which were approved by the State Board. The Du Pont Engineering Company or another firm built the school, and title was given to the State Board upon completion.[xv] By the end of 1921, the Auxiliary completed twenty-one Black schools, and had 50 under construction or planned.

Since the Auxiliary committed such large funds and energy to the necessary task of rebuilding all Black schools, early DSAA expenditures for white schools lagged far behind. The Auxiliary's apparent favoritism toward Blacks created tension between the races of which the DSAA's leadership was aware. For instance, the DSAA and the State Board had to be careful to build both white and Black schools in a particular area. The Auxiliary postponed a Black school in Seaford, because the State Board noted that there was no immediate prospect of a new white school being constructed there. [xvi]

Sometimes open hostility erupted against Black school sites. Perhaps the nastiest controversy was over four acres bought in 1920 for the Caesar Rodney consolidated Black school. Although the local school board and the State Board approved the site, the State Board twice retracted their approval because of white opposition. [xvii] White dislike of the Auxiliary for aiding Blacks was so intense that it endangered the entire reform effort. As DSAA Director Odell wrote du Pont's personal secretary, "There is a very prevalent feeling that we have already spent too much on colored schools." The feeling was especially sharp where white schools had not been built. Odell stated his fear "because it might end in a form of race hatred from which Delaware has been completely free in the past."[xviii] Odell was overly sanguine about Delaware's past, but his concerns were valid. Black schools had been burned in Delaware before by whites, and it could happen again.

There were other problems for the Auxiliary's school construction campaign. The horrible inflation of 1919 and 1920 followed by a severe business depression and high construction costs all threatened the Auxiliary's plan for rebuilding the entire Black school system. At $16,000 per room, the earliest four Black schools were very expensive. [xix] If there was a culprit, it was du Pont himself, for he had instructed his architect to take no shortcuts. However, du Pont realized that costs had to be reduced if all Black schools were to be rebuilt. Therefore, school plans were standardized and certain "frills" deleted from future schools, such as art and manual training rooms. Auxiliary-built schools after 1920 averaged a more reasonable $6,000 to $7,000 per room.[xx] The Black school construction program was virtually completed by January of 1923. Eighty schools with 148 rooms had been built at a cost of $1,025,000. Only seven schools remained to be finished. [xxi]

Probably no other foundation or fund secu red the rapid results and high-quality construction of the DSAA, not even the huge Rosenwald Foundation. [xxii] The Auxiliary's buildings used standardized pl ans, professional architects and engineers, and the most modern equipm ent available. The DSAA Black schools were solid structures expected to last forty years. They were therefore ve ry expensive for their type. Spending about $7,000 per room on mostly fram e dwellings (i ncluding sites, architect' s fees and equipment) was far above that spent else where in the South for Black schools.

The price paid for the Auxilia ry' s efficiency was that local Black parents had little influence on the location or co nstruction of their new school. [xxiii] The DSAA placed schools where their surveys told them  the most children lived within  a certain radius. Despite the lack of Black citizen control over school sites, the many thankful letters from Delaware' s Black people and testimonial di nners given to Pierre du Pont provide evidence that the Black population  was most grateful for his gifts. [xxiv]

The school surveys of 1918 and 1919 not only em phasized the need for new school build ings, but the need for consolid ation of one-ro om schools into m ulti-room, graded buildings. In fact, though, little consolidation of Bl ack rural schools took place in Delaware. Too few Black ch ildren were loca ted in sufficiently large clusters to make consolidation possible in m any districts. Another report f unded by du P ont contained an econom ic argument against effective school c onsolidation. Care m ust be taken not to disturb the distribution of the colored people,  stated the report, because "Delaware is singularly dependent on colored farm labor." Large, consolidated schools would tend to concentrate the colored population of th e state in a relatively few centers. [xxv] Population redistribution would be to the "econom ic disadvantage of the Negroes them selves" as well as to the whole state. Therefore, Bl ack schools should be consolidated only when they would be "within ready walking dist ance of the school children." Restricting consolidations to "neighborhood schools" as  a policy made effective consolidations impossible for Delaware' s black population.

Of the 81 Black schools built by 192 3, 44 were one-room  and 25 were two-room buildings. Only seven schools were consolid ated, multi-graded buildin gs: 6 five-room schools, and the seven-room  Booker T. Washington School in Dover. T he latter was the only Black school constructed with an audito rium, and at a cost of $84,749, was the most ambitious of all Black schools bu ilt by the DSAA outside of Wilmington. [xxvi] The Auxiliary generally m anaged only to repl ace the old poorly-constructed Black one-room schools with well-constructed one and two -room schoolhouses. The new schools were far superior to the old ones, with new wells , indoor toilets, dry grounds, large windows, and adequate equipm ent, lighting, and playgr ounds. The new schools w ere also nearer to the students' present homes. However, without transportation fo r elementary children, which du Pont and the State ignored, there coul d be no effective cons olidation outside of the special town districts. For all his generous gifts, totaling $1,166,000 by 1924 and $1,000,000 more for five schools in W ilmington, including a new Howard High School building, du Pont did not achieve signifi cant consolidation of rural Black schools. [xxvii]

Du Pont's philanthropy also attempted little assistance to Black secondary education outside of Wilmington, except for Delaware State College. The General Education Board team of 1919 had suggested that there was "an increasing demand among colored pupils for junior and senior high school opportunities" and it was only "just that such opportunities be provided according to the need." Therefore, they suggested that there be "at least two or three junior and senior high school centers in Sussex County," and "one or more in Kent and New Castle counties." [xxviii] Unfortunately, of the six suggestions from this report, only the secondary school expansion proposed above was disregarded. The Auxiliary Trustees agreed to support just "one colored high school for the entire state . . . located in Dover," until such time as the "educational aspirations of the colored people enlarge." Despite some gains in the number of Black secondary school students, such education remained as inaccessible to rural Blacks in 1930 as in 1918.[xxix]

One needs to remember, though, that du Pont was not primarily concerned with Black education. He moved rapidly to build schools for Blacks so that whites would rebuild their own schools. As he admitted later, the Auxiliary's function was to cajole whites into matching his gifts with increased school taxes and bonding to reconstruct the entire Delaware school system. Unfortunately for du Pont's good intentions, Delawareans were quite suspicious toward a private agency such as the Auxiliary which was not politically accountable to them. Therefore, as du Pont admitted, "We tried another tack." He offered to rebuild all Black schools so that whites, "Not wanting their children to attend poorer schools than the Negroes, immediately became interested in education." If persuasion through guilt would not work, as presented in the surveys, then perhaps embarrassment might. Whites would hate admitting that black schools were superior to their own.[xxx] Above all, by constructing all Black schools himself, du Pont believed that he had stolen one of the most pervasive arguments whites had against using public monies for schools: That white money would be used for Black children.

Pierre du Pont also realized the needs of tiny Delaware State College, founded in 1891.[xxxi] Delaware State needed help in every facet and du Pont provided $102,000 and other assistance in an altruistic but directive manner. Although blessed with 200 acres of good farm land, the institution had never received substantial aid from the state and remained dependent on federal funds from the two Morrill Acts and the Smith-Hughes vocational education act. The Delaware State Trustees asked for du Pont's assistance through his Auxiliary. Characteristically, du Pont insisted upon a complete inventory of assets and liabilities before he would commit himself. Two experts from Columbia University surveyed the College in 1919. Their report was harsh. It said that all structures desperately needed renovation if the institution was to serve an academic function, since the College had "not a single building on the grounds that could possibly be classified as a school building." For example, the original farm mansion was used as a recreation hall, boy's dorm, dining room, and kitchen. The building was so dangerous that it "should be torn down." The curriculum was also deficient, for it failed to provide a practical trade, prepare for college, or train teachers well. Even the farm was not in good repair.[xxxii]

President Jason of Delaware State College echoed the Strayer report's gloomy message. He wrote a pathetic note to H. Rodney Sharp, a DSAA Trustee and du Pont confidante, that he was "very near the situation here . . . . No one else can know so well or feel more keenly the burden of constantly increasing demands with inadequate resources and worn out equipment." Jason described leaky roofs, flooded cellars, drafty buildings, dangerous stairways, overcrowded classrooms, and a lack of proper sewage disposal or fire equipment.[xxxiii]

The report suggested that the school plant should be totally renewed. The top priority was a new classroom building with auditorium, gymnasium, and laboratories, followed by two new dormitories, industrial arts building, farm buildings, elementary school for teacher training, and modern equipment for all facilities. Also, the College needed an upgraded curriculum, a good accounting system, and agricultural research useful to Delaware's farmers. Pierre du Pont eventually fulfilled most of the report's suggestions. However, he was most concerned with the immediate safety and administrative operation of the school. In 1920, the Auxiliary took action: it hired a part-time accountant to keep the books, and asked engineers from the Delaware Safety Council to inspect the College for safety and sanitation conditions. Both actions uncovered a dangerous situation that demanded immediate attention.

A committee from the Trustees of the Service Citizens made an inventory of the College's assets so that proper accounting procedures could be instituted. By September 1920, the Auxiliary paid for a part-time bookkeeper to keep the accounts. The modern accounting system made all the more obvious in concrete terms the desperate plight of the College. Philanthropists and state authorities alike could more clearly comprehend the College's needs. However, the total lack of fire and safety standards threatened the immediate physical existence of the institution. The 55 page report of the Delaware Safety Council found "very defective" heater and stove installations, "greatly overfused" lighting systems, hazardous chemicals such as phosphorus stored on an open newspaper-covered wood shelf, oil-soaked rags strewn about and farm buildings with wood-shingled roofs that lacked fire escapes or fire extinguishers. Even common sense housekeeping procedures often did not exist. Students from the boys' dormitory disposed of ashes by throwing them from windows.

The crowded conditions exacerbated the situation. Boys slept in the same building with the laboratory, kitchen, bakery, dining room, and classrooms. The girls' dormitory contained the printing press which was powered by a gasoline engine in the basement. All water came from one uncovered well. Toilets were outside, and the sewage collected in cesspools within a few yards of the dormitories. The conditions were intolerable.[xxxiv]

The College's trustees passed at once a resolution authorizing the DSAA to "do whatever is possible to carry out these recommendations."[xxxv] The Auxiliary quickly authorized $57,889 to complete the minimum alterations necessary to put the buildings in a safe condition, including new floors, plaster, toilets, hot water heaters, pumps, fire escapes, and interior painting, along with new water and sewer systems. The DSAA also constructed a new two-room elementary school building to allow a teacher-training program to exist, and a new spartan manual-arts building. [xxxvi]

Delaware State' s assets doubled in four years due almost entirely to the direct aid of P. S. du Pont. The College' s Trustees now tried to convince du Pont and his Auxiliary to head a drive for $1,500,000 to complete a twenty-three building plan. The D SAA refused because there were only 293 Black students attending eight h grade in 1924-25 outside Wilmington, and there seem ed to be no justification for expanding the secondary school function of the College with few potential students. [xxxvii]

Still, the College grew f rom 62 students in 1919 to 174 students in 1926, eighty percent of whom were above eighth grad e, and ten of whom were norm al school students. [xxxviii] Du Pont and his cohort decided that the state m ust increase its support if the College was to grow further. After Auxiliary representatives visited the legislature, the College received state capital appropr iations for a new, la rge $125,000 manual arts training building for 1928. The Auxiliary ag reed to provide an additional $60,000 to pay for the site, architect' s fees, and equipm ent. [xxxix] The next legislature continued the capital improvements, building a new barn and teacher' s cottage. The Auxiliary campaign to gain state aid for Delaware St ate College was successf ul. The school was now a solid vocational secondary school , with the beginnings of a college.

As important as new school buildings we re, they were useless if children did not attend them. In 1915, both white and Black rural attendance was scandalously low. Average daily attendance outside Wilm ington was below 90 days annually. [xl] During the 1920s, du Pont assisted the "attendance campaign" by supporting numerous awards for high attendance. He also gave financial a nd organizational assistan ce to parent-teacher organizations so that parents would be informed about education and support their schools by ensuring that th eir child attends daily.

Du Pont also commissioned detailed atte ndance studies for each race to explain the poor attendance and suggest improvem ents. [xli] The major thesis of the studies was that low attendance closely rela ted to school failure, especial ly for rural white and Black students. The statistics belied equal e ducational opportunity, as over 38 percent of Delaware' s Black students failed to be promoted each year; m ore Black first graders failed than were prom oted to second grade; 50 percent of all Black pupils enrolled in 1920-21 were in grades one and two, and only six percent of total Black enrollm ent was above grade six. Delaware' s Black students were, on average, two years behind grade level by third grade.

Why did Black pupils m iss so much school? Non-attendance was caused by students working as farm or domestic laborers, and by parental indifference, distance from school, illn ess, frequent transfers, and failure to enro ll for the entire school year.

Rural children were expected by their parents to work whenever the various grain, fruit, and vegetable harvests occurred. Since m uch of the work began in May and continued into September, rural children were slow to enter school and quick to leave. Illness was severe in January and F ebruary, and distance from school was a form idable obstacle to regular attendance.[xlii]

The answer to parental indifference wa s strict enforcem ent of the compulsory attendance laws, said the report, although th e state legislature had abolished state attendance officers in 1921. Therefore, du Pont funded visiting teachers in each cou nty under state board control to assist rural schools.[xliii] The combination of state guid ance, increased utility of rural educ ation, and better school build ings helped to raise school attendance rapidly. By 1930, rural Black youth averaged 144 days of daily attendance a year, a 100 per cent increase in fifteen years.[xliv]

Delaware' s financial po sition improved during the 1920s as much as the school attendance figures. The 1921 school code assigned several lucrative st ate taxes solely to education, with the result that the School Fund soon had a larg e surplus. Even so, the state tax office was not well-run. When the governor appointed du Pont as State Tax Commissioner in 1925, m atters improved further. Du Pont quickly m ade the operation more efficient, and enforced tax laws pr eviously ignored. Sc hool tax collections increased at a rapid pace. Du Pont' s tax collecting ability meant tha t there was plenty of state money for the operation of schools for both races. Conditions fo r black teachers improved because state funds were available f or equalization of sala ries and supplies. Even in the depths of the De pression, Delaware had an exte nsive surplus in the School Fund.[xlv]

By 1930, Delaware public education was supe rior to that of a decade before in almost all the concrete m easurements of educational quality used by refor mers. Black youth were now located in schools that were light, warm, airy, sanitary, and rarely crowded. Furtherm ore, the state taxes were so productive that De laware was virtually able to complete the school rebuilding program during the 1930s . Partly as a result of lush tax revenues, teachers' salaries almost equalized between the races by 1930. Whereas Black teachers received on the average only 55 percent of the salary of white teachers in 1917-1918, Black teach ers outside Wilmington were just 10 percent behind white colleagues by 1929-1930. In W ilmington, Black public school teachers actually out earned white teachers.[xlvi]

In terms of equal educational opport unity, du Pont' s efforts increased the likelihood that a Black youth would com plete enough grades to becom e a literate individual in a school that was safe. What he was not able to do wa s to increase significantly either the num ber of consolidated Black sc hools or the opportunity for secondary education among Black youth in th e downstate areas where m ost of them lived. In effect, three-quarters of the Bl ack youth were consigned to more comfortable standard one-room 720 square foot boxes designed for forty pupils to replace the unsafe, inexpensive sm aller boxes which had housed them before.

One charge frequently leveled at ph ilanthropy is that it creates dependence upon outside sources of power and funds which retards the ability and desire of citizen s to govern themselves responsibly. As William Heard Kilpatrick of Teachers College, Columbia wrote to the Director of the Service Citizens: "an organization such as that of the Service Citizens . . . may indeed do a distinct harm to accustom the people to have things done for them which they should do for themselves."[xlvii] In white education, the above assertion had little appl ication to Delaware. Whites paid substantial taxes to support their new schools by 1930, by which tim e du Pont's gifts had virtually ended. Black education, however, was dependent upon philanthropy for i mprovements during the 1920s. Du Pont built almost the entire Black school sys tem in Delaware. He asked nothing from white residents except to maintain the completed structures, a task which they failed to do. Even before 1930, du Pont complained to state authorities that Auxiliary-built schools were not being m aintained properly.[xlviii] White Delawareans were grudgingly thankful that the B lack schools cost them nothing, but there seemed to be no improvement in the white attitude toward black education. If anythi ng, the reality that Blacks often had better buildings than the whites was a source of white enm ity, not contentment. In giving Delaware almost 90 Black schools, du Pont m ade more viable the wholly segregated school system s without forcing whites to take responsibility for complete equality of those system s.

Despite the unfortunate consequences for long-term integration, du Pont's contributions gave Delaware's Blacks hope for the future. He insured the rights of the Black minority to decent schooling in viable st ructures. Since the first integrated public school in the state did not take place until 1952 and no national foundation was interested in massive assistance to Delaware, there is probably no way that Blacks could have realized anything close to equality in school facilities witho ut the gifts and guidance of Pierre S. du Pont.

[i] Harold Livesay, "Delaware Blacks, 1865-1915," in Carol E. Hoffecker, ed., *Readings in Delaware History* (Newark, Del., 1973), and Stephen B. Weeks, *A History of Public School Education in Delaware*, U.S. Bureau of Education Bulletin 1917, no. 18 (Washington, 1917).

[ii] Robert J. Taggart, *Private Philanthropy and Public Education, Pierre S. du Pont and the Delaware Schools, 1890-1940* (Newark, Del., 1988).

[iii] Weeks, *History of Public School Education in Delaware.*

[iv] George D. Strayer and others, *General Report on School Buildings and Grounds in Delaware* (Wilmington, Del., 1919).

[v] Martin M. Daugherty, *Studies in Taxation; Financing Education in Delaware* (Newark, Del., 1932).

[vi] Abraham Flexner and Frank P. Bachman, *Public Education in Delaware* (New York, 1918).

[vii] P.S. du Pont to Finance Committee, Service Citizen s of Delaware, 8 August 1918, The Longwood Manuscripts, File 688-10, Hagley Museum and Library, Wilmington, Delaware (hereafter HML).

[viii] Delaware, *Laws*, XXXII, 1921, Title 11.

[ix] Daugherty, *Studies in Taxation*, p. 34.

[x] Strayer and others, *General Report*, and G. D. Strayer and others, *Report and Recommendations on Certain School Buildings of Delaware* (Wilmington, Del., 1919).

<sup>xi</sup> The Black school site survey was completed by a General Education Board team led by Frank Bachman, and announced in the Nov. 7, 1919 Wilmington *Evening Journal*. The full report was given at Dover's Black school on Nov. 14, 1919.

<sup>xii</sup>Service Citizens of Delaware, *The Wealth and Commonwealth of Delaware* (Wilmington, Del., 1924).

<sup>xiii</sup> P.S. du Pont to the Trustees of the Delaware School Auxiliary Association, 8 Oct. 1919, File 712-5, HML.

<sup>xiv</sup> George D. Strayer, *Possible Consolidations of Rural Schools of Delaware*, (Wilmington, Del., 1919).

<sup>xv</sup>Untitled Resolutions, File 712-32, HML.

<sup>xvi</sup> "Report of President to Delaware School Auxiliary Association," 13 April 1921, File 712-19, Box 2, HML.

<sup>xvii</sup> P.S. du Pont to George B. Miller, on behalf of the State Board of Education, 19 March 1920, File 712-19, Box 2, HML.

<sup>xviii</sup> Joseph H. Odell to F. A. McHugh, 8 June 1923, File 712-30, HML.

<sup>xix</sup> The Hockessin one-room school cost an exorbitant $21,000 to build, partially due to its brick construction. Ironically, the Hockessin school served as the basis for a Delaware case sent to the U.S. Supreme Court in 1952 which became incorporated into the landmark *Brown vs. Board of Education, Topeka* case of 1954.

<sup>xx</sup> State of Delaware, *Annual Report of the Department of Public Instruction*, Year Ending June 30, 1938 (Dover, Del., 1938), pp. 45-47.

<sup>xxi</sup> "Report of the President to the Delaware School Auxiliary Association," 1 January 1923, File 712-19, Box 3, HML.

<sup>xxii</sup> The Julius Rosenwald Foundation began in 1912, and helped in the construction of 4,400 Black public schools throughout the South by 1929. See Ullin W. Leavell, *Philanthropy in Negro Education* (1930 reprint; Westport, Conn., 1970).

<sup>xxiii</sup> The DSAA held local meetings for each race to obtain a consensus as to the most suitable site. However, if that site proved too expensive, the Auxiliary bought another site instead.

<sup>xxiv</sup> The testimonial dinner held at the Hotel du Pont in 1924 was the largest gathering held in honor of P.S. du Pont. Blacks also held a dinner for du Pont at Dover's new Booker T. Washington school, du Pont's largest gift up to that time for the Black population.

<sup>xxv</sup> School Site Report, File 712-17, HML.

<sup>xxvi</sup> "Colored Schools Erected to Date," 6 November 1923, File 712-19, Box 3, HML.

<sup>xxvii</sup>Service Citizens of Delaware, *What Do You Know About the Public Schools of Delaware?* (Wilmington, Del., 1924), pp. 16-18. P.S. du Pont eventually built 87 Black schools at a cost of $2,622,751.49. Jeanette Eckman, *Delaware, A Guide to the First State* (New York, 1938), p. 118.

<sup>xxviii</sup> "Report on Pierre S. du Pont Gift to Negro Schools," General Education Board, File 712-19, HML.

<sup>xxix</sup> "Consolidation of Schools for Colored Children," File 712-28, HML.

<sup>xxx</sup> Interview of Drew Pearson with P.S. du Pont, 31 August 1924, File 834, HML.

<sup>xxxi</sup> Bradley Skelcher, *Delaware State University* (Charleston, S.C., 2000).

<sup>xxxii</sup> *A Confidential Report on the State College for Colored Students*, submitted by G. D. Strayer and N. L. Englehart (September 1919), File 712-30, HML.

<sup>xxxiii</sup> W. C. Jason to H. R. Sharp, 12 April 1920, File 712-30, HML.

<sup>xxxiv</sup> "Report of Fire Protection and Exits, Safety, and Sanitation." State College for Colored Students (Dover, Del.), 6 October 1920, File 712-30, HML.

<sup>xxxv</sup> "Estimate of the Cost of Improvements at State College for Colored Students," authorized by J. H. Odell, November 1919, File 712-30, HML.

<sup>xxxvi</sup> F. A. McHugh to J. M. Odell, 5 June 1923; Mary G. Hunter to F. A. McHugh, 25 June 1923, File 712-30, Box 1, HML.

<sup>xxxvii</sup> McHugh to John Hutton, 8 September 1925, File 712-30, Box 2, HML; *Annual Report of the Department of Public Instruction*, 1925 (Dover, 1925), p. 192.

<sup>xxxviii</sup> "Information Concerning the State College for Colored Students," 1927, File 712-30, Box 1, HML.

<sup>xxxix</sup> State appropriations rose in the coming years, reaching $44,255 for current operations and $150,000 for capital appropriations in 1931. The legislature approved little else for capital appropriations until 1949

for the College. See Walter J. Satneck, "The History of the Origins and Development of the Delaware State College and Its Role in Higher Education for Negroes," Ed. D. diss., New York University, 1962, pp. 199-200.

[xl]Flexner and Bachman, *Public Education in Delaware*, pp. 65-69.

[xli] Richard W. Cooper and Hermann Cooper, *Negro School Attendance in Delaware* (Newark, Del., 1923), and R. W. Cooper and H. Cooper, *The One-Teacher School in Delaware* (Newark, Del., 1925).

[xlii] Cooper and Cooper, *Negro School Attendance in Delaware*, pp. 131, 288-89.

[xliii]Service Citizens of Delaware, *The Development of Delaware* (Wilmington, Del. 1925), pp. 37, 41-43.

[xliv] *The Annual Report of the Department of Public Instruction, State of Delaware, 1929-1930* (Dover, Del., 1930), p. 267.

[xlv] *The Annual Report of the Department of Public Instruction, State of Delaware, 1936-1937* (Dover., Del., 1937), p. 39.

[xlvi] *The Annual Report of the Delaware State Board of Education, 1917-18 and 1918-19* (Dover, Del., 1919), p. 74, and *The Annual Report of the Department of Public Instruction, 1929-1930*, p. 21.

[xlvii] W. H. Kilpatrick to J. H. Odell, 27 January 1922, File 688, Box 1, HML.

[xlviii] P. S. du Pont to State Board of Education, 22 January 1927, File 712-17, HML.

# Chapter 2
## *Brown v. Board of Education* Cases

# **Delaware**

## Challenging a Nation: Teen Contends with Segregation
Ricky Espinoza

In 1952, Ethel Louise Belton decided traveling about 50 minutes to and from school was pointless when there was a school a mile and a half away. There was only one problem: the 17-year-old was black. All-white Claymont High School was closer to home, had better facilities and teachers with higher education and offered a better variety of classes.

Belton attended the all-black Howard High School nine miles away. It was overcrowded with students forced to go to the school because of their race. At Claymont each teacher carried a teaching load of 149 students, while at Howard the teaching load was 178.

To make things worse, Belton was born with six holes in her heart, which made walking to the nearest bus stop a daily struggle. Her subsequent case, *Belton v. Gebhart*, was the fifth of five similar cases from around the nation grouped under one now-familiar name: Brown *v. Board of Education*, which sought to integrate public schools in Topeka, Kansas. The combined cases 49 years ago ended segregation in the nation's schools.

"I look at my mother as a civil rights leader," kinesiology instructor Andreia Brown said. "This case opened doors for everyone with color and disabilities."

The case hinged on the philosophy of offering separate but equal education. The Supreme Court decided May 17, 1954, that separate but equal in educational facilities meant inherently unequal.

In 1981, Belton died at age 44, leaving behind three children and a husband. "We are very, very proud to be a part of history like this," Brown said. "I think she would be very proud I am teaching at a school that is very diverse. It's something she had never seen in her time, something unheard of at the time," Brown said. "I wish it had been the same for my mother that they respected individual differences, but they didn't"

Brown's mother was very disabled. "I never wanted to live her type of lifestyle. I wanted everyone I love around me to be healthy. I live what I teach," she said.

When Belton passed away, Brown was given her mother's high school graduation ring. After graduation from high school, Brown's mother attended Delaware State University and later taught business at a junior college.

For Brown, her mother's accomplishment in high school will always stand out. "How many people keep their high school rings this long? It will be 50 years ago next year," Brown said.

When Brown returns to her m other' s hometown, people recognize the ring on her finger. "They keep it alive. Delaware is pr oud they were represen ted in that case," she said. Along with the p eople of W ilmington, Br own' s father, William, is just as proud of his wife' s accomplishments. "It was really funny. My father was my mother' s boyfriend. When she would com e on TV, he would say, ' That' s my girlfriend,' and people wouldn' t believe him ," she said.

"In a way, it made us stronger people. We are very much for human rights," Brown said. "I have a lot of my mother in me," she said. "I certainly know I have the compassion for people that I know m y mother has. I think that' s what' s great about teaching here."

Reprinted with perm ission from *The Ranger* (San Antonio College Journalism / Photography Departm ent), 2002. http://www.fou rthwrite.theranger.org/brown/

## "With All Deliberate Speed":
## The *Evans v. Buchanan* Case and Educational Desegregation in Delaware
### Samuel B. Hoff

### INTRODUCTION

Desegregation in education is an immensely important issue, of which Delaware has been a major participant, for better and for worse. This essay traces historical trends in African American education in the state; summarizes the *Evans v. Buchanan* case—which began in 1956 and stayed alive in one form or another until 1990, a thirty-four year odyssey—and examines the ramifications of of desegregation efforts in Delaware for the education system in particular and for the citizenry in general.

### BACKGROUND OF DELAWARE SCHOOLS

We can note that a half-century ensued between the first public school education in Delaware, formally established in 1829 for those of Caucasian background, and initial state government support for the education of minorities. This fact epitomizes the disparity in education between the races that Delaware has wrestled with throughout its existence.

In 1866, the Delaware Association for the Moral Improvement and Education of Colored People was founded. This organization created thirty-two schools for black students in the next decade. In 1875, the Delaware legislature passed a law to tax black citizens for support of their own schools. However, that move was reversed by general funding for colored schools in 1881.

The momentum for minority education in Delaware would not last long. In its 1896 ruling in *Plessy v. Ferguson*, the U.S. Supreme Court declared that the "separate but equal doctrine" satisfied the constitutional requirements of the equal protection clause of the 14<sup>th</sup> Amendment. Though that case dealt with transportation facilities, most states interpreted it broadly as encompassing all public accommodations. Just a year after the *Plessy v. Ferguson* decision, Delaware's new constitution instituted a segregated public school system.

The effect of separate education for the races in Delaware was evident. Between 1910 and 1920, those schools for whites received ten times the amount of state funding as those for colored students. Across a similar period, studies found that Caucasian students attended school three months longer on average than minority children. Finally, literacy rates among white students exceeded those of black students by twenty percent.

An investigation of Negro school ab sences in Delaware between 1919 and 1921 uncovered additional consequences of segregated education facilities. Illness was found to be the leadi ng reason for missing school, which was undoubtedly caused by the dearth of properl y constructed school houses, lack of ample playgrounds, and inadequate in struction on health issues.

In 1921, the Delaware General Assem bly passed a law requiring the State Board of Education to maintain separate schools for those of color, which were supposed to be uniform and equally effec tive as those for whites. However, the only high school for Negro students s upported by the state between 1912-1935 was at the State College for Colored Students in Dover. W hat the state government was unwilling to do, ph ilanthropist Pierre du Pont accomplished. He furnished $2.6 million for the construction of eighty-six school buildings for Negro pupils. Still, about a third were single-teacher schools, and none outside Wilmington offered a high school education.

There remained m any differences in education am ong the races in Delaware. A 1943 study by Geor ge Miller, referred to as "Adolescent Negro Education in Delaware," made the follo wing conclusions about the inequity of education facilities:

(1) Secondary schools for Negroes lack uniformity in organization as far as grade coverage;
(2) Progress toward better schools for blacks has been impeded by public attitudes, which reject equality and favor continuing segregation;
(3) School failures among colored students are cause d by shortcomings with teaching and curricula. The salaries for black teachers are inordin ately low com pared to those of Caucasian instructors;
(4) Health and work reasons are still among the top reasons why black students quit school;
(5) Extracurricular activities together with physical education and health classes are in need of rejuvenation;
(6) Except for Smyrna, the guidance services for black students are "pitifully in adequate."

The latter report concluded that Delawa re' s 1921 law requiring uniform and equal schools between the r aces had not been reached.

We do see that the Sup reme Court of the United States starts chipp ing away at *Plessy v. Ferguson*, and in doing so segregation as it relates to education. In 1938, the Court invalidated Missouri' s out-of-state tuition program for African American students. Twelve years la ter, the Supreme Court in validated segregation in graduate schools across the U. S. In that same year, it invalidated segrega tion in law schoo ls in the *Sweatt v. Painter* decision.

Evidently taking their cue from the federal judiciary, Delaware took a number of steps toward desegregating schools at the outset of the 1950s. For example, in 1950 the Delaware Chancellory Court ordered the elimination of all restrictions for black enrollment at the University of Delaware. Two years later, Delaware's Catholic parochial school system started to integrate. In its 1952 decisions in *Belton v. Gebhart* and *Bulah v. Gebhart*, the Delaware Chancellory Court ruled that the state's segregated schools for those of color were not equal to white schools. These cases were later incorporated into the U.S. Supreme Court's 1954 *Brown v. Board of Education* decision, which unanimously declared that the separate but equal concept was unconstitutional.

Subsequently, the Brown *v. Board of Education II* decision in 1955 affirmed the first *Brown* ruling and ordered that schools be desegregated "with all deliberate speed." There are many comparisons between *Brown v. Board of Education I* and *Brown II*. *Brown I* was said to have moral clarity but perhaps not doctrinal foundation, whereas *Brown II*, in many scholars' views, lacked both. If the first *Brown* decision redefined the equal protection clause by finding that separate but equal was unconstitutional, then the *Brown II* decision sought to identify remedies to the separate facilities which were not equal. The Court in *Brown II* refused to furnish specific deadlines for action. Because of this and the financial costs of desegregating schools, many states ignored the ruling or found ways to delay implementation. Meanwhile, groups such as the National Association for the Advancement of Colored People (NAACP) pressed for immediate action.

In a series of *per curium* decisions between 1955 and 1958, the U.S. Supreme Court invalidated segregation at state parks, beaches, bathhouses, golf courses and public transportation. The Court revisited the *Brown II* decision in its 1958 *Cooper v. Aaron* ruling. In that case, the Supreme Court rejected attempts to postpone desegregation and rebuked governors and state legislators who claimed that they could basically ignore the supremacy clause of Article VI of the Constitution. We can observe that despite these moves, a 1964 study revealed that only 2 percent of formerly segregated school facilities had in fact desegregated ten years after the Brown rulings.

THE *EVANS V. BUCHANAN* CASE

It is in this political and legal environment that the *Evans v. Buchanan* case—the premier desegregation case in Delaware—began. Contrary to a 1955 text, which declared that Delaware was one of six states having good results with desegregation, the state actually chose a strategy of obstruction and delay. In 1956, the Claymont School District said they had no plans to desegregate schools. The State School Board of Education refused requests to mandate educational integration, so Louis Redding and his associates filed a class action suit. Originally titled *Evans v. Members of the State Board of Education*, the case was renamed *Evans v. Buchanan*. Evans was Brenda Evans, one of the five original plaintiffs; her name was cited because she was the first in alphabetical order. Buchanan was Madeline Buchanan, who at the time was the President of the State Board of Education. *Evans v. Buchanan* came to be seen as unique in the histo ry of American jurisprudence at the time because, unlike oth er states whose strategic efforts to desegregate w ere aimed at city or county school boards, Redding and his associates in Delaware chose to target the State Board of Education. *Evans v. Buchanan* began in Federal District Court with a judge denying a motion to dismiss the desegreg ation order. It proceeded for thirty-four y ears and about thirty different rulings, dem onstrating the plethora of tactic s its opponents undertook to derail school integration.

In 1957, the U.S. District Court granted a summary judgment to the plaintiffs—Evans and her colleagues—in s upport of desegregation and against the members of the State Board of Education. In that same year, the Clayton district appealed the latter decision to the 3rd Circuit of the U.S. Court of Appeals. The result of that was that again Evans and those supporting desegregation won, as the appeal was found not to be legally prosecuted by the le gal board in accordance with law. There was a consolida tion of the *Evans v. Buchanan* case with six other cases in July of 1957. A U.S. District Court ordered the State Board of Education and the state superintendent to subm it a desegregation plan within sixty days. That plan was supposed to provide for admittance, enrollm ent and education on a racially nondiscrim inatory basis to alleviate those problem s with segregated facilities previously m entioned.

Over the next year the State Board and the superintendent appealed the 1957 district court order. A 1958 U.S. Appeals Court ruling in the E vans case affirmed the 1957 district court ruling. Ho wever, what seem ed like a technical win turned out to be a practical loss fo r desegregation proponen ts, as the appeals body vacated the district court' s time line for the desegreg ation plan.

Returning to the U.S. Di strict Court as a result of a latter ruling—with the change of the district court chief judge from Judge Leahy to Layton—the District Court ruled in late 1958 that the state boa rd had submit a new desegregation plan within 112 days. But the Delaware Stat e Board of Education rejected that deadline, proposing instead a grade-by -grade desegregation plan to be implemented one year at a tim e. The U.S. District Court approved that twelve-year plan in 1959. That decision was appeal ed to the U.S. Court of Appeals in 1960, which affirmed the 1957 order and rej ected the grade-by-grade approach.

In 1961, the U.S. District Court approved with modification a State Board of Education plan that allowed black st udents desiring integration to transfer immediately to white or other integrated schools, and provided a plan for integration in the future. But that ruling was criticized as one-way deseg regation of those black students to m ajority white schools. In fact, it would be another seven years before the U.S. Supre me Court would de mand two-way desegregation and use a social engineering to ol to do so: mandatory busing.

*Evans v. Buchanan* took a different track in the year 1962, when nine black students sought to tran sfer from the all-black D unlieth School, administered by the Millside School District, to the in tegrated Rose Hill Elem entary School, under the jurisdiction of the Rose Hill Minqua dale School District. This case was represented by Leonard Williams, often called a protégée of Lewis Redding, along with Irving Morris and others. In the case, W illiams and his colleag ues used the equal protection law to argue that the Constitution compelled the state to provide integrated educati on. Later in 1962, the U.S. District Court did perm it the transfer of those child ren to the Rose Hill School, but likewise sta ted that the state did not have affir mative constitutional dut y to provide integrat ed education. So once again a techn ical victory became a practical loss. Following the District Court's ruling above, a nine-year hiatus occurred in the *Evans v. Buchanan* case.

In 1965, the Delaware State Board of Education adop ted a resolution which, over a five-year period, was to close a number of the smaller schools; that plan would lead to phasing out the last so called black school district. In 1968, the State of Delaware General Assembly pa ssed the Education Advancem ent Act. This act's most significant feature was its creation of twenty-six school districts around the state. But the act excluded W ilmington from any consolidation plan and therefore from any desegregation plan. It capped as its maximum enrollm ent any school district with 12,000 students ; Wilmington had 15,000 students in its school district.

It was at this time that a number of lawyers, including Lewis Redding and his colleagues, sought support from th e NAACP Legal Defense Fund. Redding contended that the exclusion of W ilmington from desegregation efforts m eant that in fact that there were separate but unequal facilities in the state of Delaware. According to Irving Morris, NAACP Legal Defense Fund Director Jack Greenberg denied the request based on a cost -benefit analysis. Evidently, he held that there was no chance of victory in *Evans v. Buchanan*. Consequently, Redding and his colleagues sought the support of Louis Lucas, a Memphis, Tennessee, attorney, to challenge Delaware ' s Educational Advancem ent Act.

In 1971, the aforementioned act was chal lenged in U.S. District Court, and out of the ashes came *Evans v. Buchanan*. Likewise in 1971, the U.S. Suprem e Court ruled in the *Swann v. Charlotte-Mecklenburg Board of Education* case that mandatory busing could be em ployed as a device to advance desegregation.

In a series of decisions over the next five years, the U.S. District Court ruled on the substance of the complaint of the newly retoo led *Evans v. Buchanan* case. However, the seminal decision re lating to desegregation in Delaware came in the 1976 *Evans v. Buchanan* ruling by the U.S. District Court. Unhappy with the exclusion of Wilmington from desegregation efforts, the Court proposed a plan with 10- to 35-percent minority student targets within eleven New Castle school districts and mandated interdistrict busing on a substantial scale as a remedy to existing racial separateness. The breadth of the busing plan—affecting a large metropolitan area—represented the first of its kind in the nation. Over the next four years, various federal courts rejected twelve separate attempts by the State of Delaware to delay, modify, or reverse the 1976 order.

In June 1980, the Delaware General Assembly passed a law relating to reorganization, taxation, and governance of public school systems in the area of the state subject to the 1976 desegregation order. In response, the State Board of Education created four school districts in New Castle County and petitioned the District Court to modify the 1976 ruling. A December 1980 ruling by the Delaware Supreme Court found the latter law to be consistent with the Delaware constitution. A 1981 U.S. District Court decision supported the four-district setup, which was opposed by the lawyers backing the plaintiffs in *Evans v. Buchanan*. In the final decision dealing with the *Evans v. Buchanan* case, the U.S. District Court denied a 1990 attempt by the Brandywine School District to deviate from previous court orders mandating desegregation.

Over the decade of the 1990s, several other actions occurred in Delaware dealing with school desegregation. Separate U.S. District Court rulings in 1990 and 1991 found that the Red Clay School District in New Castle County failed to comply with a 1978 desegregation order. However, two U.S. Supreme Court decisions in 1991 and 1992 relaxed desegregation requirements in other states. Delaware used those decisions to advocate for looser standards of desegregation. The tactic worked, as a U.S. District Court applied relaxed desegregation procedures to New Castle County in 1995. In affirming the 1995 ruling, the U.S. Court of Appeals released New Castle County from federal supervision over desegregation in Delaware's schools in 1996. This court specifically rejected claims by desegregation proponents that the gap in performance between black and white students was caused by the longstanding segregated school system in Delaware.

Finally, Delaware entered the twenty-first century by emphasizing school reform, including the acceptance of charter schools and stringent performance standards. The Neighborhood Schools Act, passed by the Delaware General Assembly in 2000, requires every school district in the state to allow pupils to attend schools closest to their residences. If this legislation is implemented solely on the basis of geography, it is likely that a substantial majority of Wilmington-area students will be assigned to single-race schools, since approximately 90 percent of those students are either black or Latino.

CONCLUSION: MORE WORK TO DO

A 2002 report published by Delaware's Metropolitan Wilmington Urban League lamented that racial equality in the state still lags in a number of areas. Statistics on the number of black students in Delaware's nineteen school districts at the beginning of the 2003-2004 academic year show that the average percentage of black pupils per district is 28 percent, with only six of the nineteen school districts exceeding the 35-percent target for desegregation mandated by the 1976 ruling in the *Evans v. Buchanan* case. Meanwhile, some administrators and parents of white students have complained that Delaware's present school diversity has hindered achievement of performance standards, measured by test results in specific subjects such as math, reading, science, and social studies at various grade levels.

There is no denying Delaware's shameful, painful record on school desegregation. One has to wonder what could have been accomplished if the millions of dollars spent by the state's school districts on employee time, attorney fees, and court costs to block desegregation orders, and on busing to achieve equality, were instead invested to improve educational opportunities for all of its residents. Instead, Delaware has the dubious distinction of being the initial state to face a lawsuit against its board of education and court rulings mandating interdistrict mandatory busing on a large scale.

The many victories and accomplishments emanating from the *Evans v. Buchanan* case in Delaware are a tribute to the perseverance, moral principles, legal knowledge, and courage of those who refused to surrender to the forces of racism and recalcitrance. The litigants, judges, and lawyers involved in the fight to desegregate Delaware's educational system deserve commendation. Yet, as NAACP attorney Jack Greenberg has said, "Lawyers can do right, they can do good, but they have their limits. The rest of the job is up to society." Only when attitudes of prejudice are changed will racist behavior be eliminated.

This study has sought to accurately depict the historical record of the State of Delaware on a major policy area over the last 150 years, not only to uncover the past but also to learn from it and to utilize it in order to foster equality in education and throughout the state.

REFERENCES
*1978 Fact Book: New Castle County School System and History of Evans v. Buchanan.* 1978. Wilmington: Sane of Delaware.

Baker, Mary C. 1980. *A Record of the Efforts of the NAACP To End Racial Discrimination in the Public Schools of Delaware, 1951-1979.* Dover: Delaware Chapter of the National Association for the Advancement of Colored People.

Bergman, Peter M., and Mort N. Bergman. 1969. *The Chronological History of the Negro in America.* New York: New American Library.

Broyles, Randall L. 1974. *Concepts of Delaware.* West Palm Beach, FL: Universal Publishing Associates.

Cooper, Richard Watson, and Hermann Cooper. 1923. *Negro School Attendance in Delaware.* Newark: University of Delaware Press.

*Encyclopedia of Delaware.* 2001. Santa Barbara, CA: Somerset Publishers.

Fuetsch, Michele. 2003. "Del. Schools Achieve Diversity—At a Price." *Wilmington News Journal,* September 14, p. A1, 7.

Hall, Kermit L., James W. Ely, Joel B. Grossman, and William M. Wiecek, eds. 1992. *The Oxford Companion to the Supreme Court of the United States.* New York: Oxford University Press.

Hoff, Samuel B., and Bradley Skelcher. 2003. "Civil Rights and the Supreme Court in the Reagan-Bush Years." *Lincoln Journal of Social and Political Thought.* Spring, Volume 1:2, pp. 81-92.

Hoffecker, Carol E. 1977. *Delaware: A Bicentennial History.* New York: W.W. Norton.

Irons, Peter. 2002. *Jim Crow's Children: The Broken Promise of the Brown Decision.* New York: Viking/Penguin Putnam Publishers.

Miller, George R. 1943. *Adolescent Negro Education in Delaware: A Study of the Negro Secondary School and Community.* Ph.D. dissertation. New York: New York University.

Morris, Irving. 2002. "The Role of Delaware Lawyers in the Desegregation of Delaware's Public Schools: A Memoir." *Widener Law Symposium Journal.* Volume IX: 1, pp. 1-54.

Munroe, John A. 2001. *History of Delaware.* Newark: University of Delaware Press.

O'Brien, David M. 2003. *Constitutional Law and Politics, Volume 2.* New York: W.W. Norton.

*The Pace of Progress: The State of People of Color in Delaware.* 2002. Wilmington: Metropolitan Wilmington Urban League.

Patterson, James T. 2001. *Brown v. Board of Education: A Civil Rights Milestone and its Troubled Legacy.* New York: Oxford Uni versity Press.

Shull, Steven A. 1999. *American Civil Rights Policy From Truman to Clinton: The Role of Presidential Leadership.* Armonk, NY: M. E. Sharpe.

Yarbrough, Tinsley E. 2000. *The Rehnquist Court and the Constitution.* New York: Oxford University Press.

# **Kansas**

### *Brown v. Board of Education* National Historic Site

On October 26, 1992, the *Brown v. Board of Education* National Historic Site Act was signed into law. Public Law 102-525 established the context for a permanent commemorative site for this landmark U. S. Supreme Court decision. The national historic site includes the 1920s Monroe Elementary School building and its adjacent grounds. During the *Brown* era, this school was one of four segregated elementary schools attended by African American children in Topeka. In 1993, the National Park Service acquired the property, adding this site to the more than 375 national parks in the United States. Kansas now has five national parks: Fort Scott, Fort Larned, Tall Grass Prairie, Nicodemus, and *Brown v. Board of Education.*

The purposes for this national historic site are: 1) to preserve, protect, and interpret for the benefit and enjoyment of present and future generations the places that contributed materially to the landmark U. S. Supreme Court decision that brought an end to segregation in public education; 2) to interpret the integral role of *Brown v. Board of Education* in the civil rights movement; and 3) to assist in the preservation and interpretation of related resources in Topeka that further the understanding of the civil rights movement.

The *Brown v. Board of Education* National Historic Site is a place where concepts related to civil rights and equality will be effectively communicated to all people regardless of age, ethnicity, or background; where people will be educated, inspired, provoked, and challenged; and where people will understand how this historic Supreme Court decision has affected their everyday lives.

Reprinted from *The* Brown *Quarterly,* Vol. 4, No. 2, Winter 2001.

**The Preservation Effort, 1990-2003:**
***Brown v. Board of Education* National Historic Site**

The U. S. Supreme Court decision of May 17, 1954, O*liver Brown et. al. v. The Board of Education of Topeka (Kansas)* is thought to be one of the m ost significant events in the history of this country, yet it remains largely misunderstood. Prior to 1990 few attempts had been made to commemorate and interpret this history through properties associated with legal or personal aspects of the case.

The first effort to identify sites that contributed to *Brown* began in 1985 when Justice Warren Burger, former Chief Justice of the United S tates Supreme Court, called upon the National Park Service (N PS) to conduct a survey of properties associated with the U. S. Constitution. The resulting document, entitled *Constitutional Theme Study*, was published by the National Park Service in 1987 to coincide with the anniversa ry of the Constitution. To prepare this study, the author, Dr. Harry Butowsky, an historian with the National Park Service, convened a pane l of constitutional scholars and canvassed federal judges to deve lop a list of constitutional milestones.

*Brown v. Board of Education* consistently appeared am ong the top three choices. His research entailed identifying p roperties associated with thes e milestones. For his selection of sites in *Brown*, he focused on the residence of Oliver Brown (no longer standing) and Sumner Elementary, the school that had denied Mr. Brown the right to enroll his daughter solely on the basis of their race.

At that point Dr. Butowsky was unaware of the social history behind the legal history of the *Brown* case. Examinations of this case seldom deal with the com plex constitutional issues or the history that underscores the sa crifice and self-determ ination present in the African A merican comm unity. Even fewer accounts of the *Brown* decision provide inform ation about the specifics of th e Topeka case, the local leadership of the National Association for the Advancem ent of Colored People (NAAC P), the attorneys, the 13 plaintiffs representing their 20 child ren, and unknown individuals whose lives were changed by these events.

History books make little m ention that *Brown* is comprised of five cases from the states of Delaware, Kansas, South Carolina, Virginia, and the District o f Columbia. As early as 1849 with a case in Boston, Massachusetts, African American parents challenged the system of education in the United S tates that mandated sepa rate schools for their children based solely on race.

In Kansas alone there were eleven sc hool integration cases dating from 1881 to 1949, prior to *Brown* in 1954. In many instances the schools for African Am erican children were substandard fac ilities with out-of-date text books and often no basic school supplies. What was not in question was the dedication and qualifications of the African American teachers and principa ls assigned to these schools.

In response to numerous unsuccessful attempts to ensure equal opportunities for all children, African American community leaders and organizations across the country stepped up their efforts to change the educational system. In the fall of 1950, members of the Topeka, Kansas, chapter of the NAACP agreed again to challenge the "separate but equal" doctrine governing public education. The strategy was conceived by the chapter president and the law firm of Scott, Scott, Scott and Jackson. Their plan involved enlisting the support of fellow NAACP members and personal friends as plaintiffs in what would be a class action suit filed against the Board of Education of the Topeka Public Schools.

A group of 13 parents agreed to participate on behalf of their 20 children. Individuals in the Topeka case moved ahead, unaware that at the same time legal counsel for the NAACP headquarters in New York were representing plaintiffs in school cases from Delaware, Virginia, South Carolina, and Washington, D.C. When the Topeka case made its way to the United States Supreme Court it was combined with these other NAACP cases. The combined cases became known as *Oliver L. Brown et al v. The Board of Education of Topeka, Kansas*.

Children of the Topeka plaintiffs had to travel past and away from nearby schools to attend schools designated for African Americans. In the other cases outside of Kansas, African American children attended poor facilities without basic school equipment and supplies.

On May 17, 1954, at 12:52 p.m., the United States Supreme Court issued a unanimous decision stating that it was unconstitutional, violating the 14th Amendment, to separate children in public schools for no other reason than their race. Prior to 1954, Topeka, Kansas operated a dual system of public education at several levels.

First, only elementary schools were racially segregated. Second, junior and senior high schools were integrated for academics but not for extracurricular activity. Topeka operated four elementary schools for African American children compared with eighteen elementary schools for white children.

The plaintiffs in the Topeka case were parents with children in the four African American elementary schools (Buchanan, McKinley, Monroe, and Washington). Only three school buildings remain standing today. However, two have been purchased and converted for other uses.

In 1990, one of these buildings, Monroe Elementary, was to be auctioned off by its owner. At that point, the Brown Foundation interceded. The unwanted property had to be saved. The owner was unaware of its historic significance as a site associated with the *Brown* decision. Monroe Elementary School, just as its counterparts, was built solely to function as a segregated school for African American children. It had existed on the same site in various incarnations since 1868. The present structure was completed in

1927. In the 1950' s two of the plaintiffs, Oliver Brown and Vivian Scales, had children attending Monroe Elem entary during the court proceedings in the *Brown* case.

The sudden availability of this property and the sens e of urgency created by the proposed auction presented a suprem e challenge for the Brown F oundation. The Foundation was in its infancy, having been esta blished in 1988. The fi scal resources to acquire and rehabilitate the old school house were well be yond reach. C onsequently, the Foundation leadership launched a letter writing campaign. Letters were sent to wealthy individuals across the country asking for assistance. The idea was to have som eone purchase the property and agree to sell it to the Brown Foundation over a period of tim e. When that concept f ailed to generate inter est, local land speculators were contacted, again without success.

Finally, an idea was formulated based on the significance of *Brown v. Board of Education* in United States history. W ith that in mind, letters were sent to the Kansas delegation to the U. S. Congress. Seve ral members responded immediately offering suggestions of grant opportunities and organizations to contact.

The turning point of this preservation e ffort came when the Foundation was put in touch with the Afro-American Institute for Historic Preservation and Community Developm ent in W ashington, D. C. At that same time, contact was made with the author of the NPS *Constitutional Theme Study*, suggesting that there had been an oversight in his research. It was further sugge sted that he return to Topeka to research the formerly segregated African American schoo ls for inclusion in his original docum ent.

During a meeting with the au thor of the study, he suggest ed that because of the historic significance of the old school build ing and its endangered status, the National Park Service m ight be interested in preservi ng it. He spoke of this property becom ing a National Historic Site, a national park. To make that happen, the Foundation would have to enlist the support and coope ration of both the U.S. Congre ss and the U. S. Department of Interior.

Realizing the need for local support, th e Foundation developed a community task force for the purpose of brainstorm ing, letter writing, and m oral support. Contacts were made with *Brown* plaintiffs, the Monroe Neighborhood Improvem ent Association, civic and social clubs, local preservation groups, th e city econom ic developm ent office and the mayor' s offce, the local univers ity, sororities and fraternities, the state historical society, and the state legis lature.

Reprinted w ith permission from *The* Brown *Quarterly*, Vol. 3, No. 1, Spring 1999.
http://brownvboard.org/brwnqurt/03-1/03-1d.htm

# **District of Columbia**

## Unity in Struggle:
## The Washington, D.C., School Desegregation Case
Alonzo N. Smith

Like the other four school desegregation cases which the Supreme Court ruled upon in its historic May 17, 1954, decision, the Washington, D.C., case is an event in African American history which combines courageous and intrepid African American grassroots community action with the dedicated professionalism of African American attorneys. As with the cases which came from Delaware and Kansas, the physical disparities between the Black and white school buildings and equipment were not as great as in the southern states. With regard to the professional expertise and commitment of the faculty, there today is an overwhelming consensus among former students that it was superior to that offered in the Euro-American schools. Moreover, unlike the former states of the Confederacy, and like Delaware and Kansas, racist violence was not as intense, and patterns of Jim Crow were not as overwhelmingly pervasive.

At the same time, however, the rapid increase of children of African descent in the D.C. public schools from the 1930s to the 1950s, coupled with the particular method of allocating resources to the two systems, dictated that the schools they attended would remain increasingly overcrowded and understaffed. Moreover, as in all of the areas, African Americans seeking to get an education frequently had the experience of being excluded from the school nearest their home and forced to attend one a farther distance away. Wherever Jim Crow education existed, the demands of Black parents for the integrated education of their children stemmed less from a desire to see them interact socially with white people and more from the realization that state-mandated segregation was for the purpose of subordinating them, and they were determined that their tax dollars be used to provide a quality of education that was equal to that of the white children. Thus, the struggle for integrated education must be viewed in the light of the broader African American struggle for freedom and justice in the United States.

As jobs opened up in the federal government during the Second World War, Black people streamed into the city of Washington. But despite this dramatic surge in the city's African American population, by1950 white people were still about 60% of the total population. Although some areas such as public transportation were free of Jim Crow, racial segregation was a pervasive fact of life for Black Washingtonians.

Towards the end of the War, the D.C. Department of Recreation actually instituted segregation in swimming pools and playgrounds where none had existed before. Anacostia was a largely white neighborhood where the local residents staged a noisy protest when African Americans attempted to integrate a swimming pool. An interracial organization, the National Committee to End Segregation in the Nation's Capital, was formed, but it met with stubborn resistance from local white citizens' associations and their southern allies in Congress. In 1948 this group published a report, *Segregation in Washington* that exposed the contradictory existence of racial discrimination in the capital of the so-called "free world."

As in many cities around the countr y, Jim Crow in the District was *de facto* rather than *de jure*. During the Reconstruction era, pub lic accommodations laws had been enacted, but these "lost laws," as they were re ferred to by local civil rights activists, were never enforced. The postwar period saw a ri se in local civil rights activity, with demonstrators targeting People' s Drug Stores (now CVS), the National Theatre, and Thompson' s Restaurant. They were joined by the venerable Mary Church Terrell, who at the age of 88 walked picket lines in downtown Washington. One of the results of these actions was the bringing of two cases before the U.S. Supreme Court. *Hurd v. Hodge* (1946) was argued by Black attorney Charles Hamilton Houston, and in this case the Court ruled that racial restrictive cov enants were not enfor ceable. In 1953 the high court ruled in the Thom pson Restaurant case that public facilities in the natio n' s capital could not discriminate on the basis of race. [xlix]

In the early part of the twentieth c entury, African American public education in the nation' s capital, while segregated by la w, was nevertheless of a relatively high quality. The M Street School, later known as Dunbar High School, boasted teachers with advanced degrees and produced su ch commun ity leaders as Kelly Miller and Charles Hamilton Houston. Howard University not only graduated m any leaders but also exercised a powerful cultural and political influence among Black Washingtonians. But after the 1920s, the combined effe cts of the Depression, continued m igration, and the refusal of the southern congr essmen who controlled the pub lic school system to provide adequate funding all m eant that the quality of the African American public schoo ls began to slip. Under this "dual system," as it was known, all Division One schools were headed by a white superintendent, and all Division Two schools were headed by a Black Assistant superintendent.

The method of allocating funds to th e dual school system was based on each decennial census, but because of the rapid e xpansion of the African Am erican population, this meant that the current apportionm ent was always out of date and Black children were always short-changed. By 1947 per pupi l expenditures were $160.21 for the Euro-Americans and $120.52 for the African Am ericans. Many African Americans had no access to kindergarten at all, and nearly 44% of the black primary school classes contained over forty children. Black child ren often passed under-capacity white schools to attend schools where there were often two, a nd sometimes three, shifts of students per day. [l]

In 1947 the all-Black Browne Junior High School switched to a two-shif t system, where students had to arrive earlier in th e morning and leave around m id-day but still with reduced hours. A ngered by these conditions and led by local NAACP activist attorney Belford Lawson, Black parents filed a lawsuit in the nam e of Marguerite Carr, daughter of the president of the Browne PT A, against Hobart Corning, the Division One Superintendent. The basis of the lawsuit was a departure from the current strategy of the NAACP, which was still to dem and equal faciliti es rather than to directly challenge the separate-but-equal principle laid down in *Plessy v. Ferguson* (1896). Black parents in

*Carr v. Corning* demanded immediate integration, and the case was eventually decided in 1950 by the Court of Appeals for the District of Columbia in favor of segregation. As with some other previous cases of this nature it was the dissenting opinion that was the most prophetic in the long run. In his dissent, Judge Henry Edgerton struck at the heart of the matter:

> ..School segregation is humiliating to Negroes. Courts have sometimes denied that segregation implies inferiority....Segregation of a depressed minority means that it is not thought fit to associate with others. Both whites and Negroes know that enforced racial segregation in schools exists because the people who impose it consider colored children unfit to associate with white children.[li]

But three years before this court defeat, another initiative was taking shape that was destined to become a part of history. One of the African American community people who was skeptical of the NAACP's efforts was Gardner Bishop, a barber with a shop in the "U" Street community, in the heart of Washington's business and cultural center. Although himself the parent of a Browne student he was not active with the PTA because he doubted its effectiveness. African Americans in the Nation's Capital were divided along socioeconomic, complexional, and other lines; and Bishop not only despised the racism of white people, but he also distrusted the leadership of the established Black people, who, he felt, could not adequately represent what he referred to as "the little people," who made up the overwhelming majority of the city's population. At the same time, however, Bishop was a pragmatist who was able to utilize the talents of many different kinds of people in his battle against segregation. Gardner Bishop was the principal leader in the local school desegregation movement, and he is one of the major unsung heroes in the history of Washington's African American community.

His daughter, Dr. Judine Bishop Johnson, now a professor of education, was a pupil at Browne at the time. In a recent interview, she recalled her father. A man who did not bite his tongue, "he became enraged about this situation, and could not understand why more black folks in Washington, D.C., were not enraged also." Although most of the Black schoolchildren came from modest backgrounds, he was able to mobilize their parents. "They were the children of working parents, poor parents, blue-collar parents, but he was able to convey..his sense of outrage and concern and anger..to those parents."[lii]

D.C. school authorities attempted to designate two rundown former white primary schools to handle the overflow of students at Browne. The annexes were several blocks from the main building, and students were asked to take different classes in different buildings. This stopgap measure fanned the growing resentment of African American parents, and it became a symbol for everything else all that the Board of Education was doing to the Black children of Washington. As Bishop later, recalled, "...we were mad at everyone—the whites, the highfalutin' blacks, the Board of Education—everyone." [liii]

Out of this resentment grew a new organization, the Consolidated Parents Group, and their first action was to show up unannounced at a school board meeting, where Bishop informed the flabbergasted board members that no one would be in school the next day. "They sat there like a bunch of fools," Bishop remembered, "not believing a word they heard." Any of those doubts were removed the next day when almost all of the 1,800 students stayed out of class. School board members attending meetings were confronted by demonstrating parents carrying signs telling them that "Our children are our jewels, give them the best education" and "There are enough good schools for all, discard the bad ones." Bishop presented a petition signed by 160 parents who protested the fact that the 1,800 students at Browne were in a facility built to accommodate 880. The parents told the board that,

> We shall withhold our children from [the] use of Blow and Webb
> Elementary Schools and the Browne Junior High School until the
> Board of Education justly performs its duty by designating for...
> our children adequate relief..inflicting no jeopardy on life, limb
> or health of our children. [liv]

Community churches such as Jones Memorial Methodist lent their facilities to help organize the strike. But as the weeks went by, support for the strike began to wane. Some of the parents felt that it was "better to have [children] go to some school than none at all." It looked to Bishop that they might "lose the fight and lose everything." He convinced skeptical Parent Group members to give him permission to approach Charles Hamilton Houston, an activist attorney. [lv]

Charles Houston is another figure in African American history whose visibility has not been in proportion to his contributions. Next to Thurgood Marshall, he is without question the most significant attorney in the African American freedom struggle in the courts. Born in Washington, D.C., in 1890, Houston attended Dunbar High School and later Amherst College, where he graduated cum laude. During the First World War he served as a lieutenant in an artillery unit, where the discrimination he encountered established his determination to use the law to help his people.

After the war, the young veteran received his legal education at Harvard Law School, and in 1924 he returned to Washington where he joined his father's law firm. Four years later, he was called by Howard University president Mordecai Johnson to head its School of Law. Under his leadership, the school was transformed from a part-time, unaccredited night school to a full-time, accredited institution whose focus was to utilize the legal system to advance the Black freedom struggle. In addition to offering the first civil rights course in a law school, Howard produced Thurgood Marshall, Oliver Hill, Harold Boulware—all of whom argued numerous civil rights cases, including those that became *Brown v. Board of Education.*

Although Houston by his background epitomized the kind of African American leader whom Bishop distrusted, he overcame his distaste, and in February of 1948 he approached Houston at a rally at Jones Memorial. After his self-introduction the civil rights attorney said, "I know you, Bishop, and I'd like to help," and he put his arm around the U Street barber. The two men developed a relationship based on deep mutual respect and devotion to the struggle. Bishop was convinced that Houston was "..terribly concerned, and terribly ignorant about us. He had never been associated with our kind of people before." Nevertheless, he informed Bishop that "..you've got yourself a lawyer."[lvi]

Houston's first step was to announce the calling off of the strike, assuming for himself the responsibility for taking this action, so the parents could save face. Rejecting the frontal attack on segregation strategy, Houston filed during the next two years a total of four lawsuits against the D.C. School Board, demanding equal facilities in primary to high schools. He argued that the so-called "strike" of Browne students had really been a lockout of the African American school children by the white school officials because when they attempted to enter the building at Browne, they were directed to the inferior satellite classes at the two dilapidated formerly white grade schools. While the administrators attempted to make Browne serve all of the African American school children of Northeast Washington, as well as those in Southeast, they were building a new facility, Sousa Junior High School, for the then still-sizeable but declining Euro-American population of Anacostia in Southeast Washington. Bishop and the Consolidated Parent Group covered the Black community, gathering depositions and other information in support of Houston's courtroom campaign. However, even as the Black parents supported Houston's equalization strategy for the public schools, at the same time they conducted demonstrations to desegregate swimming pools and playgrounds

As usual, Houston immersed himself in his civil rights work, despite serious health problems. In 1948, the same year the series of equalization lawsuits began against the D.C. School Board, he argued and won *Shelly v. Kraemer*, a Supreme Court case striking down the enforcement of racial restrictive covenants. The Consolidated Parent Group became a formally incorporated organization, with a constitution and a slogan, "Give the Child a Fair Chance."[lvii] One of the major struggles was over Central High, a Division One school. Cardozo Senior High School was a Division Two facility, over 40 years old, where the students attended classes in triple shifts and were forced to sit in the hallways and the auditorium to receive instruction. Moreover, Cardozo had no home economics class, no workshop, and only one studio arts class for 1,700 students. Central High was newer, had better facilities and was at three-quarters capacity, even though its student body included a junior high school. Paul Cooke, the president of American Federation of Teachers Local 27, the Black teachers' union, was a principal leader in this struggle, and he demanded that Central be transformed into a school for students of African descent. Central had long been the flagship campus of the D.C. high schools, with many prominent members of the local white power structure among its alumni. The Central Alumni Association locked horns with the school board and the Black community activists, but in the end Paul Cooke got what he demanded.[lviii]

It was in part the activism of the Consolidated Parents Group that helped to produce a comprehensive study of the Washington, D.C., public schools in 1949. George D. Strayer, a professor of education at Columbia University, was commissioned by the Board of Education to conduct a study of the system. While the report did not specifically attempt to evaluate school segregation as a public policy, it contained extensive revealing data on the Black and white schools. For example, the report noted the low score of Dunbar High School on a rating of school buildings. This institution, which had produced a generation of Black leaders and had been the envy of many whites, still rated the highest of the three Black high schools but below the lowest white high school. "The educational adequacy of the senior high schools for colored students..stands out in sharp contrast with the scores of the senior high schools for white pupils. Only one of the regular senior high schools, Dunbar, scores near the 500 mark; Armstrong dropping to a score of 353."[lix]

As in the South, victories by Black activists stirred white hostility. The Federation of Citizens Associations, the leading segregationist group, called for Bishop's arrest for leading the strike. In July of 1949 John Connaughton, president of the Federation, responded to Bishop's invitation for a public debate with a refusal that was dripping with racist venom:

> You represent a small minority group of Negroes in Washington which recently conducted a student strike against attendance of your children, which attendance is for the benefit of your children..so you do not have the proper relationship to community responsibility and respect for law to justify any other group to discuss any subject with you....When the Negro people of Washington have cleaned your race of its high percentage of criminals,..and when your race has eradicated its high percentage of venereal disease and other communicable diseases, then come back to us with a proposal..You are now asking social intermingling on play grounds and swimming pools, and we do not intend to join you in this social relationship.[lx]

Bishop's response, while it reflected the imperfect English of a self-educated man, was nonetheless a penetrating and cogent summary, not only of the desegregation controversy but also of the entire state of race relations in postwar America, and thus it is worth quoting at length. The following is an excerpted and edited version:

> The Consolidated Parents Group's telegram, inviting your federation to an open discussion on the abolition of segregation in all play areas in this the nation's capital, was sent in good faith....For reply you chose to ignore the Consolidated Group and address a vilifying letter to me personally. Nothing you could have done could possibly have demonstrated more forcibly that you have run out of ideas and reasons and have nothing to fall back on except your irrational prejudice...In

your own little corner y ou see a lot of people labeled "White." When will you wake up to the fact that th ese people exist in the p resence of a nonwhite w orld which holds the balan ce of world power?...Your clichés about crimes and disease are thread bare and outmoded. Ne groes have a higher crim e rate than Whites in p art because White policem en arrest Negroes for crimes they let White people get away free on. What else except a high official crim e rate can Negroes expect, when W hite hoodlum s attack Negroes minding thei r own business at a federally owned swimming pool and W hite police arrest the Negro victim s and let the aggressor White hoodlum s go free? Negroes had no venereal disease until the White m an brought it to Africa. Now Whites like you deny them decent housing, d ecent schoo ls, adequate medical care and fair employment opportunity so they cannot pay for m edical care. Then you in your prejudice com plain about some Negroes having diseases that you brought to them....The Negro fights for democracy to protect all people..the federally owned swi mming pools..belong to all the people. If you have any fears about our wishi ng to associate with people like you, please disabuse yourself. However we do not propose to be denied our public rights because of your lik es and dislik es. This reply is in hopes that some semblance of intelligenc e may penetrate the false shell of egotistical greatness you have so foolishly wrapped around yourselves. Please be rem inded that prejudice, racial hatred and the belief of superiority of one race caused the last war... [lxi]

Houston' s support of the Consolidated Parents Group was able to open previously closed doors to Bishop; and Bishop' s dynamic personality, fo rceful style of expression, and community roots furnished Houston with the troops he needed for a m ovement. Again, Dr. Johnson rem embers: "I remember Mr. Houston just worked with Daddy for three years..before he becam e very ill. And I k now when he died m y father cried. He really did because they had becom e very, very close friends. Two people, a barber and a lawyer." [lxii]

In leadership, m embership, and style, the Consolidated Parents Group reflected a cross-section of W ashington, D.C.' s African American comm unity. While Bishop was the president, the vice pr esident was Burma Whitted, also a leader of the local chapter of Jack and Jill, an African American children' s social group. Although the NAACP chapter did not support the Parents Group until it pressed for full desegregation, several individual m embers lent their assistance. Prominent physicians and Howard faculty members and their wives included Dr. and Mrs. Kline Price, p arents of Hugh Price, the recent pr esident of the National Urban League; and Mrs. Dorothy Porter, the principal developer and direct or of the Moorland-Spingarn Library of Howard University. Church groups included both the Methodist and Baptist m inisterial alliances as well as ind ividual chu rches such as Jones Memorial Methodist Church and Metropolitan Baptist Church, which regularly provided m eeting sp aces. In addition to Jack and Jill, social clubs included the St. George' s Men' s Club, the Club Fifteen, the

Ramblers Club, and the Oldest Inhabitants. Greek-letter societies such as Alpha Phi Alpha and Omega Psi Phi also played a prominent role. Fundraising activities ranged from chitterling parties to bake sales to more formal occasions for the more affluent. [lxiii]

As the movement picked up support from Washington's black business and professional people, it also attracted support from liberal whites. Recognizing the need to reach out to Washington's liberal, cosmopolitan leaders, Bishop addressed an open letter to the members of the diplomatic community. In the late 1940s DuBois and other progressive Black leaders attempted to embarrass the United States by pointing out the hypocrisy of anti-communist Cold War rhetoric in the face of continued racism in this country. Petitions were presented to the United Nations accusing the U.S. government of violating the United Nations charter by tolerating segregation and racial violence. Bishop attempted the same strategy at the local level in Washington, D.C. On June 17, 1949, he circulated a mimeographed open letter, which read as follows:

> To their Excellencies – the Ambassadors and Ministers Plenipotentiary Accredited to the Government of the United States: May we as American citizens apologize for the recent decision of the Board of Recreation for the District of Columbia on racial segregation which discredits our nation before the world and is bound to prove embarrassing to our Government in its foreign relations....We recognize the inconsistency between the United States insisting on democracy abroad while it tolerates racial segregation on public playgrounds in its own capital. It is precisely because this inconsistency is irreconcilable that we apologize to you and to the nations you have the honor to represent. [lxiv]

The Washington, D.C., school desegregation movement was dealt a severe blow by the death of Charles Houston in April of 1950. But from his hospital bed in Freedmen's Hospital, a few weeks before he succumbed to the final heart attack, he instructed Bishop to "Go tell [George E.C.] Hayes and Jim Nabrit they owe me and [to] take your case." It was Burma Whitted who helped facilitate Bishop's initial contacts with the two prominent civil rights lawyers and who assumed many of the administrative tasks of organizing and fundraising.

Eventually, James Nabrit's legal team included George E. C. Hayes, Harry B. Merican, George Johnson, Julian R. Dugas (currently professor emeritus at Howard University Law School), Herbert D. Reid, Sr., and James A. Washington, Jr. In the other four "state cases" that made up *Brown v. Board of* Education, the strategy was to show inequality between the white and Black schools, with the hope that the Supreme Court would strike down the principle of separate-but-equal as a policy that was impossible to maintain. But Nabrit decided to argue that the inequality of the dual system was beside the point, that segregation *per se* was unconstitutional. At Nabrit's insistence, and following the shift in policy from the NAACP's Legal Defense Fund in New York, the Parent Group abandoned the equalization strategy in favor of an all-out attack on segregation, which would focus on the new all-white Sousa Junior High School. In the fall of 1950 the *Washington Daily News* reported that "Anacostia's junior high schools are target s for a new move by Negroes….The Consolidated Parents Group requests..an integrated sch ool system." Bishop, Whitted, and the pastor of Campbell AME Church, along with other community leaders, arranged to have the Capital Taxicab Company provide transpor tation for eight children who presented themselves on Septem ber 11, 1950, to register for the school year at the new, under-capacity Sousa Junior High. Turned down as they expected, they filed suit and thus began *Bolling v. Sharpe*, one of the five cases consid ered by the U.S. Supreme Court in *Brown v. Board of Education*.[lxv]

As with the lis ts of plaintiffs in the othe r cases, the names were arranged alphabetically; and so the person whose nam e appeared first on the lis t was 12-year-old Spottswood T. Bolling, Jr. The defendant in th is case was Melvin Sharpe, the D.C. school superintenden t. The young Bolling' s widowed m other held a $5 7.60-a-week job as a bookbinder for the General Services Adm inistration. Denied admittance to S ousa, he enrolled at Shaw Junior High, a 48- year old school whose science laboratory consisted of one Bunsen burner and a bowl of goldfish. Like the other schools it was so overcrowded that som e in Washington' s Black community ref erred to it as "shameful Shaw." But as one of his former grade-schoo l teachers remembers, Spottswood was a good-looking, personable youth, whose fam ily were members of an historic African American church in Georgetown. [lxvi]

From a technical legal standpoint, the W ashington, D.C., case can be considered a "companion case" to the other four "state cases" that made up *Brown v. Board of Education*. *Bolling v. Sharpe*, although it was eventually included in the Supreme Court' s historic May 17, 1954, decision, was not a part of the cases argued by the NAACP' s Legal Defense Fund. The other four cases, from Topeka, Kansas; Clarendon County, South Carolina; Prince Edward C ounty, Virginia; and W ilmington, Delaware were argued on the basis of the Fourteen th Amendment, which states that "..no *state* [italics author' s] shall deny equal protection of the laws." Since Washington, D.C., was not a state, Nabrit and the other lawyers had to argue on the basis of the Fifth Amendment, which stipulates that the fede ral government must guarantee due process of the law. Thus, the legal strategy in the four "state cases" was significantly different from the Washington, D.C., "companion case." Since the due process clause of the Fifth Amendment was broader and less precise than the equal protection clause of the Fourteenth Am endment, Nabrit adopted a line of argument that was stronger and more daring. In the four state cases, the NAACP attorneys attempted to prove that school facilities in each of the f our states were unequal, thus proving that there was no way that separate-but-equal could ever be struck down.

The lawyers also claim ed that the Reconstruction Era legislation setting up segregated schools in the Dist rict of Columbia seemed to imply that segregation of pupils might be by parental choice rather than mandatory, as the leg islation in the Dee p South explicitly stated. They also attempted to prove that racial discrimination was contrary to federal policy.[lxvii]

In addition to *Bolling,* which asked that the U.S. District Court issue a permanent injunction ending D.C.'s segregated schools, the attorneys filed *Ex parte Cogdell,* asking the Court to rule on the constitutionality of the dual system. Both suits were dismissed by the U.S. District Court, and the attorneys prepared to bring the case to the U.S. Court of Appeals. At this point the Supreme Court stepped in, and informed them that Chief Justice Fred Vinson wished to hear the D.C. case along with the four state cases. This was an invitation to apply for a writ of certiorari, bypassing the Court of Appeals and coming directly before the Supreme Court. Even though Nabrit had received relatively little in legal fees and Hayes had received nothing, it was necessary for the Parents Group and the lawyers to raise money for court costs of about $24,000, a considerable sum in the 1950s, to bring the case before the highest court in the land.

They proved equal to the task. By this time, the civil rights activists had established an extensive network in Washington, D.C. One example of this was a daylong meeting at Howard University, held on January 20, 1951, titled "A Workshop: Planning for Democratic Schools in the Nation's Capital". The event was sponsored by the Women's Action Committee of the Consolidated Parents Group, which included Burma Whitted; Jewel Mazique, wife of a prominent physician; noted scholar Margaret Just Butcher; Marjorie Lawson, wife of attorney Belford Lawson; and Frances Payne and Marie Smith, Howard faculty wives. The workshop was opened by Gardner Bishop and speakers included George E. C. Hayes and Paul Cooke, the latter of whom by this time was a professor of English at Miner Teachers College. Discussion leaders included Charles H. Thompson, Dean of Howard's Graduate School, and E. Franklin Frazier, the noted sociologist. A summary and recommendations for action were presented by Alex Weinstein, Director of Community Relations of the Anti Defamation League of B'nai B'rith. Bishop continued to raise funds at the grassroots level, and the Parents Group also sponsored events such as a reception held on April 15, 1953, at the Alpha Phi Alpha fraternity house.[lxviii]

*Bolling v. Sharpe* was first argued before the Supreme Court on December 10-11, 1952, reargued December 8-9, 1953, and decided May 17, 1954. Noting that the Washington, D.C., case was decided on different grounds from the "state cases," Chief Justice Earl Warren said that, "..the concepts of equal protection and due process, both stemming from our American ideal of fairness, are not mutually exclusive." Closing an important possible loophole that might be open to segregationists, Warren went on to say that, "In view of our decision that the Constitution prohibits the states from maintaining racially segregated public schools it would be unthinkable that the same Constitution would impose a lesser duty on the Federal Government."[lxix]

The movement begun by the U Street barber in 1947 had finally come to fruition. Gardner L. Bishop's singular achievement was that from a modest educational background and income status, he mobilized people from varied walks of life, including working-class parents and children as well as talented university professors and civil rights attorneys. The heroic band of Washington, D.C., brothers and sisters who formed the Consolidated Parents Group had confronted injustice and become part of the greatest legal victory in American history. As Bishop later recalled, the movement bridged class and color divisions and was not "done by any [one] class, any [one] kind of people" but "so many people from so many varied walks of life," who, in the words of historian Genna Rae McNeil, "demonstrated a level of ideological clarity which made unity in struggle possible."

[xlix] Dennis B. Fradin and Judith B. Fradin, *Fight On! Mary Church Terrell's Battle for Integration* (New York, Clarion Books, 2003), chapters 11-13.

[l] Richard Kluger, *Simple Justice: The History of* Brown v. Board of Education *and Black America's Struggle for Equality* (New York: Knopf, 1976), p. 517.

[li] Kluger, *Ibid*, p. 517.

[lii] Judine Bishop Johnson, interviewed by Dave Lacey, July 16, 2003. This interview was conducted under the auspices of Hillman and Carr, a visual communications firm which is producing a video component for the National Park Service's forthcoming exhibition on *Brown v. Board of Education*, scheduled to open in Topeka, Kansas, in May 2004. Used with permission of Hillman and Carr.

[liii] Kluger, *Ibid*, p. 514.

[liv] Kluger, *Ibid*; Genna Rae McNeil, "Community Initiative in the Desegregation of District of Columbia Schools, 1947-1954: A Brief Historical Overview of Consolidated Parent Group, Inc., Activities from *Bishop* to *Bolling*," *Howard Law Journal*, 23:1(1980), p.27.

[lv] McNeil, *Ibid*, quoted from Gardner L Bishop interview, March 2, 1972.

[lvi] Kluger, *Ibid*, p. 515.

[lvii] McNeil, *Ibid*, pp. 31-32.

[lviii] Sara C. Kaplan, "The Desegregation of the District of Columbia Public Schools: *Bolling v. Sharpe* to *Hobson v. Hansen* (unpublished NEH Younger Scholar paper, September, 1990), p. 9., in the Washingtoniana Section of the Martin Luther King, Jr., District of Columbia Public Library. Also in this section are papers of Paul Cooke relating to the Cardozo-Central controversy.

[lix] George D. Strayer, *The Report of a Survey of the Public Schools of the District of Columbia*, n.p., Washington, D.C., 1949, p.318.

[lx] Howard University, Moorland-Spingarn Research Center, Manuscript Division, Record Group 19, Consolidated Parent Group, Box 1, Folder 12. John H. Connoughton to Gardner L. Bishop, July 5, 1949

[lxi] *Ibid*, Gardner L. Bishop to John H. Connoughton, July 11, 1949.

[lxii] *Ibid*, Judine Bishop Johnson interview.

[lxiii] McNeil, *Ibid*, p.33.

[lxiv] Consolidated Parent Group Papers, Box 1, folder 12, Letter to the Washington diplomatic community, June 17, 1949.

[lxv] McNeil, *Ibid*, pp. 36-37.

[lxvi] Kluger, *Ibid*, p. 521; Telephone interview with Mrs. Catherine Dodson, June 4, 2003.

[lxvii] Kluger, *Ibid*, p. 521; Kaplan, pp.17-21.

[lxviii] Consolidated Parent Group Papers, Box 2, folder 27.

[lxix] *Bolling v. Sharpe*, 347 U.S. 497 (1954).

# **South Carolina**

*Briggs v. Elliott*: Clarendon County's Quest for Equality—A Brief History

## Part I

## BACKGROUND

On May 17, 1954, the United States Supreme Court handed down the decision that segregation in public schools violated the Fourteenth Amendment of the United States Constitution. The first of the five cases filed with the Supreme Court that resulted in this historic decision was *Briggs et al. v. Elliott et al.* from Clarendon County, South Carolina. The Court's ruling directly affected school systems and educational practices in seventeen states that had laws either requiring or permitting racially separate schools. Indirectly, this decision has affected almost every facet of American society.

After the Civil War, many people did not think former slaves should have equal rights and protection. So discriminatory laws, referred to as "Black Codes" were enacted. To protect former slaves and their descendants from the "Black Codes," other laws and some amendments to the Constitution, including the Fourteenth, were passed. To avoid complying with the Fourteenth Amendment, the southern states passed laws that permitted or required "separate but equal" facilities for Americans of different races.

The "separate but equal" doctrine can be traced back to the 1849 case of *Roberts v. City of Boston*. That case started because five-year-old Sarah Roberts had to walk past five white elementary schools to reach the elementary school she attended. The Massachusetts judge who heard the case ruled that the segregation law was founded "on reason" and so he did not rule against school segregation. Even though *Roberts* predated the Civil War and the Fourteenth Amendment, it set a legal precedent that was used to justify the subsequent "separate but equal" laws enacted in the nineteenth century. In 1896, the *Plessy v. Ferguson* case legitimized the "separate but equal" doctrine when the Supreme Court ruled that the practice of having separate but equal rail facilities was constitutional.

"Separate but equal" became the law of the land after *Plessy*. It continued as such until the decision of May 17, 1954. The 1954 decision, generally known as *Brown v. Board of Education*, was actually based on five cases argued concurrently before the Supreme Court. *Briggs v. Elliott* was one of these cases. Like *Briggs* and *Brown*, two of the other cases challenged the constitutionality of "separate but equal" schools under the Fourteenth Amendment of the Constitution. The fifth, *Bolling v. Sharpe*, made the challenge under the Fifth Amendment.

## Part II

## ORIGINS OF _BRIGGS V. ELLIOTT_

### A. Life in Clarendon County Around the End of WW II

The first lawsuit to reach the Supreme Court in challenge of the constitutional ity of school segregation in the United States and to demand equal status for black children originated in Clarendon County, South Carolina. Through a quirk of history, _Brown v. Board of Education_ generally gets this credit. However, if were not for a lawsuit—nam ely, _Briggs v. Elliott_—that began in Clarendon County, racial segregation in the United States may have continued for many years longer.

In the 1940s the majority of people livin g in Clarendon County were bl ack. This situation had existed for perhaps 200 years, ever since boatlo ads of slaves had been bro ught from Africa to work on plantation fields. Although more than 70 years had passed since the slaves were freed, the black people in Claren don County continued to be poor and uneducated. Few of the adults had even fini shed fifth gra de.

Over the y ears, many black people cont inued to wor k on farms or as household help. A few fortunate blacks were lan downers and some ha d even acquired large hol dings, but most black farmers were sharecroppers. They lived and worked on farms owned b y other people. Instead of paying rent, they shared the money from selli ng crops with the farm' s owner. Since many sharecroppers were illiter ate, landowners could easil y cheat them. Furthermore, if the owner of the farm was not happy with the sharecropper, the sh arecropper could be t hrown off the property with no place to go.

It was a hard life for farmers. They worked from sunup to well past sundown, s craping out a meager living. They had no tractors, no washing machines and even no electricity. Probabl y none of the black people i n Clarendon Co unty even knew that a thing called tel evision had been invented. On Saturday s, families piled onto a hor se-drawn wagon or truck, if there was one, and rode into t own to buy supplies and see other peopl e. On Sundays, everybody went to church, the closest thing there was to a community center.

Things were so mewhat better for black peopl e who lived in the small towns. The women were maids, housekeepers and laundresses. They toiled long hours doing housework for someone else, then went hom e to take care of their own families and do their own h ousework, often b y lamplight. The men worked in low-paying positions at service stations, stores, cotton gins and tobacco warehouses. The y came home at night to th eir rented houses, worn out fr om heavy lifting and backbreaking work .

Life was far from easy for black people, whether the y lived in town or on a farm. Although some whites treated black s well and with respect , the prevailing social custo ms demanded that blacks always treat whites with de ference. Black people alway s had to be alert, to know their place and to stay in it. The consequences of doi ng the wrong thing could be severe.

Clarendon Count y blacks were poor and inadeq uately educated, but they were not dum b. They totally understood their plight and were constantly seeking way s by which they could improve themselve s. The women who cleaned kitche ns for white people or washed their clothes didn't work just to earn a living for themselve s. They were quick to say that they also worked to afford an education for their children so the ne xt generation would not have to suffer the sa me indign ities.

In 1945, World War II came to an end. Like soldiers fro m all over the United States, black men from Clarendon County were coming hom e after fighting for freedom and democracy on foreign soil. The black veterans had a new awareness of the kinds of things they should be able to enjoy, but they came home to the same segregated place they had left. Home to stores they could not enter, to toilets they were not allowed to use, to state parks that were off limits to them , to water fountains marked "whites only" or "colored." Home to a place where the incomes of black s ranked among the lowest of the United States. Home to a place where it was still hard for a black person to get an education.

## B.   Clarendon County' s Schools in 1945

In the early part of the twentieth century, it was very difficult for children who lived on farms to get to school.  In the 1920s and before, all elementary children went to little one-, two- or three-room schools that were scattered all over the county.  Even with so many schools, some children still lived far from the nearest school. Clarendon Count y solved part of its school problem by consolidating some schools. Instead of having several small sch ools all over the county, consolidated schools—with better fac ilities and m ore resources—were built in a few locations. But they were only for white children.

State law in South Carolina made it a crime for black and white children to go to the same schools.  At the end of the Second World War, the quality of all schools, black and white, varied greatly, but ever ywhere the schools for black children were the worst ones. The school buildings were shabbier. They had fewer educa tional resources and frequentl y their school year was shorter.  Some rural schools were in session for only three to five months during the cold season. That was the time of year when children didn 't have to work in the fields. However, even when black children were free to attend school,  transportation to and from school was often a limiting factor for their education.

The many ramshackle el ementary schools for black children rema ined loosely organized, divided into some 40 different school districts. Only a few of these schools h ad been built with public funds.  Most were started in the twenties and thirties by church groups, fraternal organizations or philanthr opic foundati ons. By the early nineteen forties, however, all were considered to be part of Clarendon Count y's public school system.  Nevertheless, public f unds sometimes supplied nothing m ore than teacher s' salaries and a few old textbooks.  Maintenan ce and upkeep—bu ying coal, lighting fires in the stoves that heated the room s, patching the tin roofs and fixing the wooden steps—wer e left up to the teachers, the st udents and their parents. And prior to 1948, even the sala ries of black teacher s were inferior to those of white te achers.

After the white schools were consolidated, black children continued to go to small, broken-down schools.  No school buses picked th em up on cold, wet mornings. If they went to school at all, they walked over the unpaved roads, muddy or dusty dependin g on the weather. Their socks had holes in the heels, their shoes had holes in the sole s and their coats were thin and threadbare.  They arrived at classrooms heated by the firewood they collected or by the coal their parents or their teachers bought.  There were no janito rs, and no one was paid to light the fires for heat, to sweep the room s, to wash the chalkboards, to patch the roofs or to fix the steps. All of these things had to be done by the teachers, the students and their parents.

In spite of all of this, black parents wanted their children to go to school to get an education. But for many students, the obstacle s were formidable and it was easy to be discouraged. Classes were overcrowded, material s were in short supply and the daily round trip to a high school could mean many miles of walking.

## C. School Bus Transportation

In 1945, school buses took Clarendon Count y white children from rural areas to the county' s centralized white schools. No bus servi ce was available for black child ren, a number of whom lived m ore than ten miles away from their assigned school. The situation left four options available for these black students: (a) they could wa lk to school, a rriving tired, cold and dirty; (b) they could, if they were am ong a very "lucky" few, occasionally get a ride to school on somebody' s truck or mule and wagon; (c) they could board in town with relatives or friends; or (d) they could drop out of school.

To keep their children from dropping o ut of school, a group of black parents who lived i n the Davis Station area decided to bu y a bus in 1945. The bus was supposed to take their children to various schools as far as away as Summerton (a little more than 10 miles). The bus cost $400.00. It had been jun ked by the white school sy stem. Before the black parents bought it, it was being used for hay storage, but the parents probably thought anything was better than nothin g. By 1946, the old bus was in such bad shape that it could no longer be used. The hopeful parents bought a second bus for $700.00.

Rev. Joseph Armstrong (J. A.) De Laine was a long-time friend of some of the Davis Station parents, particularly Hammett Pearson and his brother Levi. Rev. De Laine, a college graduate, was the pastor of two local ch urches. It was probably because of discussions between Rev. De Laine and the Pearson brot hers that the idea for obtaining a school bus became a reality. Over a number of years, Rev. De Laine's activities had inspired confidence and the ki nd of leadership many of the people appreciated. He became the spokesperson for the blacks of Davis Station, not only because of his education and re ligious status but also because of his apparent willingness to take risks and provi de sustained lead ership throughout stressful situations. Rev. De Laine wa s also a landowner. All in all, he was somewhat less dependent on whites for his livelihoo d than were most Clarendon Co unty blacks.

While the Pearsons and other Davis Station pa rents were try ing to find a dependable way to get their children to school, a young man drowne d near Society Hill A.M.E. Church, just seven or eight m iles away. He was in a boat, trying to cross an arm of the newly formed Lake Marion made lake where the bridge had been washed out. The accident happened on a Sunday and the person was not going to school. Howev er, the same boat was regularly used by black children to get and from school.

The drownin g upset black parents for miles around. They could imagine so mething bad happening to their own chi ldren while tr ying to get to school. The Davis Station parents became more determined than ever to have bus transportation for their children.

There are dreams, and there is reality. No matter how great the desire, people like the Davis Station parents could not afford to keep buying gas and paying for expensive bus repairs. It had been hard enough to get enough money to buy the buses. The parents were confident that their present reality and their future reality did not have to be the same. Someone else could be convinced to help them maintain the bus. Rev. De Laine was delegated to ask the County Superintendent of Schools for assistance.

The request was denied.

New plans had to be made.

## D. *Pearson v. Clarendon County*

During the month of June 1947, while enrolled in the Benedict College-Allen University Summer School (in Columbia, South Carolina), Rev. De Laine heard the chairman of the South Carolina Conference of the NAACP, Mr. J. M. Hinton, speak at a university general assembly. Mr. Hinton challenged the audience by saying, "No teacher or preacher in South Carolina has the courage to get a plaintiff to test the school bus transportation practices of discrimination against Negro children."

Bingo! Here was a chance to turn dreams into reality.

Rev. De Laine took the challenge as a personal one. He returned to Davis Station and made a proposal to the parents. In response, the Pearson brothers and several other families decided to stop trying to get action on a local level and to turn their request into a court challenge. The idea of a court challenge seemed promising in light of the recent District Court decision that the state must pay its teachers, black and white, equally for equal qualifications.

A group of black Clarendon County residents approached leaders of the South Carolina conference of the NAACP. They made the request that a lawsuit, with Mr. Levi Pearson as plaintiff, be filed against Clarendon County for school bus transportation for black students. The state NAACP officials agreed for their legal counsel to represent the parents. However, the Clarendon County parents were advised that the NAACP could not finance the case. The state conference had spent all of its money on the recent lawsuits for voting rights and teachers' pay. The Palmetto State Teachers Association, a black teacher organization, volunteered to finance the lawsuit. It is not known whether the Association was asked to do so by the NAACP or whether its members knew that the NAACP needed funds and wanted to see the case go forward. In any case, with the financial backing, legal actions could be set in motion. On March 16, 1948, the case (*Levi Pearson v. Clarendon County and School District No. 26*) was filed in the U.S. District Court on behalf of one of Mr. Pearson's sons who attended high school in Summerton. The legal journey that became *Briggs v. Elliott* and ended with segregation being declared illegal by the U.S. Supreme Court had begun.

The objective of *Pearson v. Clarendon County* was to have the court "force" the school board to provide school transportation for the county's black children. The case was scheduled to be heard on June 7, 1948. However, during the discovery phase it was found that, although Mr. Pearson's house literally straddled the lines of two black school districts, he paid taxes in a different district from the one that he was trying to sue.

The case had to be withdrawn.

Despite the setback caused by *Pearson* being withdrawn, the parents were by no means ready to give up. According to Mr. James L. Miller, a pact had been made among several men involved in the purchase of the Davis Station school bus. He said they vowed that they would not withdraw their support from the quest for better facilities even under the threat of death. Their agreement was that, even if one of them were to be killed or forced to withdraw, others of the group would continue the struggle.

### E. Transition from *Pearson* to *Briggs*

In January 1949, Rev. De Laine and Mr. Pearson conferred with NAACP Attorney Harold Boulware concerning how to proceed. Less than three months later, on March 12, 1949, Mr. Thurgood Marshall, a lawyer for the national NAACP's Legal Defense Fund, met with a group from Clarendon County. He informed them that the NAACP had decided it would no longer argue cases that were not class-action cases or whose only goal was to obtain bus transportation.

The Clarendon County group was not willing to let the matter drop. Too many things were wrong with their children's schools. For example, Scott's Branch School in Summerton had two outhouse toilets to serve almost 700 elementary and high school students as well as their teachers. Drinking water was obtained from a row of faucets out in the school yard, and there were not enough classrooms for the students. After being urged by Rev. De Laine and the other representatives from Clarendon County to reconsider, Mr. Marshall finally agreed to an alternate action plan. He would ask the other NAACP officials to back a group of Clarendon County "parents who wanted to sue for Equal Educational Opportunities and Facilities for Negro Children"—if such a group could be found.

The Clarendon County group returned home, wanting to waste no time in starting legal action. With the NAACP's assistance, four strategic meetings were scheduled at different churches. As a result, over two hundred persons expressed interest in becoming plaintiffs. In May 1949, the staff of the NAACP set forth the following conditions to be satisfied if it were to accept the Clarendon County case and to proceed with it:

- Only one school district could be involved, and it had to be possible to directly compare that district's white and black high schools.

- The list of plaintiffs had to be limited to families living in that school district. Rural families whose children attended the school were not acceptable unless they were actually residents of the district.

In this way District 22, the Summerton District, was selected, and Scott's Branch School became the focal point of the effort to obtain better educational facilities for blacks.

This action marked the transition of efforts from *Pearson* and school bus transportation to what would become *Briggs v. Elliott* and finally a part of *Brown et al. v. Board et al.*

*Briggs v. Elliott* was filed in U.S. District Court, suing for equal educational opportunities for black children. The plaintiffs were t wenty parents or guardians suing on behalf of 46 minors. The defendants wer e members of the Board of Trustees of School District 22 and other offic ials of Clarendon County's educational system, including the superintendent of education. The surname of the first plaintif f was Briggs; Elliott was the surname of the Chairm an of the Board of Education.

The presiding District Co urt Judge was J. Waties Waring. At the pre-trial hearing in November 1949, Judge Waring questioned why the plaintiffs wer e suing for "separate but equal" schools when they were already said to have them. He suggested they rethink what they should be suing for. The NAACP's legal staff took heed and withdrew the case.

With this one action, a white southern ju dge had changed the approach that the NAACP would use to rectify inequities between black and white citizens of the United States.

The case was refiled in U.S. District Court, but this time it challen ged the constitutional ity of the long-held "separate but e qual" doctrine. The Clarendon County group had become the first to make this challen ge to public school segregation. *Briggs v. Elliott* had become a spearhead for wi de-reachi ng changes. In its new form, *Briggs v. Elliott* threatened "the long established..way of life [that] South Carolina [had] adopted and practiced and lived since..the institution of human slavery."

Before they first signed the petition, the plain tiffs had been warned of the pos sibility of severe and perhaps dangerous repercussions because of their challenge to the status quo. Alm ost all of the plaintiffs directly depended on white c itizens in Clarendon Count y for their livelihoods. An effort had been made to avoid allowing the most vulnerable blacks (i.e., the sharecroppers) to be plaintiffs. The male plaintiffs were m ostly land-owning farm ers or workers in town while the female plaintiffs were cooks, maids or childcare providers. Desp ite the early warnings, it was (and still is) inconceivable to im agine the extent to which the blac k people of Clarendon Count y would be made to suffer for suing for rights guara nteed to them by the Constit ution of the United States. Over the course of the next 15 years, they lost jobs, homes, opport unities for hi gher education and even lives. They were refused service in stores, credit for farm essentials and rental of farm equipm ent. They were hounded and harassed. In short, they paid dearly for the privileges no w enjoy ed and taken for gr anted by every American.

In May of 1951, the case was heard. Since it was asking a federal court to issue a judgm ent against the state's laws, it was necessary for the case to be heard by a panel of three federal judges. The judges were Circuit Court J udge John J. Parker, District Court Judge Georg e B. Timmerman and Distri ct Court Judge J. Waties Waring. In June, they rendered a split decision that supported the constitutionalit y of the "separate but equal" doctrine. Judge Waring, however, wrote a remarkable dissenting opi nion. As part of its decision, the court did rul e that Clarendon County had failed to pr ovide equa l educational opportunities for i ts Negro students and was thus violating their rights. This decision put the entire state in a position that it had to improve the black schools.

It was a foregone conclusion that the NAACP would appeal. Because *Briggs v. Elliott* was a constitutional challenge, the NA ACP was able to appeal directly to the U.S. Supreme Court on behalf of t he Clarendon Count y plaintiffs, by passing the Court of Appeals.

At the Supreme Court, *Briggs v. Elliott* went as far as the discovery proceedings. Then, on January 28, 1952, the Supreme Court returned it to District Court for a report on progress made toward equalizing educational facilities a nd opportunities in response to the 1951 District Court ruling.

By the time *Briggs v. Elliott* was returned to the Supreme Court, four other NAACP cases (all claiming that segregation in public schools was a violation of constitutional rights) had also reached that level. The five cases were argued concurrently. For some reason, perhaps to show that the segregation issue did not apply to only the Deep South, the cases were put forth under the title *Brown et al. v. Board of Education of Topeka, Shawnee County, KS, et al.* in the fall term of the 1952 Supreme Court session. The cases were argued Decem ber 9 through 11 of 1952.

Excerpt reprinted with per mission from O. Gona Press (Pine Brook, New Jersey), April 2002 (Please go to the lesson plans to see the Curri culum Guide accompanying this booklet.)

# **Virginia**

### *Brown v. Board of Education* (1954) in the Stream of U.S. History:
### The View from Virginia, 1930s-1960s
Peter Wallenstein

The U.S. Supreme Court decided the case of *Brown v. Board of Education* some fifty years ago. Looking back now, it is hard to comprehend how much changed—how very different the world became—as a result. Yet it is hard also to comprehend how much difficulty it took to secure even a little change. Why this paradox? If we take a tour of Virginia through the 1930s, 1940s, 1950s, and 1960s, we can get some idea of how the 1954 decision came about and also how much of a challenge there was to make the court victory produce real change in the schools.

Before the Civil War, Virginia had no system of public schools, and in fact there was a law against permitting black Virginians—slave or free—to attend any school at all. Virginia began its system of public schools during Reconstruction, in 1870. Schools were soon open to black students and to white students. Yet, from the very beginning, the state legislature insisted that the schools remain absolutely segregated, with white students attending one set of schools, and black students attending another set. Teaching the white students were white teachers, never black teachers. At first, many of the teachers in the black schools were white, but in time all the teachers and principals in the black schools were black. So black students had black teachers, just as white students had white teachers.

In 1902, Virginia placed the segregation requirement—separate schools for black students and for white students—in the state constitution. In the years to come, far more money was spent on public schools than before, but the increase was very unevenly divided. The state divided up state money for schools according to the number of school-age people in each county. When the money arrived in each county, the school board divided it up among the schools. In the western counties, where the black population was small, the black schools received almost as much money per black student as the white schools received per white student. In the eastern counties, though, where the black population was large (in some cases a substantial majority), the school boards took much of the money that had been apportioned on the basis of black students and gave it to the white schools. So the schools with the most state money per student were the white schools in the east—far more than the black schools in the east or any of the schools, black or white, in the west.

With far less money available for black schools in the east—where most black Virginians lived—black teachers there were paid far less than were white teachers, the school year was shorter, the average class size was larger, the facilities were more limited, and—certainly in the higher grades—the course offerings were more restricted. The fact that schools were segregated made these sizable differences possible. So did the fact that, even though the money was apportioned on the basis of the total number of children, white school boards got to decide how to spend the money, so black taxpayers had no say. In the city of Richmond in the early 1940s, the highest paid black teacher—a man who had an advanced degree and m any years of experience and also served as school principal—was paid at least one do llar less than the leas t experienced white female teacher. (Teachers, white or black, were paid more in those days if they were men than if they were wom en.)

By the late 1930s and the 1940s, black Virginians began to develop a strategy to get a larger share of the school m oney. In the city of Nor folk, a teacher named Aline Black, from Booker T. Washington High School, we nt into state court to sue to get pai d as much as she would be paid if she were wh ite. Instead of winning her suit, she lost her job when the school bo ard refused to renew he r teaching job. Then her colleagu e Melvin Alston stepped in. He sued, but he went to federal court, where he eventually won, and over the next few years the sc hool board put a new salary schedule into place, so that black teachers and white teach ers—if they had identical education, experience, and responsibilities—would earn th e same salaries. During the 1940s, similar changes took place elsew here in Virginia, at least in the cities, including in Richm ond.

But salary differences were hardly the only examples of racial discrim ination, and they were h ardly the on ly areas in which black Virginians went into f ederal court in the 1940s to try to get things changed. If the white school had a gym nasium, a cafeteria, indoor plum bing, and a library full of books, pe ople in the black community argued that they should have the sam e in the black schools. If white students could go to a high school where they could take courses that w ould prepare them for college, black parents thought their children should, too. If school bus es took white children to white schools, black parents and students though t there ought to be buses th at took black children to school, too. As it was, school buses picked up white children but drove right past black children, and black children so metimes had to walk past white schools on their way to their own, more distant schools.

So black Virginians w ent to court. The people who were involved in these actions in court included the teachers, who wanted higher pay—they argued that it was not right that they be paid a lower salary just because they were black. They also included other m embers of the community, like the parents who feared for the safety of their children walking to school and who re sented the privileges their children were denied solely because they were black inst ead of white. And they included black civil rights lawyers like Thurgood Marsh all and Oliv er Hill, classmates at Howard University Law School who graduated in 1933. Marshall sometimes came to Virginia from his office in New York City with the National As sociation for the Advancem ent of Colored People (NAACP). Hill lived in Richmond.

District Court Judge Sterling Hutches on, a native white Virginian, ruled the way he saw the U.S. Constitution requiring. Years later, after *Brown*, he balked at pushing the process of desegregation along, but in March 1948 he ruled, for exa mple, that the school board in Surry County was discrim inating in teachers' salaries, bus transportation, physical facilities, and curricular offerings. There was more than one way to equalize, though. Ordered the next m onth to remedy such a deficiency in King George County, the school board there equalized the w hite high school and the black "training school" by cutting chem istry, physics, biology, and ge ometry from the white high school' s curriculum. Then it was white students an d their parents who protested the school board' s actions.

By 1950, Thurgood Marshall, Oliver Hill, and their colleag ues had fought m any court cases over racial discrim ination in the Virginia schools. Often they won, but they had to keep fighting. Although som e equalization under "separate but equal" did take place, the changes were difficult to obtain and uneven in p ractice. Always there were more issues to fix and m any remaining places that had not yet begun to equalize opportunities for black and white teach ers and students. Regardless, the po licy of segregation—the "separate" in "separate bu equal"—eon tinued to grate.

In 1950, the NAACP de cided that it was not going to keep struggling to equalize segregated schools. Instead the organizatio n would take cases that argued against segregated schools at all. If they were successful, as they saw it, black students and white students would attend the sam e schools. All the people in a comm unity' s schools, black or white, would have the sam e school facilities, the sam e curricular opportunities, and the same salary schedules.

NAACP attorneys planned to argue that segregation itself vi olated the Equal Protection Clause of the Fourteen th Amendment of the U.S. Constitu tion. They anticipated that the state of Virginia would argue that much had already been accomplished in equalizing teachers ' salaries, progress was being made in such areas as physical facilities and cu rricular offerings, and the Supreme Court' s holding *in Plessy v. Ferguson* in 1896—that segregation its elf did not violate anyone ' s rights—should be left in place.

In 1951, a sophomore named Barbara Johns and her classmates at Robert Moton High School in Farm ville, Virginia, in Prin ce Edward County, went on strike to protest the inadequ ate facilities at their school. They contacted O liver Hill in Richm ond, and he stopped by a big meeting held by black citizens in Farmville. He explained that he and his colleagues were not taking cases any m ore that simply tried to sec ure more of the "equal" in the old formula of "separate bu equal," but if the black citizens in Prince Edward wanted to go to court to protest sc hool segregation—to challen ge the polic y that restricted black students to Moton High School —then he could help them. And so it was agreed.

The case was in the courts for a long tim e. At first they lost, but the U.S. Supreme Court agreed to hear their case. At about the same time, the Supreme Court agreed to hear similar cases from South Carolina, Kansas, Delaware, and the District of Columbia. In fact, all five cases were argued at the Supreme Court together, and we know them by the nam e of the case from Kansas: *Brown v. Board of Education of Topeka.* In May 1954, the Supreme Court ruled th at a state policy of segregation was unconstitutional, that it violated the Equal Pr otection Clause. Under this ruling, states could no longer segregate public schools or maintain all-white or all-black schools, whether Booker T. Washington High School in the city of Norfolk or Robert Moton High School in Prince Edward County.

A year later, in May 1955, the Supreme Court followed up its 1954 ruling ( *Brown I*) by issuing broad guidelines that it thought were designed to govern the transition in every segregated state to a new, non-segregated system of public schools. According to the 1955 ruling (*Brown II*), the lower federal courts—th e district courts—would m onitor progress and oversee the change (and an occasional court order to desegregate one sch ool or another might be necessary). In the *new* non-segregated system, it was thought, black teachers and white teachers alike would teach in the same schools, and white studen ts and black students alike would attend those schools and take thos e classes. White students and black students would ride together on the sam e buses to the same schools, and there they would enjoy the s ame facilities and the same curricular opportunities. And the changes would take place soon.

In most places across the segregated states, things did not work out that way. In Virginia, in fact, nowhere did they work out that way. Instead, the state legislature adopted policies designed to keep desegregation from occurring at all. For one thing, the legislature adopted a policy that was called "m assive resistance." According to it, the governor was directed to close down any school that a court or dered desegregated. Better no school, this policy declared, than a desegreg ated school. For another thing, the sam e legislature passed other new laws that were designed to destroy the ability of the NAACP to bring cases in the continuing effo rts to get schools desegregated.

Nowhere in Virginia, in elem entary school or high school, did black students and white students attend public school togeth er in 1954 or 1955—or in 1956, 1957, or even 1958. Massive resistance came directly into play in the school year 1958-1959. Most schools in Virginia rem ained open all that year, still segregated. Some schools, though, having been ordered desegregated—for exa mple, schools in the city of Norfolk—had to close rather than open on a desegregated basis.

In January 1959, two courts overturned the policy of m assive resistance. A state court pointed out that the stat e constitution con tinued to require that Virginia maintain a system of public schools, so the state c ould not begin shutting schools down. A fe deral court ruled that the policy of massive resistance violated the Fourteen th Amendm ent and the ruling in *Brown v. Board of Education*. When the public schools reopened in the city of Norfolk, six high schools th at had previously enrolled no African Americ ans enrolled a total of seventeen black student s. (It was rare that any white students began attending previously black schools.) Sim ilar small changes took place in Char lottesville, in W arren County, and—before m any months had passed—in a few other places, too.

Well into the 1960s, though, m any school systems in Virginia rem ained entirely segregated. The m ost flagrant example of defiance cam e in Prince Edward County, the place that Virginia's share of the *Brown* case had originated. The state policy of massive resistance had been turned back by the cour ts, but white leaders and their followers in Prince Edward County acted out a local versio n of massive resistance in 1959. When a federal court ordered the school s there desegregate d, the county decide d to stop funding public education. A private school, Prince Ed ward Academy, was established, and most white students began attending it. For the remaining white students—and for all of the black students—no local schools were open. Not until 1964 were the Prince Edward public schools reopened, and when that happened m ost white students continued attending Prince Edwar d Academy, while bl ack students attended the "desegregated" public schools.

Resistance to desegregation did not end in 1964. Various jurisdictions in Virginia—th e city of Richm ond for one, Ne w Kent County for another— were still in the courts for the next few years fighting over segregation and desegregation. Yet some change had taken place. Gone was the policy, in place thro ughout the state for so m any years, of absolute segregatio n in all the public schools. Moreover, playgrounds and other public facilities were often desegreg ated as a result of the logic of *Brown*. Yet the Prince Edward model prevailed at so me recreation facilities. Some public swimming pools, in particular, were closed in stead of desegregated.

The rules that the Supreme Court announced in *Brown v. Board of Education* in 1954 were a long time coming. In Virginia, the policy of segregation had prevailed from 1870 to 1954, and the new policy took a lo ng time being im plemented. Massive resistance died when th e courts intervened and when a major ity of white Virgin ians decided that they would rather have desegr egated schools than no publ ic schools at all. Massive resistance triumphed, however, to the degree that it postponed the beginnings of desegregation. And desegregat ion not only cam e later but also caused less change in the end than had been expected by Oliver Hi ll, Thurgood Marshall, or the U.S. Supreme Court.

How typical was Virgin ia on matters of race and schools? Virginia's record of inequality, striking though it was, was actually less than the norm across the South during the Age of Segregation. That is, teachers' salaries, for example, were less unequal in Virginia than they were in a num ber of other southern states. Regardless, compared with other southern states, Virginia supplies a fu ller record of litigation challenging unequal schools in the 1940s, so it illustrates very well the discriminatory na ture of segregated schooling in America in the ye ars before *Brown*. The struggle after *Brown* ran much the same kind of course in Virgin ia as it did in the other southern states. Moreover, the persistence of largely segr egated schools long after *Brown* could be found across the nation, outside the South as well as w ithin the region.

Exercises

1) Play different roles in ha nding out the state school fund in a segregated world in which schools are racially separate and black Virgin ians have no political say—for example, in

the 1930s. Let someone be the Virginia stat e school superintendent; a m ember of the local schoo l board, one east of the Blue Ridge and one west of it; and a black teache r or a white teacher, one each in the east an d the west. What have you learn ed?

2) Play different roles—black or white, teacher or shop owner, elem entary school student or high school student, college applicant or college gradu ate, migrant from farm to city in Virginia or from the South to the North—in considering the conse quences of the great inequality that took place under "separate but equal"—for exam ple, in the 1920s. What have you learned?

3) Play different roles arguing a case in federal court, for or against, a series of possible changes: (in the 1940s) equalizi ng salary schedules, equalizi ng curricular offerings, or equalizing p hysical facilities; or (in the 1950s) dismantling segregation. What arguments do you adopt? Why? What are the chances th at you will win?

4) Play different roles, alte rnating between black and white , in a newly "desegregated" formerly white high school in the 1960s: th e football quarterback, a cheerleader, the football coach, a math or French teacher, th e senior class president, the principal. How do you feel? W hat do you see?

Bibliography

Irons, Peter. 2002. *Jim Crow's Children: The Broken Promise of the* Brown *Decision.* New York: Viking.

Kluger, Richard. 1974. *Simple Justice: The History of* Brown v. Board of Education *and Black America's Struggle for Equality.* New York: Random House.

Patterson, James T. 2001. *Brown v. Board of Education: A Civil Rights Milestone and Its Troubled Legacy.* New York: Oxford University Press.

Wallenstein, Peter. forthcom ing, 2004. *Blue Laws and Black Codes: Conflict, Courts, and Change in Twentieth-Century Virginia.* Charlottesville: U niversity of Virginia Press.

## Barbara Johns: A Student Leads the Way to the Highest Court
Cheryl Brown Henderson

"Some of the boys in the vocational program visited the shop at the white school and came back telling us how nice their whole school was...I remember thinking how unfair it was. I thought about it a lot in bed that night, and I was still thinking about it the next day."—Barbara Johns

More than two hundred plaintiffs and lawyers were involved in the *Brown v. Board of Education* case decided by the United States Supreme Court on May 17, 1954. Their cases were combined in a sweeping strategy by the National Association for the Advancement of Colored People (NAACP) to end the era of "separate but equal."

Who were these petitioners? Were these women among them? We need to recognize the achievements of black women in the civil rights movement. *Brown v. Board of Education* is another example of our patriarchal view of history. In three of the five cases represented by *Brown* the principal petitioners were women from Delaware, Virginia and Kansas.

In Virginia, the NAACP filed a class action suit in May of 1951 on behalf of 117 African American students enrolled at segregated Moton High School. For these students in deteriorating buildings without access to many academic options, social activism became a matter of survival.

Enter Barbara Johns, a junior at Moton High School. Barbara was a bright African American teen who read about an America that seemed just outside of her reach. What she saw was not available to her reach. What she saw was not available to her, solely because she was African American. Her school was supposed to prepare her for citizenship and participation in the political and economic life of her country, but she saw that white America was not interested in her future. Her school was an inadequate structure so overcrowded that several tarp aper "shacks" stood outside as overflow classrooms.

Barbara Johns was already a student leader. Articulate and persuasive, she was convinced that any action for change would have to come from the African American students. Whites controlled the wages, jobs, farm mortgages and credit. For black parents, acceptance was a way of life.

NAACP leaders and the school principal had been unsuccessful in proposing a new facility to replace the overcrowded and deteriorating Moton High. After months of official inaction, Barbara rallied support for what she believed to be their only course: a student strike.

Knowing that across town white students attended a well-equipped, well-appointed high school had become a discontent too large to contain. A student strike organized by Barbara Johns began in April of 1951. Students assembled in the school auditorium to hear Barbara speak. She asked the faculty to leave and told her classmates that "it was time that Negroes were treated equally with whites, time that they had a decent high school, time for the students to do something about it."

With her words of challenge, the students left the building with instructions not to leave the school grounds. Some carried signs asking for better facilities. When the strike was underway, Barbara Johns and Carrie Stokes sought legal counsel from the NAACP. With the promise of action, the students agreed to return to school. A month later, the NAACP filed suit in federal court on behalf of some of the students including the strike leaders. Their case would travel all the way to the Supreme Court.

If you would like to know more about Barbara Johns and the Virginia case, read Bob Smith's book, *They Closed Their Schools: Prince Edward County, Virginia, 1951-1964,* published in 1966.

Reprinted with permission from *The* Brown *Quarterly,* Vol. 2, No. 3, Spring 1998.
http://brownvboard.org/brwnqurt/02-3/02-3b.htm

# Chapter 3
## Beyond *Brown*

# Capturing Forgotten Moments in Civil Rights History
Jean Van Delinder


The names of Claymont, Delaware, Farmville, Virginia, or Summerton, South Carolina do not come to mind when thinking about the 1954 *Brown v. Board of Education of Topeka* school desegregation case. However, these communities were as significant a part of this famous case as Topeka, Kansas. You may have heard that in September 1950 a man named Oliver Brown took his little daughter Linda to Sumner Elementary School in Topeka, Kansas, and tried to enroll her in classes. But there were twelve other African American parents in Topeka trying to enroll their young children in schools across the city on that same day. At the same time, African American parents were doing the same thing in the communities of Summerton, South Carolina, Farmville, Virginia, and Claymont, Delaware.

Over forty years ago, in elementary and high schools around the country, African-Americans challenged segregated education in their communities. Many state and local laws had been written in such a way as to exclude African American children from attending certain schools because of their race. Seven-year-old Linda Brown attended Monroe Elementary School in Topeka, Kansas, which was twenty blocks away from her home. There was a school three blocks away, called Sumner Elementary, but she could not attend it. Only white children could go there.

In the early 1950s, the law of the land said it was legal to keep African Americans and whites in "separate but equal" institutions. From the time this law was first put into practice in 1896, its effect was to exclude African-Americans from the same opportunities that were automatically given to white citizens. Fifty years later, in the 1950s, African-Americans took steps to change this law. It took more than one person to do this. It took many people, in many places to overturn segregation.

There really *was* an African-American family named Brown who lived in the city of Topeka, Kansas, who were brave enough to challenge segregation in the early 1950s. But they were not alone. There were twelve other families who volunteered to participate in a lawsuit against the Topeka school board. We know this because of extensive interviews made with many of the participants of desegregation. These interviews, or oral histories, help us to discover "footsoldiers" missed by the history books. Oral histories are gathered by personal interviews of persons who lived through the events surrounding these cases, many of them were eyewitnesses. These interviews serve as a link between the legal issues and the participants' personal experiences.

In 1991, the Kansas State Historical Society, in cooperation with the Brown Foundation and Washburn University Law School, developed a proposal to create an oral history collection focusing on the people involved in and those affected by the *Brown* case and other related cases around the United States. These oral histories will be used to provide a human dimension to the *Brown v. Board of Education* National Historic Site now being developed in Topeka, Kansas. This collection of oral histories will remind future visitors coming to the National Historic Site that Topeka did not act alone in trying to bring about desegregation. It will also tell stories recounting personal struggles to fight segregation.

These stories of personal struggle include African Americans in Summerton, South Carolina and Farmville, Virginia. In Summerton, South Carolina, school enrollment attempts were met with violence. One of the major participants in the school litigation, Reverend J. A. De Laine, fled his residence in the middle of the night in fear of his life. His house was later burned to the ground. Defendant Harry Briggs, the first named plaintiff on the case that would later be called *Briggs vs. Elliott*, found he could no longer get his cotton ginned anywhere in the county. He eventually left South Carolina seeking work in Florida. Annie Gibson not only lost her job as a maid in a local motel, but her husband was forced off land his family had sharecropped for over fifty years. In recounting these events forty years later, Annie said that if the segregated schools had had desks for her children to sit in, she never would have signed her name to the petition demanding better educational facilities.

Just before graduation in April, 1951, students attending Robert Moton High School in Farmville, Virginia, walked out of class and went on strike for two weeks protesting the use of poorly constructed shacks for classroom space. Attorney Oliver Hill of Richmond, Virginia, remembers receiving a telephone call from one of the student leaders in Farmville asking for help. Hill was a Howard Law School classmate of Thurgood Marshall and had handled numerous civil rights cases for the National Association for the Advancement of Colored People (NAACP) in Virginia. He was also familiar with the overcrowded conditions in the segregated schools in Prince Edward County, the school district where Farmville was located. He doubted that the strike would have much effect on current district policies, but he did agree to meet with the students and assess the feasibility of filing a lawsuit in Farmville. His legal assistance, combined with the determined efforts of community residents, resulted in the school desegregation case called *Davis, et al. v. Prince Edward County*. This lawsuit was reviewed by the United States Supreme Court along with the *Brown* case.

The *Brown* lawsuit in Topeka received its name from Oliver Brown, who took his eldest daughter Linda and tried to enroll her in Sumner Elementary School, a few blocks from their home. He was not alone. Mrs. Lucinda Todd with her daughter Nancy and Mrs. Lena Carper with her daughter Catherine attempted to enroll in Randolph Elementary School. Mrs. Sadie Emmanuel tried to enroll her young son James in Lafayette Elementary. Throughout Topeka the story was similar. In all these cases the children lived within four to five blocks of a white neighborhood school, but were bussed ten to twenty blocks to one of the four segregated schools. A total of thirteen African-American parents tried to enroll their grade school children into neighborhood schools that fall in Topeka, Kansas.

The children remember their experiences, even today, of waiting in hallways for their parents to return from hushed conversations with school officials. Linda rem embers waiting outside the principal's office while her father went inside to speak to Frank Wilson, the principal of Sumner Elementary. She doesn't remember much else about that day except afterward, when they were walking home, her father held her tightly by the hand, hurrying her with his long strides. Frank Wilson remembers Oliver Brown arriving at his office that September morning. He remembers a quiet, dignified looking man. Mr. Wilson wasn't surprised by the arrival of this reticent man with his eldest daughter standing shyly next to him. Mr. Wilson had been expecting such a visit since early summer when he was warned by Topeka School Superintendent Kenneth McFarland that the local NAACP would attempt to enroll African-American children in schools that were reserved for white Topekans. Wilson, like principals of white schools across Topeka encountering African-American parents that fall, politely received Oliver Brown and listened to his request to enroll his daughter, and politely refused to allow it. The law was clear: African-American children had their own schools to attend.

Under existing law, Topeka was within its rights to segregate elem entary schools on the basis of race. The scene played out just as Superintendent McFarland had planned. The threat of legal action did not deter McFarland in his mission to keep the segregation status quo in Topeka. He had been named as a defendant before in lawsuits. McFarland, and Wilson too, knew they probably would later be named as defendants in the *Brown v. Board of Education* case. This did not alter either of their courses of action. For one reason or another, each in his own way felt responsible for maintaining segregation.

Other states had similar laws. For example, Delaware also prohibited African Americans from attending school with whites. In the fall of 1951, the family of Spencer Robinson was one of several African American families living in the unincorporated community of Claymont, Delaware. Spencer Robinson remembers that his parents tried to enroll him in Claymont High School, less than a mile away from his home. Robinson had to ride a city bus two hours each way in order to attend classes at the closest school that admitted African Americans: Howard High School in the city of Wilmington, Delaware. The State of Delaware appealed a decision to integrate state schools in the fall of 1952. Pending that action, Claymont School Superintendent Stahl was told to disenroll the African American children already attending classes. Unlike his Kansas counterpart, Mr. Stahl refused to make the students leave, and for two years African Americans attended Claymont High School in violation of state segregation laws. Stahl saw no sense in disrupting the students' academic career. Robinson remembers School Superintendent Stahl as being a strict disciplinarian and that he would not tolerate any actions by white students to make African Americans feel unwelcome. Robinson went on to graduate from Claymont High School in the spring of 1954, within a few weeks of the *Brown* decision making school segregation unconstitutional.

We now know the names of many forgotten people who were involved in changing school segregation in the 1950s. Also important to remember are the decisions made by school administrators such as Mr. Wilson in Kansas and Mr. Stahl in Delaware, who shaped the way school integration would happen in their local communities. The men and women mentioned in this article, as well as many others, were the footsoldiers of the civil rights movement. Their contributions are now being recaptured through oral history interviews. The knowledge gained from talking to these eyewitnesses to history provide a broader understanding of the numerous personal sacrifices African Americans made to change the law from segregation to integration. These stories from Summerton, South Carolina, Farmville, Virginia, and Claymont, Delaware are as essential to the *Brown* story as the events that happened in Topeka. Through oral history interviews, these forgotten moments in civil rights history provide an essential insight into how history was made.

## SUGGESTED STUDENT LEARNING ACTIVITIES

1. Are there forgotten moments in civil rights history in your own community? One way to find out is to go to your local library and ask for historical information about your community. Another way is to ask your parents or grandparents if they remember anything related to civil rights that happened forty or fifty years ago.

2. Doing historical research is a lot like being a detective. You have to search for clues and hidden messages that have been covered up by time. Libraries usually have old newspapers and they are a good place to begin your investigation. Make a list of the dates you think might be important to the civil rights movement, such as May 1954, when the *Brown* case was decided. Once your list is complete, ask for copies of old newspapers and search for stories related to the subject of civil rights.

3. Once you have collected stories about the Civil Rights Movement, make a poster listing names, dates and a brief description of what happened. Who was the first African American in your community to attend an integrated school? Register to vote? Sit at a lunch counter and be served?

Reprinted with permission from *Cultural Resources Management* (*CRM*), Vol. 19, No. 2, 1996. *http://brownvboard.org/brwnqurt/03-1/03-la.htm*

### The Struggle Against "Jim Crow" and "Bantu" Education
### in the United States and South Africa
Bradley Skelcher

Growing impatient with the school authorities to equalize the segregated Robert R. Morton High School in Farmville, Virginia, Barbara Rose Johns led a walkout of 450 high school students in a protest to desegregate education in Prince Edward County on April 23, 1951. Johns was the niece of Reverend Vernon Johns, pastor at the Dexter Avenue Baptist Church in Montgomery, Alabama, which took the lead in the 1955 Montgomery Bus Boycott. Johns took her case to NAACP Legal Defense and Educational Fund attorneys Oliver Hill and Spottswood Robinson III, who eventually filed suit against segregation in *Davis v. County School of Prince Edward County* in 1951. Along with four other cases, the Prince Edward County suit was combined in *Brown v. Board of Education of Topeka, Kansas*. On May 17, 1954, the United States Supreme Court rendered its landmark decision ruling "separate but equal" in education "inherently unequal."[lxx]

Reminiscent of the student protest against segregation in Prince Edward County in Virginia on June 16, 1976, over 10,000 students in Soweto, a township near Johannesburg, rose up against apartheid education, called "Bantu education" by the Nationalist regime in South Africa. Inspired by the Black Consciousness Movement, inspired by Stephen Biko, students were protesting the recent decision to teach secondary education in Afrikaans, the language of the white oppressors. Andries Treurnicht, Under-Minister for Bantu Education, issued this order focusing mainly on mathematics instruction to be delivered in Afrikaans. In response, Bantu and white police forces responded to the protesting students with violence, killing an estimated 1,000 youths.[lxxi]

Like Johns in Virginia, Stephen Biko in South Africa understood the value of education equal to the one offered to white students. Biko emerged as the leader of student protests against South Africa apartheid as a youth growing up in Eastern Cape. Because of his "anti-establishment" behavior, Biko was forced to move to Durban where he eventually entered medical school at the University of Natal in the black section. He eventually joined the National Union of South African Students and later founded the South African Students' Organization. Biko believed that educated people should serve the community to uplift it, contrary to the notion of education held by the Nationalist regime. To further this end, he founded the Black Peoples Convention in 1972, leading to the emergence of the South African Student's Movement influential in the Soweto Uprising in 1976. In 1977, South African authorities arrested him as a terrorist. He later died in police detention resulting from brutal beatings by his guards.

At the same time when the NAACP Legal Defense and Education Fund attorneys were presenting their cases to desegregate education in the U.S., the Nationalist regime in South Africa moved to do the opposite. They instead began the legislative process of establishing a national policy of apartheid, or racial separation, building upon earlier laws. In many respects, white South Africans used "Jim Crow" segregation laws in the

United States as their model for apartheid. After coming to power in 1948, the Nationalist Party in South Africa passed the Bantu Education Act of 1953 providing for the first time funding for the education of non-whites in South Africa. Hendrik Verwoerd, Minister of Native/ Bantu Affairs and later Prime Minister, introduced this Act to the Senate, which outlined the future of education in South Africa for almost forty years. Based upon recommendations in the 195 1 Eiselen Report, Verwoerd em placed the cornerstone of white suprem acy in South Africa to ensure against non-white "equality with Europeans."[lxxii]

Whether discussing apartheid in South Afri ca or segregation in the Unite d States, white supremacists believed people of color to be intellectually inf erior and capable of learning only vocational skills. Following the American Civil W ar, many educational systems established for Afri can Americans tended to fo llow the philosophy of General Samuel C. Armstrong, founder of Ha mpton Normal and Industrial Institute in 1868 located in Ha mpton, Virginia. Like Ve rwoerd, Armstrong thought African Am ericans lacked the intellectual capacity to achieve beyond the vocational skills. He wanted to teach them "respect for labor..to build up an industrial system for the sake..of intelligent labor."[lxxiii] Others, like W.E.B. Du Bois, believed this type of educational philosophy held African Am ericans back, keep ing them in a servil e position servin g the needs of the oppressors.

In South Africa, Verwoerd thought th at the liberal education stressed by missionary education gave Black people false hope of aspiring beyond their intellectual capacities similar to Armstrong' s belief. Verwoerd believed this would lead to frustration and social unrest. Instead, he believed Bantu education should stress skills leading to employm ent that would serve whites in South Africa. Once he becam e Prime Minister in the 1960s, Verwoerd led the apar theid regime to promote white suprem acy through efforts such as banning book s with sinister titles like *Black Beauty*.[lxxiv]

In 1959, the Nationalist regim e extended the apartheid system into higher education with the passage of Act 45, the Exte nsion of University Education Act. This Act ended the adm ission of non- white students and their removal from white universities. It replaced integra ted institutions of higher educ ation with s eparate schools for coloreds, blacks, and Asians. This resulted in the creation of separate schools for each group in places like Durban, where three s chools ex isted for Asians, blacks, and whites. It also led to the establishm ent of Technikon vo cational training schools for blacks.

The Extension of University Education Ac t of 1959 resembled the Se cond Merrill Land Grant College Act of 1890 pas sed by the United States Congress. This Act was in response to financially ailing institutions of higher education created from the First Merrill Land Grant College Act of 1862. To encourage higher educ ational opportunities for African Americans, Congress stipulated that states must admit them to existing schools or create new ones for Afri can American students. Southern states opted for the latter in an era of growing legal segregation, which in tensified following the U.S. Supreme Court decision *Plessy v. Ferguson* in 1896, upholding "Jim Crow" segregation laws. The result led to the establishment of higher educational institutions aim ed at providing agricultural educationa l opportunities for African Am ericans. Many criticized these schools as perpetuating the idea that African Americans could only aspire to vocational training.

South Africa and the United States follo wed sim ilar paths regarding separate educational opportunities for black people a nd white people with the intention of suppressing the form er. In South Africa, the Nationalist regime openly proclaim ed its intention to lim it the educa tional opportunities of black South Africans while white Americans defended segregation as based in tradition or *defacto*, claiming educational systems as "separate but equal." Am erican segregation began to break down under the pressure of the NAACP Legal Defe nse Fund le gal challenges, resulting with the 1954 Brown decision overturning the "separate but equal" doctrine stemm ing from the 1896 *Plessy* decision. The rem edy, however, was de layed with Brown II in 1955 declaring integration "with all deliberate speed ." White resistance led to decades o f challenges to desegregate education in the U.S. Like South Africa, African Am erican youth took the lead through the formation of the Student Nonviolen t Coordinating Comm ittee, which took the lead in attacking segregation through "sit-ins" and voter registration drives. Similarly, the movement in the United States has shown success in breaking down segregation, as had the youth m ovement in South Africa.

In 1994, South Africans ushered in a new governm ent led by the African National Congress and President Nelson Mandela replaci ng the apartheid regim e. Under majority rule, the new South Afr ican gove rnment desegregated educati onal institutions leading to white resistance harkening to the days following the *Brown* decision in 1954 in the U.S. Additionally, desegregation of white schools has left histori cally black schools in sim ilar difficulties as ones in the United S tates. Many had already suffered from years of neglect and underfunding like the University of Zulula nd in KwaZulu-Natal. Others are being closed like the Technikon vocational schools . In formerly all-white schools like University o f Natal in Durban, white students are leaving in the wake of black and A sian students entering. Black and As ian students currently are prot esting against racist white faculty upset with the lack of preparation of the new students enteri ng the University of Natal. South Africa also lacks universal educa tion, prompting U.S. A.I.D. to offer assistance in accomplishing this.

In comparison, schools in the U.S. increa singly are becom ing more segregated through *defacto* segregation in residentia l patterns. Some argue that education is more segregated now than it was in 1954. W ith school funding reliant upon local property taxes, many African Am erican schools are fa lling further behind than their white counterparts with higher incom es and property values. Additionally, with integration of higher educational institutions, historically black colleges and universities (HBCUs) face growing questions regarding their relevancy. Public HBCUs are suffering from declining budgets passed by state legislatures.

In closing, both South Africa and the United States followed a history of oppression to reinforce white suprem acy. Both saw education as a means to their ends of creating societies based upon the inferiority of black people a nd the superiority of white people. Education was a m eans of uplifti ng one group while holding another down with the idea of perform ing a service for the superi or group. When challenged, the system s of segregation and apartheid fell in both the United States and South Africa. The challenge facing both countries no w is to fulfill the pr omise of equal education al opportunities for all by creating equal edu cational opportunities.

[lxx] James T. Patterson, *Brown v. Board of Education: A Civil Rights Milestone and Its Troubled Legacy*, (New York: Oxford University Press, 2001), 27-29.

[lxxi] Robert Ross, *A Concise History of South Africa* (Cambridge, U.K.: Cambridge University Press, 1999), 141-143; Zubeida Desai, "Democratic Language Planning and the Transformation of Education in Post-Apartheid South Africa," in *Education in a Future South Africa*, edited by Elaine Unterhalter, Harold Wolpe, and Thozamile Botha (Trenton, NJ: Africa World Press, 1992), 119-120.

[lxxii] "Apartheid and Education," *The History of Education and Childhood* (1997-2001) <http://www.socsci.kun.nl/ped/whp/histeduc/apartheid.html> [July 26, 2003]; Neil Parsons, *A New History of South Africa* (London: Macmillan Education, 1982), 291-293.

[lxxiii] Samuel Chapman Armstrong, *Twenty-Two Years' Work of the Hampton Normal and Agricultural Institute* (Hampton, Virginia: Normal School Press, 1893), 6.

[lxxiv] "Apartheid and education"; Ross, *A Concise History of South Africa*, 134.

**Personal Perspective: *Brown v. Board of Education*' s 50ᵗʰ Anniversary**
Cheryl Brown Henderson

Our nation is fast approaching a watershed year. In Kansas, as well as all over the country, we will witnes s the 50ᵗʰ anniversary of the landm ark U. S. Supreme Court decision in *Oliver L. Brown et. al. vs. the Board of Education of Topeka (KS), et. al.* on May 17, 2004.

We should pay particul ar attention to the *Brown* decision because of the weight placed on its importance by legal scholars and historians alike. With *Brown*, the high court issued a definitive interpretation of the 14ᵗʰ Amendment to our Constitution, making it clear that every indiv idual in this country was entitled to "equal protection under the law" without regard to race, ethnicity, gender, disability, age or any other circumstance. In addition, their decision had a profound impact on our society by m aking it illegal to practice racial segregation. *Brown* laid a foundation for ending legal discrimination on any basis as evidenced by the legislation that followed a decade later beginning w ith the Civil Rights Act of 1964.

In order to prepare and educate our state and nation and bring a better understanding of the com ing anniversary of *Brown*, we created a 50ᵗʰ Anniversary state coalition. This coalition will plan programs to focus our attention on Brown' s role in race relations, education and access to public accommodations. The goal is to have a better-inform ed citizenry with respect to this historic m ilestone. This group began its public programs in 2001 by hosting a national tour ing exhibit "Marching Toward Justice: The History of the 14ᵗʰ Amendment and a Tribute to Thurgood Marshall." Other programs include a fall visiting Oliver L. Brown Scholar for Diversity Issues at Washburn University, African Am erican History Month lectures and a May comme moration of the *Brown* decision.

In order to ensure a federal presence in the 50ᵗʰ anniversary of *Brown*, the Brown Foundation worked along with our Kansas Congr essional delegation to pass legislation which esta blished a *Brown v. Board of Education* 50ᵗʰ Anniversary Presidential Commission. President Bush signed this bill on Septem ber 18, 2001. After appointments to this body were confirm ed in August of 2002, the Commission began its work. Meetings will convene in each of the five st ates that presented cases co mbined under the heading of *Brown*, as well as Massachusetts, the site of the first docum ented school case in the country. The Commissi on will plan commemorations and engage in program s for the purpose of educating the public about the significance of the *Brown* decision. We are networking with organizations like the Natio nal Bar Association and the American Bar Association about the possibi lity of sponsoring "Moot Court" opportunities in 2004 for high school students in tribut e to attorneys Charles H. Houston and Thurgood Marshall.

The centerp iece of the 50ᵗʰ anniversary commemoration will be the grand opening of the *Brown v. Board of Education* National Historic Site, a unit of the National Park Service. This opening is scheduled to co incide with the date of the Suprem e Court decision, May 17<sup>th</sup>. The National Park Service will make certain that the *Brown* decision is interpreted for generations to com e.

On a personal note, my fa mily, much like the country, ca me to gradually understand the im portance of the *Brown* decision. It became most evident with the passage of legislation like th e Civil Rights Act of 1964, the Voting Rights Act of 1965 and Title IX in 1972 because each of these Ac ts are based on the Court's edict of equal protection under the law. My father was recruited by his childhood friend, who at the time was legal counsel for the Topeka NAACP, and joined 12 other pa rents as plaintiffs in this class action suit. We bear this legacy proudly. Being the fa mily of the na mesake of this judicial turning point comes with a responsibility to teach and never let the country forget what it took for some of its citizens to be afforded their constitutional rights.

Finally, I categorize the im portance of *Brown* in this way: it rep resents three critical aspects in the pursuit of our democratic ideals. First, education reform because education is funda mental to citizenship. Second, *Brown* required the country to acknowledge and define race relatio ns. Third, the Court ultimately directed th e country in what course it had to follow with r espect to the inclusive intent of the 14<sup>th</sup> Amendment to the Constitution. *Brown* asserted the rights of African American people to be full partners in social, politic al and communal structures.

The *Brown* decision and the civil rights movements in the United States inspir ed and galvanized hum an rights struggles around the world. The *Brown* federal commission hopes to catalogue the thousands of comme morative programs that will occur in communities, school dis tricts, universities and organizations across the country.

The *Brown* decision was merely a catalyst. Positive relations require more than one willing participan t. For many of us, this is a once-in-a-lifetime opportunity to have a national platform for conveying to the citizens and l eaders of our country that the heart of positive race relations is a sense of unity, respec t and acceptance.

The year 2004 also marks the following anniversaries: the 150<sup>th</sup> of territorial Kansas, the 150<sup>th</sup> of the city of Topeka and the 200<sup>th</sup> of the Lewis and Clark expedition.

Members of the state *Brown v. Board* 50<sup>th</sup> Anniversary Coalition include: The Brown Foundation, *Brown v. Board of Education* National Historic Site, City of Topeka, Kansas African American Affairs Comm ission, Kansas Humanities Council, Kansas State Historical Society, Mayor's Council on Diversity, NAACP of Topeka, Topeka Black Home Reunion, Topeka Convention and Vi sitors Bureau, Topeka Public Schools, Washburn University and the University of Kansas.

Reprinted with permission from *The* Brown *Quarterly*, Vol. 5, No. 3, Winter 2003.
http://brownvboard.org/brwnqurt/05-3b.htm

# Chapter 4
# Learning Resources
# (Lesson Plans and Curriculum Units)

# **<u>Elementary Level</u>**

## *Brown v. Board of Education*
### Irene Owens

To celebrate *Brown v. Board of Education* suggest an African American Fair with implications for social studies, math, English, and literature. This lesson presents the geography and the English aspects.

Lesson Title: *Brown v. Board of Education*

Grade Level: Elementary K-5

Length of Lesson: 2-4 class sessions

Standard(s) Addressed: Types of Writing, Speaking and Listening, Reading, Analyzing, and Interpreting Literature, Math Calculation

Learning Goals and Objectives:
- x To identify the two-letter postal designation for Kansas
- x To determine the distance between two geographic points
- x To record one African American site of interest in two states entered between beginning point and ending point to or from Topeka, Kansas
- x To help students develop and maintain personal, reality-based math connections

Activities: Identify the state in which you live and locate it in an atlas. You are going to travel to Topeka, Kansas, to interview Linda Brown, the daughter of Oliver Brown, the Topeka father who was the plaintiff in this historic case, which went to the Supreme Court of the United States. With the assistance of a partner, you will determine how far you live from Topeka using the guidelines in a text or using an on-line service such as mapquest.com.

Trace or sketch an outline of the state of Kansas and approximate where Topeka would be located.

Complete the cloze procedure.

Complete the *Brown v. Board of Education* word search.

Instructional Materials Needed: Internet access for a website such as puzzlemaker.com; a U.S. atlas such as <u>National Geographic United States Atlas for Young Explorers</u> or <u>The Young People's Atlas of the United States;</u> a cloze procedure similar to the example provided.

A Sample Cloze Procedure

The number of miles you must travel from your house to Topeka, Kansas is _____. You consider writing to the tourist bureau of Topeka before you begin your trip. The two capital letters that represent the postal designation for Kansas are _____. As you travel along the highways of Kansas, look for a sighting of its state bird, which is the _____. As you pass through the countryside and towns, you notice three things that stand out. One of these is the state song, _____, which you begin to hum as you listen to it on the radio. Another is that one of its cities, _____, is known as the "Center of the Wild West." Thirdly, the state ranks number one in the production of _____, perhaps due to its rich, fertile soil.

Assessment:    Create a fact-finding travel bookmark of interesting sights and places of interest that may include restaurants, parks, museums, libraries, etc. See sample using Ellison die. These bookmarks will be displayed and later exchanged with classmates.

Variations:    Younger children, kindergarten and first graders may glue on pictures provided by teachers for bookmarks. For cloze procedure, teachers may take students on a walk through the school, where items relative to Kansas have been displayed by teachers prior to the walk. Students can fill in sentences orally with teachers acting as their guides.

Collateral Readings:

Baker, C., ed. 2003. *Footsteps: African American History.* Peterborough, NH: Cobblestone.

Coles, R. 1995. *The Story of Ruby Bridges.* New York: Scholastic.

## An Interview with a Plaintiff in *Brown v. Board of Education*
Irene Owens

Introduction:    Linda Brown is the daughter of Oliver Brown, the Topeka father who was the plaintiff in the historic *Brown v. Board of Education* case of 1954, the Supreme Court decision that desegregated schools. The interview form at allows elementary students an opportunity for a creative venue of self-expression.

Lesson Title:  An Interview with a Plaintiff in *Brown v. Board of Education*
Grade Level:  Elementary 3-5

Length of Lesson:  2-3 class sessions

Standard(s) Addressed:  Types of Writing, Reading, Speaking and Listening, Visual Art

Learning Goals and Objectives:
- To acquire a recognition vocabulary by identifying, researching, and correctly using words, symbols, and artifacts to internalize the significance of *Brown v. Board of Education* via web/e-mail interview, conference call interview or in-person interview;
- To listen and record accurately responses to interview questions;
- To read and interpret research summaries of *Brown v. Board of Education* on reserve and identify the key participants in the case;
- To construct a visual representation of one of the principles in the case.

Activities:    Construct an interview information card that includes the following contact information:

        Name of person interviewed:
        Address:
        Phone no:
        e-mail:
        FAX:
        cell phone no:

Interview Questions:

        When and where were you born?
        Tell us about your family:
                A. Do you have siblings? If so, what two fun things did you enjoy doing with them?
                B. Of what did your favorite meal consist?
                C. Describe one of your favorite cousins.

Tell us about your elementary school:
   A. Its name is?
   B. Describe your first day of school.
   C. How far was it from home?
   D. How did you get to school?
   E. What things did you notice along the way to school?
   F. Who was your favorite teacher?  Favorite subject?  Favorite activity?
   G. Did you buy lunch or take a bag lunch?
What is the best or worst memory you have of childhood?
 How did you celebrate your favorite holiday as a child?
What do you remember about 1954?
The person you would consider your hero or heroine as a child was _____?
In three words, describe yourself.

Thank You

After reading the *Brown v. Board of Education* case summary on reserve in your library and the three (3) selections from the classroom vertical file, create a portrait of Linda Brown, the primary focus of the case, or of her father, Oliver Brown, the chief plaintiff, using torn/cut strips of paper. What color are their eyes, hair, and skin? Is their hair long or short, straight or curly? For the face, trace or draw a circle or oval and cut it out. Next, tear/cut bits of construction paper for hair and glue to circle. Cut out colored paper for eyes and glue to face. For nose, fold a piece of paper in half and shape; then glue to center of face. Use red paper to cut shapes for lips and glue. Tear/cut pieces for eyebrows and glue. Eyelashes, teeth and cheek color may also be added. Sign and label as shown in finished sample.

Instructional Materials Needed:  Interview questions; a notebook or journal to record responses; three summary articles on *Brown v. Board of Education*. For portrait, a supply of brown bags (free grocery bags will do); construction paper in colors of red, white, black and brown; pencils, glue sticks, scissors, circular template

Assessment:  Using a briefcase die (Ellison Co.), compile photos, newspaper clippings, website addresses, correspondence, symbols, comments, quotes, etc. to design a portfolio book. The briefcase can be decorated first and laminated before the pages are inserted. Students can share their compilations and have an interesting artifact of the case to take home.

# Middle – High School Level

# Teacher Talk:
## Lesson Plan on School Segregation Before *Brown*

**Measurable Objectives:**
1.  Students will use information on school segregation by state to create a color-coded map of the United States.
2.  Students will recognize trends in segregation and begin to consider reasons for regional differences in segregation practices.
3.  Students will know if school segregation was practiced in their home state.

**Materials Needed:**
- x  Copies of map activity page for each student
- x  Colored pencils or markers

**Teacher Preparation:**
- x  Map activity page for students with discussion questions
- x  Historical background for students

**Vocabulary:**
- x  **required by law**: actions that are required to be done because a law or laws make those actions mandatory
- x  **prohibited by law**: actions that are illegal because laws have been enacted that specifically identify those actions as being illegal
- x  **permitted by law**: actions that are legal because they have not been legally prohibited

**Instructions:**
1.  Give each student a copy of the map activity page that lists the state names in four categories.
2.  Determine a color code for each of the four categories: segregation required, segregation permitted in varying degrees, segregation prohibited, and no specific legislation on segregation. Have students record those color codes on their papers.
3.  Have students locate each state on the map and color that state according to its appropriate color code.
4.  Have students answer the following questions.

**Worksheet or Discussion Questions:**
1.  What forms of segregation might have been allowed under "segregation permitted in varying degrees?"
2.  What are the similarities between states that allowed or required segregation and states that prohibited it?

3.      What was the status of segregation in 1950 in your home state? Explore the history of segregation in the states that surround where you live. How were they similar? How were they different?

4.      What information surprised you about segregation in the United States in 1950? Why?

5.      What trends did you notice in the geographic distribution of states with segregation legislation?

**Segregation Required:**
Alabama, Arkansas, Delaware, District of Columbia, Florida, Georgia, Kentucky, Louisiana, Maryland, Mississippi, Missouri, North Carolina, Oklahoma, South Carolina, Tennessee, Texas, Virginia and West Virginia

**Segregation Permitted in Varying Degrees:**
Arizona, Kansas, New Mexico and Wyoming

**Segregation Prohibited:**
Colorado, Connecticut, Idaho, Illinois, Iowa , Indiana, Massachusetts, Michigan, Minnesota, New Jersey, New York, Ohio, Pennsylvania, Rhode Island, Washington and Wisconsin

**No Specific Legislation on Segregation:**
California, Maine, Montana, Nebraska, New Hampshire, North Dakota, Oregon, South Dakota, Utah and Vermont

**Advanced Activities:**
1.      Study the laws of your state in 1950. Is segregation mentioned, and if so, how? What specific laws mentioned segregation and for what public areas?

2.      Use census information to investigate the population statistics for states in 1870 (when the 14<sup>th</sup> Amendment was passed) and for the same states in 1950. Make a graph comparing the total population (percentage of people identified as white, "colored," or African American). How might these numbers have affected a state's decision to ratify the 14<sup>th</sup> Amendment?

3.      Select two states from the above categories. What was the economic base for these states in 1870? In 1950? How might the economics of a state affect segregation laws?

4.      What was the ratio of states requiring or allowing segregation compared to states prohibiting it? What was the ratio of states with segregation legislation compared to states with no laws regarding segregation?

Printed with permission from *The* Brown *Quarterly*, Vol. 4, No. 2, Winter 2001.
http://brownvboard.org/brwnqurt/04-2/04-2g.htm (go on website to get map)

# *Brown v. Board of Education* National Historic Site
## EDUCATOR'S GUIDE

## CURRICULUM EDUCATION PROGRAM

# What is the National Park Service?

The National Park Service is a bureau within the U.S. Department of Interior. The Organic Act of 1916 established the National Park Service "to conserve the scenery and natural objects and wildlife therein and to provide for the enjoyment of the same in such manner and such means as will leave them unimpaired for the enjoyment of future generations." In other words, it is the mission of the National Park Service to protect and maintain our cultural and natural resources for all Americans—today and for generations to come.

There are over 387 units of the National Park system nationwide. These units include parks, historic sites, recreation areas, preserves, seashores, lakeshores, scenic rivers, and scenic trails. Thus, the National Park Service is the steward of the nation's natural and cultural heritage. It holds in trust not only the awesome splendor of the Grand Canyon and majesty of Mount McKinley, but ancient Native American ruins and hallowed battlegrounds as well. The preservation of these national symbols depends on the successful interpretation of their messages to each generation of Americans.

Here at Brown v. Board of Education National Historic Site, our mission is to preserve, protect, and interpret for the benefit and enjoyment of present and future generations the places that contributed materially to the landmark United States Supreme Court decision that brought an end to segregation in public education.

While at the park, most visitors will spend their time with the interpretive park rangers. These are the women and men you will find conducting tours and staffing the visitor center. Their gray and green uniforms, topped off with Stetsons (Smoky Bear hats) best identify them. Besides the duties above, they perform many behind-the-scene duties i.e., volunteer coordinators, education specialists. Park rangers are just a part of the overall staff that keeps the park running smoothly. If you have any questions or want to learn more about the park or the National Park Service, feel free to ask one of the rangers.

# United States Department of the Interior
### NATIONAL PARK SERVICE
Brown v. Board of Educati on National Historic Site
424 South Kansas Avenue Suite 220
Topeka, Kansas 66603

Dear Educator:

We are pleased to welcom e you to Brown v. Bo ard of Education National Historic Site and offer you *Stories in Stone,* a curriculum-based educational program established in partnership between the National Park Servi ce and Topeka Public Schools. Our joint goal is to bring history aliv e for students throughout Topeka . Our objectives in reaching this goal are to introduce students to historical objects and artif acts, to stimulate historical experiences, and to explain the benefits of preserving this historic site.

This packet of materials describes the *Stories in Stone* program and provides details f or the particular programs you have requested. Bringing your classes to Brown v. Board of Education National Historic Site to take pa rt in a non-traditional learning experience will give your students a special opportunity for exploring our nation' s history.

One of our primary challenges at Brown v. Bo ard of Education NHS is to show students that they, as U.S. citizen s, can be active st ewards of these historical resources and can participate in their protection and preservation. W ith your help, the *Stories in Stone* program can help us meet this challenge by stimulating your students' awareness and interest in our nation' s cultural resources. From this awareness and intere st will grow an appreciation of their cultur al heritage and a sense of belonging to their com munity.

We hope that you have an enjoyable school year.

Sincerely,

Stephen E. Ada ms
Superintendent

# ABOUT *BROWN v. BOARD OF EDUCATION* NHS

On May 17, 1954, the United States Supreme Court, in the case, *Oliver Brown v. et. al. Board of Education of Topeka, Kansas, et. al.*, unanimously declared that "separate educational facilities are inherently unequal" and violated the Fourteenth Am endment's guarantee of "equal protection of the laws" for all citizens. The Court's decision reversed its 1896 ruling in Plessy v. Ferguson, which ha d established the doctr ine of "separate but equal."

The story behind the *Brown v. Board of Education of Topeka* decision speaks to what it means to be an American and is a chapter in the maturation of our nation. The Brown decision reaffir med the sovereign power of the American people to protect their rights against arbitrary limits and restrictions imposed by the fe deral and local governm ents. This legal engagem ent, spearheaded by attorneys from the NAACP's Legal Defense and Education Funds, clarified the right of all citizens not to be subjected to arbitrary restrictions and led to the de nial of equal treatm ent of African Americans in areas like transportation, housing, and education.

To comme morate this landm ark decision, the U.S. Congress passed Public Law 102-525 on October 26, 1992, creating the B rown v. Board of Education National Historic Site in Topeka, Kansas. The site consists of the Monroe School, one of the four segregated elem entary schools for African Am erican children in Topeka, and the adjacent grounds. The site was established to interpr et the role of the *Brown* decision in the Civil Rights Movement and to assist in the preservation and interpretation of related resources that further our understanding of the struggle for racial equality and basic human rights.

Each case was unique, but addressed the sa me question: W as segregation in public education a violation of the C onstitutional right to equal pr otection? Here is a brief synopsis of each case.

### *Oliver Brown et. al. v. Board of Education of Topeka*

African American parents in Kansas began challenging the sy stem of segr egated public schools as early as 1881 with the case of *Tinnon v. Ottawa School Board*. However, the first documented schoo l case in the country took place in Massachusetts, *Roberts v. the City of Boston* in 1849. In Kansas there were eleven school integration cases dating from 1881 to 1949 prior to *Brown* in 1954. These early cases reached the State Suprem e Court, and they challeng ed a Kansas law passed in 1879, which perm itted segregated elem entary schools only in firs t-class cities of 15,000 or more residents. Consequently, African Americ an parents who sued in sm aller communities won
their cases based on their residence in s econd-class cities. For African American children, elem entary school included grades K through 8. It was not until 1941 that grades 7 through 9 were integrated.

In response to several un successful attempts to ensure equal educa tional opportunities for all children in larger Kansas communities, African American organizations stepped up efforts to change the segregated educationa l system. In the fall of 1950 mem bers of the Topeka chapter of the N ational Association for the Adva ncement of Colored People (NAACP) agreed to again challenge the "s eparate but equal" doctrine governing public education. For a period of two years, fr om 1948 to 1950, chapter president McKinley Burnett attempted to persuade the Topeka Bo ard of Education to integrate their schools since Kansas' s law permitted but did not require segregated public schools. Burnett' s efforts met with continu ed resistance. Challenging the Board of Edu cation in court was a measure of last resort.

## Case Strategy

McKinley Burnett, along with NAAC P secretary Lucinda Todd and attorneys Charles Scott, Sr., John Scott and Charles Bledsoe, de veloped the strategy for a court case. Their plan involved enlisting the support of fello w NAACP members and personal friends as plaintiffs in what would becom e a class action suite filed against the Board of Education of Topeka Public Schools. Lucinda Todd was th e first to volunteer to serve as a plaintiff on behalf of her daughter. A group of 12 parent s were recruited to join her on behalf of their children (19 children). Individuals in the Topeka case moved ahead unaware that at the same time lega l counsel for the NAACP headquarte rs in New York was repres enting plaintiffs in school cases from Delaware, Virginia, South Carolina, and W ashington, D.C.

Children of the Topeka plaintiffs had to tr avel past and in the opposite direction from their neighborhood schools. They could only attend the 4 schools designated for African Americans. Topeka operated 18 elem entary schools for white child ren.

In the fall of 1950, each plaintiff was inst ructed by the NAACP to watch the local newspaper to determ ine the appropriate enrollm ent dates, then take their child o r children along with a witness to a white school near est to their home. Once they attem pted enrollm ent and were denied, the next step was to report back to the NAAC P. Their experiences provided attorneys with docum entation needed to file a lawsu it against the Topeka Board of Education.

On February 28, 1951, NAACP attorneys filed their case as *Oliver L. Brown et. al. v. the Board of Education of Topeka.* Mr. Br own was selected to serve as lead plaintiff principally because he w as the only man among the roster of plaintiffs. The plaintiff roster included Mrs. Darlene Brown (no relati on to Oliver), Mrs. Lena Carper, Mrs. Sadie Emmanuel, Mrs. Marquerite Emmerson, Mrs. Shirla Fleming, Mrs. Zelma Henderson, Mrs. Shirley Hodison, Mrs. Maude L awton, Mrs. Alma Lewis, Mrs. Iona Richardson, Mrs. Vivian Scales and Mrs. Lucinda Todd.

During court proceedings, several facts m ade this a defining test case . First, the African American schools appeared equal in facili ties and teacher salaries although som e programs were not offered. Secondly, fewer elem entary schools for African Am erican children m ade attending neighborhood schools impossible. Their challenge was aimed solely at elem entary schools because junior and senior h igh schools were integ rated. The Federal District Court under the leadership of Presiding Judge Walter Huxm an, former Governor of Kansas, ruled in favor of the Topeka Board of Education. N AACP attorneys immediately filed an app eal to the U.S. Supreme Court. When the Kansas case reached the high court, it was combined with othe r NAACP cases from Delaware, South Carolina, Virginia, and the District of Colum bia. The court heard the com bined cases under the heading of Oliver L. *Brown et. al. v. the Board of Education of Topeka, et. al.* Historic speculation suggests that the *Brown* case led the docket because Kansas is not a southern state.

The court' s decision in the *Brown* case began the process of dism antling segregated public schools system s in 16 states that required separate facili ties as well as the Dis trict of Columbia, and four states, including Kansas, that permitted the racially divisiv e practice. These segregated system s had been based on the "separate but equal" doctrine established in 1896 by the U.S. Supreme Court' sdecision in *Plessy v. Ferguson.* In this opinion the court stated that segregation did not conflict w ith the Fourteen th Amendment (equal protection under the law) as long as separate facilities for "Negroes" were equal to those for whites. The *Brown* decision overturned the court' s earlier decision in the *Plessy* case.

At the time of the *Brown* ruling, 625 African Am erican pupils attended four segregated elem entary schools in Topeka (Buchanan, McKi nley, Monroe and W ashington). All f our of those schools were subsequently closed. Three of the buildings are still standing and are no longer owned by Topeka Public Schools. Buchanan is now used as an office building, McKinley is used as a warehouse, the National Park Service owns Monroe, and Washington was dem olished to allow the land to be used as a flood control corridor. White pupils in Topeka attended their choice of 18 schools. Seven of those were nam ed in the original *Brown* case. Two of those seven s chools, Randolph and Quincy, are still open and now serve all children. The rem aining segregated white schools nam ed in the original *Brown* case have either been dem olished or sold for private use.

### *Belton v. Gebhart* (*Bulah v. Gebhart*)

African American students in Delaware rode the bus nearly an hour to attend two black-only schools, Howard High School in W ilmington and a one-room elementary school in Hockessin. The school buildings w ere substandard, lacked appropriate instructional material, and were located in a crowded, i ndustrial area of town. Moreover, teachers' training and pay lagged f ar behind white teachers. The black child ren' s parents demanded e qual transportation to their one-room school and improvem ents to the building. Their requests were denied. In the combined cases, the plaintiffs sought equality in teacher training, pup il-teacher ratio, extracurricular activities, physical plant, and time and distance involved with traveling to and from school.

### *Bolling v. Sharpe*

The petition in this case was on behalf of 11 African Am erican junior high youths who were refused adm ission to all-white schools. Their school, grossly unequal in term s of physical con dition, was located in a rundown pa rt of the city and lacked ad equate educational materials. Led by local activist Gardner Bishop, a suit was filed on behalf of these studen ts in 1951. Unsuccessful in th e lower courts, their case was appealed to the U.S. Supreme Court. Directed by attorn ey Charles Houston from NAACP' s Legal Defense Fund, Bishop sued on behalf of the Consolidated Parents Group, Inc. Although the case was consolid ated into *Brown*, it was decided separately, si nce it origin ated in the District of Colum bia. After reviewing the *Brown* case, the Supreme Court ruled in *Bolling v. Sharpe* that "segregation in the public schools ...is a denial of the due process of law guaranteed by the F ifth Amendment."

### *Briggs v. Elliot*

Of the five desegregation suits, conditions were clearly the wo rst in Clarendon County, South Carolina. Schools for the 6,500 African American students were assessed at less than one-third the value of the schools for the 2,300 white students. The school board provided on ly for the African-Am erican teachers' salaries, at two-thirds the rate of white teachers and nothing for supplies o r building maintenance. There were no school buses for the African Am erican students, and few coul d walk the nine m iles to the high school. Mandatory school attend ance was not enforced because the students were needed in th e white farmers' fields at planting and harvesting tim e. Harry Briggs filed a lawsuit against Roderick W. Elliott, chairman of the school di strict in the hop e of securin g equal scho ol facilities for the children of South Carolina. The case invo lved 20 African Americans who sought better educational facilities than wooden shacks a nd poor transportation. They sought qualified teachers and educational provisions th at met the needs of their children.

### *Davis v. Prince Edward County*

On April 23, 1951, senior Barbara Rose Johns and 117 African Am erican high school students chose to boycott classes rather than attend school in a building that lacked indoor plumbing and was in need of repair. The st udents initially wanted a new building with indoor plum bing to replace the old school. Strike leader Barbara Johns enlisted the assistance of the NAACP attorneys. Their e ffort evolved into a lawsuit filed on their behalf in 1951. The U.S. District Court orde red equal facilities to be provided for the black students but "denied the plaintiffs admission to the white schools during the equalization program." Attorneys for the NAACP filed an appeal with the U.S. Supreme Court.

## The Decision

The Supreme Court ruled in favor of the plaintiffs in the *Brown* case, which overturned the 1896 *Plessy v. Ferguson* decision. The Supreme Court concluded that separate facilities are inherently unequal, thus denying the legal basis for segregation in the 21 states with segregation laws and segregated school rooms and starting a revolution in the legal status of black Americans that continues to this day.

The *Brown* decision had, and continues to have, ramifications in virtually every community and state in this country as well as throughout the world. It is one of the foundation blocks for the Civil Rights Movement.

# EDUCATIONAL OPPORTUNITIES

With such vast, diverse re sources available within *Brown v. Board of Education* National Historic Site, there are lim itless opportunities to u se the site as "classrooms away from school." We offer four curriculum-based education program s that meet the Kansas Public School System Social Studies Curriculum Guide objectives.

### *Defined by Color* (included in *Stories in Stone*)

The decision rendered by the U.S. Suprem e Court in the case of *Brown v. Board of Education of Topeka, Kansas*, was a landmark in American History. Discover the people and events that led to this hist oric case and discu ss its significance.

### *Footprints—The Struggle for Eq uality* (included in *Stories in Stone*)

Trace the history of the Afri can American struggle for civil rights. Find out how Kansas played a crucial role.

### *Struggle for Equal Rights* (separate curriculum guide available upon request)

This curriculum guide developed for 4t h through 6th, interm ediate, and middle school grad es students will s erve to expand oppor tunities to educate the p ublic about the history of the *Brown Case*.

### *What Does a Park Ranger Do?* (included in *Stories in Stone*)

The National Park Serv ice is entrusted with caring for our nation' s cultural and natural treasures. Find out how ranger s help to care for these treasures.

### Junior Ranger Programs (available upon request)

Teachers can schedule g roups of children between the ages of 9-13. To find out more, contact the Junior Range r Coordinator at (785) 354-4273.

# THE STORIES IN STONE PROGRAM

The National Park Service provides educational opportunities for students at sites across the country through its **Parks as Classrooms** program. *Brown v. Board of Education* NHS wanted to develop a local program in the **Parks as Classrooms** mold. It is clear that Topeka is dotted with stone buildings that play important roles in the *Brown v. Board* case. It is also clear that these silent bits of stone hold the secrets of our national heritage. The objective became obvious: reading these stories in stone can reveal history.

*Brown v. Board of Education* NHS developed the *Stories in Stone* educational program in conjunction with Topeka Public Schools. Turning to Topeka's social studies curriculum, a team of teachers and National Park Service educators worked together to determine which curriculum objectives could be addressed when taking classes to visit *Brown v. Board of Education* NHS. They then developed activities to help teach and reinforce these objectives.

The results of all this planning, testing, and evaluating are in this packet of materials. Teachers will benefit from the *Stories in Stone* program by having a lively way to approach their curriculum objectives and by taking advantage of the expertise of the National Park Service rangers. Students benefit by learning in a historical setting. The site will benefit by meeting their educational objectives and by having their message delivered to our nation's young citizens.

The chart on the next page lists the Topeka required curriculum objectives that can be addressed while visiting our site.

# TRIP TIPS

Here are a few suggestions for a successful visit:

* **Be Prepared:** Provide some background information for your students so they will know what to expect. Make sure they understand the purpose of their visit.

* **Plan Ahead:** Be sure to check your route and to allow plenty of time for travel to and from the site as well as for the visit itself. If your trip runs through lunchtime, be sure to identify a place to buy food or eat bag lunches. We do not have facilities available at the site.

* **Make ID Tags:** It is a good idea for students to wear nametags during their visit. This will help keep them together and will also help the ranger make the visit more personal for each student.

* **Dress:** Make sure the students dress appropriately for the weather.

* **Stick Together:** For a safe and successful visit, make sure the students stay together as a group, except when directed to explore freely under the guidance of you or the ranger.

* **Keep It Safe:** Always watch for traffic when getting on or off buses and when crossing streets. Remember that steps and sidewalks can be very slippery and wet, snowy, or icy conditions.

* **Be Considerate:** Teachers and adults accompanying the students are responsible for the behavior and conduct of the group and providing assistance while the park ranger conducts the program. There should be at least one adult per 10 students.

* **Show Respect:** To help preserve the natural and cultural resources, we do not allow any collecting or removal of any objects. Suggest to your group that they take photographs, write in a journal, or draw pictures if they wish to have a memento of their trip.

* **Parking:**
30-minute and 1-1/2 hour parking is available at the front of the U. S. Federal Post Office Building on both sides of Kansas Avenue.

* **Comfort Stations:**
Public restrooms are available in the National Park Service visitor center. Facilities are available for people with special needs.

# Reservation Form

Teacher Information: (PRINT CLEARL Y)

Teacher Name_____School Name_____

Address_____ City_____State_____

Contact Person_____Requested From_____Grade_____

Phone Num ber_____Size of Class_____Date_____Time_____

# of Adults_____Date of Confirmation_____

Select Program:

A. *Defined by Color* (4-6 grade)

B. *Footprints—The Struggle for Equality* (4th-6th grade)

C. *What Does a Park Ranger Do?* (K-12th grade)

D. *Struggle for Equality* (4th through 6th, interm ediate, and m iddle school)

Junior Ranger Program (K-3rd grade)

Other Information: (special needs; speci al focus: curriculum, location; onsite; or classroom)

_____

_____

Please schedule your field t rip at least a week in advance of your planned visit by calling 785-354-4273 between 8:00 a.m. and 4:00 p.m., Monday through Friday. You may schedule a program by mailing the enclosed reser vation form to *Brown v. Board of Education* National Historic Site, 424 South Kansas Avenue, Suite 220, Topeka, KS 66603. There is no charge for these programs. Programs are availabl e Monday through Friday. The site is cl osed on federal holidays. Programs are one hour in length; the first program starts at 9:00 and the last program ends at 3:00.

# VOCABULARY LIST

In order to prepare your students for their visit to the *Brown v. Board of Education* National Historic Site, please review this vocabulary list and definition s with your students.

**Civil Liberties**
Fundamental individual rights such as freedom of speech and religion, pro tected by law against unwarranted governm ental or other interference.

**Civil Rights**
Rights belonging to a person by virtue of his or her status as a citizen or as a member of civil society.

**Constitutional**
Being in acc ordance with or author ized by the Constitution of the United S tates or any state.

**Desegregation**
To abolish segregation.

**Discrimination**
The unequal treatm ent of a person or persons on a basis other than individual m erit.

**Emancipation Proclamation**
A proclamation issued by President Abraha m Lincoln, effective January 1, 1863, freeing all enslaved people in territory still at war with the Union.

**Freedom**
Liberty of a person from slavery, oppression, or incarceration.

**Integration**
The act or process of incorporating people as equals into society or organization of individuals of different groups regardless of ethnicity, ra ce, gender, or disability.

### Jim Crow Laws

Laws and customs put in place in the South during the period of segregation that required separate facilities for African Americans.

### Racism

The notion that one's own ethnic group is superior.

### Reconstruction

The period (1865-1877) during which the Federal government controlled the states of the former Confederacy before they were readmitted to the Union.

### Segregation

The policy or practice of imposing the social separation of the races in schools, housing, employment, transportation, and public accommodations.

### Unconstitutional

Not in accord with the principles set forth in the constitution of a nation.

# For Further Reading
Teachers

Beals, Melba Patillo. 1994. *Warriors Don't Cry: A Searing Memoir of the Battle to Integrate Little Rock's Central High*. New York: Pocket Books.

Greenberg, Jack. 1994. *Crusaders in the Courts*. New York: Basic Books.

Kluger, Richard. 1975. *Simple Justice*. New York: Alfred A. Knopf.

Martin, Waldo E., Jr. 1998. *Brown v. Board of Education: A Brief History with Documents*. Boston: Bedford.

McNeil, Genna Rae. 1983. *Groundwork: Charles Hamilton Houston and the Struggle for Civil Rights*. Philadelphia: The Univers ity of Pennsylvania Press.

Orfield, Gary, et al. 1989. *Status of School Desegregation, 1968-1986: A Report of the Council of Urban Board of Education and the National School Desegregation Research Project*. Chicago: The University of Chicago.

# For Further Reading
Students

Drisko, Carol F., and Edgar A. Toppin. 1967. *The Unfinished March: The History of the Negro in the United States, Reconstruction to World War I.* New York: Doubleday.

Dudley, Mark E. 1994. *Brown v. Board of Education (1954).* New York: Twenty-first Century Books.

Fireside, Harvey, and Sarah Betsy Fuller. 1994. *Brown v. Board of Education: Equal Schooling For All.* Springfield, NJ: Enslow.

Haskins, James. 1994. *Thurgood Marshall: A Life for Justice.* New York: Henry Holt.

Smith, Bob. 1965. *They Closed Their Schools: Prince Edward County, Virginia, 1951-1964.* Chapel Hill: University of North Carolina Press.

# Chronology of Events

| | |
|---|---|
| **1793** | U.S. Congress adopted the first Fugitive Slave Law, which increased the possibilities for the extradition of slaves and made it a criminal offense to protect a fugitive slave. |
| **1822** | Denmark Vesey, a free black, organized slave rebellion in Charleston, S.C. |
| **1831** | Nat Turner rebellion. |
| **1849** | *Roberts v. City of Boston* declared separate black and white schools legal (later overturned by state law). |
| **1850** | Compromise of 1850 strengthened 1793 Fugitive Slave Law. |
| **1857** | Dred Scott decision denied U.S. citizenship to African Americans. |
| **1861** | Civil War began. |
| **1861** | Kansas becomes a state. |
| **1862** | President Lincoln issued Emancipation Proclamation, which takes effective January 1, 1863. |
| **1865** | Thirteenth Amendment abolished slavery. |
| **1865** | Freedman's Bureau founded. |
| **1865** | Reconstruction began. |
| **1868** | Fourteenth Amendment guaranteed civil rights to all Americans. |
| **1869** | Fifteenth Amendment guaranteed male citizens the right to vote. |
| **1873** | Slaughterhouse Cases narrowly defined federal power and emasculated the Fourteenth Amendment by asserting that most of the rights of citizens remain under state control. |
| **1877** | Reconstruction ended. |

| | |
|---|---|
| **1883** | Civil Rights Cases invalidated provisions of the Civil Rights Act of 1875 and declared that the Fourteenth Amendment did not prohibit discrimination by private individuals or businesses. |
| **1896** | *Plessy v. Ferguson* decision established doctrine of "separate but equal." |
| **1899** | In *Cumming v. Richmond County Board of Education*, the Supreme Court ruled that public school education is within the purview of the states rather than the federal government. |
| **1908** | In *Berea College v. Kentucky*, the Supreme Court ruled that private educational institutions must abide by the segregation laws of the state. |
| **1909** | National Association for the Advanced of Colored People (N ACCP) was established. |
| **1914** | World War I began in Europe. Second Great Migration began in the United States. |
| **1917** | United States entered World War I. |
| **1929** | Charles Hamilton Houston became Vice Dean of Howard University Law School. |
| **1933** | NAACP began to attack segregation and discrimination in education at the graduate and professional levels through legal suits; its first case, lost on a technicality, was a suit against the University of North Carolina on behalf of Thomas Hocutt. |
| **1934** | Charles Hamilton Houston appointed NAACP Special Legal Counsel. |
| **1935** | NAACP decided to launch a full-scale campaign against legal injustices suffered by African Americans. |

1936        In *University of Maryland v. Murray*, the
Maryland Supreme Court ordered that a
black student be admitted to the state's white
law school. Thurgood Marshall joined NACCP legal staff.

1938        In *Gaines v. Missouri*, Charles Hamilton
Houston successfully argued before the
United States Supreme Court that the
State of Missouri must either build a law
school for blacks or desegregate the white one.

1941        United States entered World W ar II.

1950        Supreme Court decisions in  *McLaurin v.*
*Oklahoma State Regents for Higher Education*
and *Sweatt v. Painter* established that segregation in higher education is unconstitutional.

1952        Initial oral arguments in *Brown* were heard before the Suprem e Court.

1954        *Brown v. Board of Education* Supreme Court decision declared separate-
but-equal schools unconstitutional.

1955        The *Brown II* decision of the U.S. Suprem e Court
implemented the 1954 ruling by requiring desegregation
"with all deliberate speed."

1955        Rosa Parks was arrested because she refused to give her bus seat to a
white man in Montgomery, Alabam a; this action started the Montgom ery
bus boycott.

1957        13-year-old Emm ett Till beaten and killed.

1957        Common Civil Rights Act establishe d U.S. Commission on Civil Rights.

1958        First black students enro lled at Central High School in
Little Rock, Arkansas.

1960        John F. Kennedy, a Demo crat, elected president.

1961        President Kennedy named Thurgood Marshall to the
Federal bench, the Second Circuit Court of Appeals.

1962        President Kennedy assassinated in Dallas, Texas.
Vice President Lyndon B. Johnson assum ed the Presidency.

| 1963 | The March on Washington was held . Dr. King delivered the fa mous "I Have a Dream" speech on the steps of the Lincoln Mem orial. |
|------|---|
| 1964 | Lyndon B. Johnson elected president in his own right; signed into law the Civil Rights Act of 1964, stronger than that of 1957. |
| 1965 | Voting Rights Act passed. |
| 1967 | Thurgood Marshall nom inated by President Johnson and confirm ed by the Senate to become the first African Am erican Supreme Court Justice. |
| 1968 | Martin Luther King, Jr., assassinated in Memphis, Tennessee. |
| 1969 | Lyndon B. Johnson chose not to run for re-election as president. Richard M. Nixon, Republican of California, defeated Vice President Hubert H. Humphrey for the Presiden cy. |
| 1970 | In *Alexander v. Holmes County [Mississippi] Board of Education*, the Supreme Court ended the "all deliberate speed" timetable for integration, ruling that "the obligation of every school district is to terminate dual school systems at once and to operate now and hereafter only unitary schools." |
| 1971 | The Supreme Court ruled th at busing of students to achieve racial integration is constitutional in *Swann v. Charlotte-Mecklenburg [North Carolina] Board of Education.* |
| 1972 | Congress passed the Em ergency School Aid Act, a desegregation assistance program . Richard M. Nixon reelected to the P residency. |
| 1973 | In its decision in *Keys v. Denver School District No. 1*, the Supreme Court ruled that the Denver, Colorado, school board acte d to intentionally segregate its system and ordered it to take steps to achieve integration. Denver was the first city outside the South to implement a court-ordered busing plan. |

| | |
|---|---|
| **1974** | President Richard Nixon resigned under threat of impeachment. Vice President Gerald R. Ford assumed the presidency. |
| **1974** | The Supreme Court's decision in *Miliken v. Bradley* limited to achieve desegregation and thus drastically limited the possibility of substantial and lasting desegregation in the urban North. |
| **1976** | Jimmy Carter, a Democrat from Georgia, elected President. |
| **1980** | Ronald Reagan, a Republican from California, defeated Jimmy Carter for the presidency. Reagan and his administration preferred neighborhood schools and actively sought to dismantle earlier desegregation policies. |
| **1988** | Republican George Bush, Vice President under Ronald Reagan, was elected to the presidency. |
| **1990-1992** | In separate decisions involving Oklahoma City, Oklahoma; DeKalb County, Georgia; and Kansas City, Kansas, the Supreme Court made it easier for school districts to be released from desegregation orders and limited their responsibilities to foster desegregation. |
| **1992** | Bill Clinton, Democrat from Arkansas, was elected president. Conservative Republicans won a majority of seats in Congress. |
| **1994** | The number of blacks in the nation's public schools grew by 178 percent and the number of Hispanics by 14 percent; the number of whites fell by 9 percent. |
| **1995** | A Federal district court judge released the Denver, Colorado, public schools from federal supervision and court-ordered busing. Officials in Pittsburgh, Pennsylvania; Seattle, Washington; Indianapolis, Indiana, and elsewhere sought to end local busing plans. |
| **1999** | Topeka, Kansas, released from Federal District Court supervision. |

# INTRODUCTION

*Brown v. Board of Education* National Historic Site invites you and your class to visit the site. The Educator's Guide included in this packet provides details about the site.

See Educator's Guide for trip tips and some background information about the *Brown v. Board of Education* NHS. A *Brown v. Board* site brochure is also enclosed in this packet for your convenience. These two references will explain how to get to the site and what you can expect to find there.

This site guide provides the framework for specific *Stories in Stone* educational program for fourth through sixth grade classes. By teaching your class about the landmark *Brown v. Board of Education* case, you will be able to address these Kansas Public Schools curriculum objectives for your grade level:

Trace the events that led to the 1954 Supreme Court decision.

Explain how this decision affected the lives of Kansas.

Provide understanding of the legal framework that supported equal educational opportunities for all children.

Explain the role that public opinion played in ending racial discrimination.

Develop and interpret charts, tables, timelines, graphs, diagrams, and other graphic aids.

Examine a sequence of events and identify cause-and-effect relationships.

Provide related events in chronological order.

Compare and contrast different stories or accounts about past events, people, places, or situations and identify how they contribute to our understanding of the past.

Recognize the significance of the Supreme Court decision in *Oliver Brown et. al. v. Board of Education.*

# WHAT'S INSIDE

Here is a look at what we have included in this Site Guide:

* Lesson Plans: These describe activities that a National Park Service ranger will conduct for your class on-site. There are also suggested pre-visit and post-visit activities. Whenever possible, a park ranger will come to your class to conduct these activities as well. In the event this classroom service is not possible, a ranger will make arrangements to deliver any necessary material and to offer guidance so that you can conduct the classroom activities yourself. The goals and objectives provided in the lesson plan are those of the National Park Service for *Brown v. Board of Education* NHS.

* Bibliography: There is a list of suggested resources for finding more information about the landmark *Brown v. Board of Education* case. It includes references that may be helpful in providing further research for both you and your students.

* Appendix: Chronology of events related to *Brown v. Board of Education* NHS and copies of the United States Constitution will be supplied to students for use during the on-site visit.

* Registration Form: In order to participate in the *Stories in Stone* program, you must register by mail at least four weeks in advance. There is a reproducible registration form in the guide. For each program, make a copy of this form; fill in the appropriate information, and mail it to the address provided on the form. A park ranger will then contact you to confirm the date of your visit and go over any special arrangements.

* Evaluation Form: After you and your class have participated in this program, please take a few minutes to tell us what you think. Copy the form, answer the questions, and send to the address provided. We appreciate your feedback.

* Site Brochure: As already mentioned, we have enclosed a *Brown v. Board of Education* NHS brochure in this packet. This brochure will provide some background information on the *Brown v. Board of Education* case.

# STORIES IN STONE
## LESSON PLANS

## Defined by Color

**Pre-Visit Activity**

**Post-Visit Activity**

# PRE-VISIT ACTIVITY

Green and Blue
"Separate and Unequal"

**Objectives:**
Students will be able to:
* Analyze the issues of separate but unequal.
* Compare and contrast separate but equal.

**Materials**
* Box with green and blue tags.
* New school books (new version)
* Old school books (old version)

**Time**
1 Class period.

**Procedures**
1. Place open box where everyone can see it. Have each student choose a tag and put it on.

2. Students with blue tags will sit at desks, and students with green tag students will sit on the floor.

3. Ask students to turn to chapter_____ in the book.

4. Instruct a student wearing a green tag to begin reading.

5. Instruct a student wearing a blue tag to begin reading where the other person stopped.

6. Have at least four students from each group read.

**Questions to ask the students:**
Ask the green group how they felt having to sit on the floor while blue group sat at their desks.

Ask the green group how they felt being given outdated textbooks.

Let the group know that the textbooks given to blue group are updated textbooks.

Explain to the students that black students were given outdated textbooks to read and learn from.

Explain to the students that even though black students went to separate schools, which were supposed to be equal, schools were unequal.

# PRE-VISIT ACTIVITY

### The Meaning Behind the Struggle

This activity will be conducted by a National Park Service ranger at *Brown v. Board of Education* NHS the day of your visit. The students will use the provided vocabulary list to match words with their meanings.

**Objectives:**
Students will be able to:
* Compare/contrast by using the vocabulary list
* Analyze issues through using the vocabulary list
* Evaluate historical events and perspectives
* Present historical information
* Recognize historical perspective

**Material**
* Laminated cards with vocabulary words
* Laminated cards with vocabulary definitions

**Time**
1 hour

**Procedures**
1. Class will be greeted by a park ranger at *Brown v. Board of Education* NHS. The ranger will provide an introductory presentation about the *Brown* case and about the site and its relevance to our society.

2. The class will be divided into two teams. Each team will be given 14 laminated cards each.

3. Each team will have to match the word with the correct definition or definition with the correct word.

4. After matching all words with their definitions, the students will be videotaped reciting the U.S. Supreme Court decision. The class can keep the videotape and play it back later in the classroom.

# POST-VISIT ACTIVITIES

DEAR RANGER...

Soon after their visit to the *Brown v. Board of Education* NHS, the class may want to send a letter to the park ranger who worked with them . Have students write letters that describe what they thought and felt about the trip. What did they learn about the *Brown* case? Students in grades three through six can draw a picture of their school.

# EVALUATION FORM

Please photocopy, fill out, and return this 2-page form after your participation in Brown V. Board of Education NHS *Stories in Stone* program. Send to Education Coordinator, 424 South Kansas Ave. Suite 220 Topeka, Kansas 66603

Circle the number that best reflects your feeling about each statement.

|  | Strongly Agree | | | | Strongly Disagree |
|---|---|---|---|---|---|
| **For the Pre-Visit Activity:** | | | | | |
| 1. National Park Service objectives were met. | 5 | 4 | 3 | 2 | 1 |
| 2. The activity prepared the students for the site visit. | 5 | 4 | 3 | 2 | 1 |
| 3. The activity was appropriate for my class. | 5 | 4 | 3 | 2 | 1 |
| 4. I could teach the lesson effectively without a park ranger. | 5 | 4 | 3 | 2 | 1 |

|  | Strongly Agree | | | | Strongly Disagree |
|---|---|---|---|---|---|
| **For On-Site Activity:** | | | | | |
| 1. National Park Service objectives were met. | 5 | 4 | 3 | 2 | 1 |
| 2. The park ranger was well prepared and effective. | 5 | 4 | 3 | 2 | 1 |
| 3. The activity was age-appropriate. | 5 | 4 | 3 | 2 | 1 |

|  | Strongly Agree |  |  |  | Strongly Disagree |
|---|---|---|---|---|---|

For the Post-Visit Activity:

| | | | | | |
|---|---|---|---|---|---|
| 1. National Park Service objectives were m et. | 5 | 4 | 3 | 2 | 1 |
| 2. The activities reinforced the s ite-visit lesson. | 5 | 4 | 3 | 2 | 1 |
| 3. The activities were appropria te for my class. | 5 | 4 | 3 | 2 | 1 |
| 4. I could teach the lesson effectively without a park ranger. | 5 | 4 | 3 | 2 | 1 |

Please give your candid co mments on the following:

1. What did you like best about the program ?  Explain.

2. What aspects about the program would you change?  Explain your answer.

3. Were you able to address your curriculum objectives through the program s? Why or why not?

4. How did your students respond to the program?

5. Would you recomm end this pr ogram to other teachers?

Additiona l Comments:

# *STORIES IN STONE*
## Lesson Plan

## *What Does a Park Ranger Do?*

**Pre-Visit Activity**

**Post-Visit Activity**

# *STORIES IN STONE*
## LESSON PLANS

## *Footprints—The Struggle for Equality*

### Pre-Visit Activity

### Post-Visit Activity

# PRE-VISIT ACTIVITY

## "Time Will Tell"

**Objectives:**
Students will be able to:
* Create and use a timeline
* Recognize historical perspective
* Present historical information.

**Materials**
* Time chart (without years)
* Flashcards with year
* Flashcards with historical chronological text relating to Kansas and civil rights.

**Time**
1 Class period

**Procedures**
1. Time line chart is placed on the floor.

2. Divide the class into two groups of seven and one group of six.

3. The two groups of seven are given flashcards with year or historical chronological text.

4. The third group is given historical overview of the struggle for civil rights in Kansas.

5. Students from group three will take turns reading the historical overview.

6. When a significant year is read, the students with flash cards with that year will go and stand on the time chart. (Students will begin with 1879)

7. Students holding historical chronological text cards will stand and read from the card that pertains to that particular year.

8. This sequence will continue until the reading of the overview is completed.

**Questions to ask the students:**

Ask students if they understand the sequence of hi storical events in Kansas that led to the *Brown* case.

Ask students if they understand the signifi cance of "The Struggle for Equality."

Ask students to identify two events on the time line that led up to the *Brown* case.

# PRE-VISIT ACTIVITY

**"Putting the Pieces Together"**

This activity will be conducted by a National Park Service ranger at *Brown v. Board of Education* NHS the day of your visit. The students will use provided photographs, United States maps, and historical overview of the five cases that were involved in *Brown v. Board of Education.*

**Objectives:**
Students will be able to:
* Cause and effect.
* Story retelling.
* Evaluate historical events and perspectives.
* Present historical information.
* Recognize historical perspective.

**Material**
* Laminated photographs of plaintiffs from the five cases
* Laminated historical overview of the five cases
* Laminated United States maps

**Time**
1 hour

**Procedures**
1. Class will be greeted by a park ranger at *Brown v. Board of Education* NHS. The ranger will provide an introductory presentation about the creation of *Brown v. Board of Education* NHS and its relevance to our society.

2. The class will be divided into three groups: two groups of five and one group of the remainder of the class.

3. Group one will be given five laminated photographs of plaintiffs from the five cases.

4. Group two will be given five laminated copies of the historical overview of the five cases.

5. The remaining students will be given laminated copies of the United States maps.

6. A student from group one will step forward with their photograph.

7. Students from group two will step forward and read from the card that tells the story about the case.

8. The remaining students will locate on their map what state the case was filed in.

9. This sequence will continue until all the cards are presented and states are identified.

**Questions to ask the students:**

Ask students if they understand the need for the parents to file lawsuits in the four states and the District of Colombia.

Ask students if they understand the significance of "The Struggle for Equality."

# POST-VISIT ACTIVITIES

DEAR RANGER...

Soon after their visit to *Brown v. Board of Education* NHS, the class may want to send a letter to the park ranger who worked with them. Have students write letters that describe what they thought and felt about the tr ip. What did they learn about the *Brown* case?

# PRE-VISIT ACTIVITY

### "Rangers Work in Different Kinds of Parks"

This activity will be conducted by a National Park Service ranger at *Brown v. Board of Education* NHS the day of your visit. The students will use provided photographs, NPS systems maps, and historical overview of the creation of the National Park Service

**Objectives:**
Students will be able to:
Identify the National Park Service (NPS) uniform.
Identify five National Parks.
Identify three divisions within the NPS and their functions.

**Material**
NPS logo and badge
Pictures of five National Parks and map of NPS system
Walkie-talkie radios, Leave No Trace rules and regulations, and backpack with trail guides and junior ranger program

**Time**
1 hour

**Procedures**
1. Class will be greeted by a park ranger at Brown v. Board of Education NHS. The ranger will provide an introductory presentation about the creation of the National Park Service and its relevance to our society.

**Questions to ask the students:**

1. Ask students to name five national parks.

2. Ask students what do they think of when they think of a park.

3. Ask students if they have ever been to a national park.

4. Ask students if they knew that not all parks are nature parks (some parks are historical sites).

# POST-VISIT ACTIVITIES

DEAR RANGER...

Soon after their visit to *Brown v. Board of Education* NHS, the class may want to send a letter to the park ranger who worked with them. Have students write letters that describe what they thought and felt about the trip.

Printed with permission from the National Park Service *Brown v. Board of Education* National Historic Site, Topeka, Kansas.

## Origins of *Briggs v. Elliott*

### Preface

This curriculum guide and teacher resource booklet was prepared by descendants of a few determined black people who lived in Clarendon County, South Carolina, during the 1940s. Their actions in trying to get their piece of the "American Dream" changed the course of United States history.

The series of events that they initiated ultimately became the legal case of *Briggs et al. v. Elliott et al.* This was the first of five cases challenging segregated educational facilities to reach the United States Supreme Court. *Briggs v. Elliott* was ultimately argued before the Supreme Court as a part of *Brown et al. v. Board of Education, Topeka, Kansas.*

The Supreme Court decision for these five cases marked the beginning of a new era of social awareness in the United States. It set the stage for the practice of equal opportunities for all persons—whether they are racial or ethnic minorities, women, disabled persons, senior citizens, or disease victims. Yet few people have heard of the other four cases.

The booklet's purpose is to present an actual case history that teachers can use to help students in South Carolina schools: (a) to understand more of their state's history and (b) to appreciate the roles of the U. S. Constitution, of individual action and of due process of law in the United States' democratic society. As a result of following the curriculum, the student will become acquainted with a critical chapter in South Carolina's history.

The guide provides suggested approaches for using *Briggs v. Elliott* in classroom instruction and a resource specifically for the teacher as well as resources that can be photocopied for student use.

Instructional strategies are presented as Suggested Student Activities designed to encourage critical examination of one chain of events that demonstrates the roles of the U. S. Constitution, of individual action and of due process of law in the United States' democratic society.

*Briggs v. Elliott* is a resource for both teachers and students.

## Part I - Curriculum Guide

## A. PROCEDURES

**Suggested Number of Teaching Periods**

4-6 class periods (50 minutes each)

### Social Studies Standards (South Carolina) Addressed

See Section B.

### Teacher Preparation

1. Review the curriculum, including the questions.
2. Read the resources. Photocopy them for students as necessary.

## Background

On May17, 1954, the United States Supreme Court handed down a ruling that segregated public schools we re in violation of the Fourteenth Amendment of the United States Constitution. This ruling directly affected school system and educational practices in seventeen states that had laws requiring or permitting racially separate schools.

After the Civil War, many people did not thi nk that former slaves should have equal rights and protection. So laws were m ade that were referred to as the "Black Codes." To protect the former slaves and their des cendants from the Black Codes, other laws and several amendments to the Constitution, including the Fourteen th, were passed. To avoid complying with the Fourteenth Amendment, the southern states passed laws that permitted or required "separate but equal" facilities for African Americans.

The "separate but equal" doctrine ca n be traced back to the 1849 case of *Roberts v. City of Boston.* Five-year-old Sarah Roberts had to walk past five white elem entary schools to reach the elem entary school sh e attended. The Massachusetts judge wh o heard the case ruled that the segregati on law was founded " on reason" and did not rule against school segregation. Even t hough this case predated the Civil W ar and the Fourteenth Am endment, it set a legal precedent that was used to justify subsequent "separate but equal laws" in the nineteen th century. In 1896, the *Plessy v. Ferguson* case legitim ized the "separate but equal" doctrine with the Suprem e Court's ruling that the practice of separate but equal rail facilities was con stitutional.

"Separate but equal" became the law of the land after *Plessy*. It continued as such until the *Brown v. Board of Education of Topeka, Kansas,* decision in 1954.

Actually, *Brown v. Board* consisted of five cases that were combined for argument before the Supreme Court. One of these cases, *Bolling v. Sharpe* from Washington, D.C., challenged the constitutionality of "separate but equal" schools under the Fifth Amendment of the Constitution. The other four cases were challenges to the Fourteenth Amendment. They were:

- *Belton et al. v. Gebhart et al.* (Delaware)
- *Briggs et al. v. Elliott et al.* (South Carolina)
- *Brown et al. v. Board of Education of Topeka et al.* (Kansas)
- *Davis et al. v. County School Board of Prince Edward County, Virginia, et al.* (Virginia)

All except B*elton v. Gebhart* went to the Supreme Court on direct appeal from U. S. District Courts. The *Belton* case was appealed from the Delaware Supreme Court by the State of Delaware.

## Student Preparation (Outside of Class)

1. All students read resource, "Genesis of *Briggs v. Elliott*"
2. One group of students find photographs of schools, both rural and city, that were built in their state more than 55 years ago and a picture of an old (from before 1940) school bus (Suggested Student Activity 1, Part A).
3. One group of students interview an older person (Suggested Student Activity 2, Part A).

## Classroom Activities

1. Discuss changes in schools and bus transportation (Suggested Student Activity 1, Part B; Suggested Student Activity 2, Part B).
2. Read and discuss Preamble and selected Amendments to the Constitution (Suggested Student Activity 3; Suggested Student Activity 6).
3. Read the following three items and follow with a discussion:
   -Dissenting Opinion of Judge J. Waites Waring in *Briggs v. Elliott* (see http://www.nara.gov/educational/cc/brown.html, List of Documents #1, pages 18-21)
   -Judgment of *Brown v. Board*, 1954
      http://caselaw.lp.fidlaw.com/scripts/getcase.pl?court=US&vol=347&invol (List of Documents #3)
   -Judgment of *Brown v. Board* 1955 (Reargued)
      http://caselaw.lp.findlaw.com/scipts/getcase.pl?court=US&vol=349&invol
4. Act out a skit showing discrimination (Suggested Student Activity 4).
5. Explain how *Briggs v. Elliott* has affected minority rights.
6. Discuss ways in which discrepancies between the reality and the ideals of American constitutional democracy can be reduced (Suggested Student Activity 5).
7. Discuss the concept of "states' rights" (Suggested Student Activity 7).
8. Identify the three branches of government and the way a civil lawsuit reaches the Supreme Court (Suggested Student Activity 8).

**Additional Approaches:**
1.  Write a letter inviting an official to discuss a recent case of discrimination (Suggested Student Activity 6).
2.  Identify a news event from the last 12 months that demonstrates some kind of prejudice (Suggested Student Activity 5).
3.  Watch the made-for-television movie, *Simple Justice* (Public Broadcasting System),

    dramatizing the events leading to the landmark decision of *Brown v. Board*, in which the *Briggs v. Elliott* case led the way. It starts with the *Briggs* case and describes the long journey to *Brown v. Board*. The film can be used to motivate interest and spur lively discussions with students.

    After viewing the film, analyze and discuss it in light of the actual facts of the *Briggs v. Elliott* case. Pose the following questions to students: If you were a filmmaker today, how might your film about B*riggs v. Elliott* be different? Why do you think the film was made the way it was? Who were the characters in the film that stood out for you? How did the decisions they made affect their own lives as well as the lives of those in and beyond their community as well as your life today?

**Teaching Activities:**

Tapping Into Prior Knowledge:

Explain to students that this unit focuses on one aspect of South Carolina's history and on the roles of the U. S. Constitution, of individual action and of due process of law in the United States' democratic society. Further explain that in the unit they will learn about: (a) events that occurred in South Carolina that contribute to equal rights for all citizens, (b) U. S. District and Supreme Court decisions that contributed to these events, (c) opposition to the decisions and (d) the kinds of effects these decisions have had on the practice of American democracy. Begin by assessing the extent of students' knowledge about the lives of people in the 1940s. Follow Suggested Student Activities 1 and 2, Part A.

Expanding Knowledge:

Select four or more of the Suggested Student Activities, introducing different parts of the activities as desired.

Reinforcing Knowledge:

Select six or more learning outcomes from the list of Suggested Tests of Knowledge to be emphasized.

**B.**    **SOUTH CAROLINA SOCIAL STUDIES STANDARDS ADDRESSED**

5.4    The learner will demonstrate an understanding of government, its origins and functions, including civi c life and politics.

  5.4.1    The student should be able to explai n representative government, the rule of law, majority rule, minority rights, and popular sovereignty.

5.5    The learner will demonstrate an understanding of the foundations of Am erican democracy, including its basic principles and the basis of the American political system.  The student should able to:

  5.5. 2    describe diversity in the United States and its benefits and challenges, and

  5.5.5    discuss events that dem onstrate and promote principles of Am erican democracy.

8.7    The learner will demonstrate an understanding of the role of the citizen in American democracy, including personal a nd civic rights and responsibilities. The student should be able to:

  8.7.2    differentiate between personal,  political, and econom ic rights;

  8.7.4    identify the factors th at enhance the effectivenes s of citizens and prom ote the functioning of Am erican constitutional dem ocracy;

  8.7.5    describe the m eans by which Am ericans can monitor and influence politics and governm ent; and

  8.7.7    explain the struggles for equity in th e political arena that affected African Americans, women, and other ethnic and religious groups.

12.2    The learner will dem onstrate an understanding of the major developm ents in the United States and South Carolina from th e end of W orld War II to the present.

  12.2.5  The student should be able to evalua te the struggle for racial and gender equality and the extensio n of civil lib erties.

  12.3    The learner will dem onstrate an understanding of governm ent, its origin and functions, including civic life  and politics.  The student should be able to:

    12.3.3    compare and contrast the term s "rule of law" and "rule of man"; and

    12.3.4    explain the various pu rposes that constitutions serve.

  12.4    The learner will dem onstrate an understanding of the foundations of Am erican democracy, including its basic principles and the foundations of the Am erican political system .  The student should be able to:

    12.4.10    identify some im portant American ideals and explain, using historical and contem porary examples, discrepancies between American ideals and the realities of political and s ocial life; and

12.4.11    identify and give exam ples of ways in which discrepancies between the reality and the idea ls of American constitutional democracy can be reduced by indi vidual action, social action and political action.

12.5    The learner will dem onstrate an understanding of the role of the U. S. Constitution in American democracy, including the ways in which the U. S. governm ent established by the Constitu tion em bodies the purposes, values, and principles of Am erican dem ocracy.  The student should be able to:

12.5.1    evaluate, and take and defend positions on issues regarding the distribution of powers and res ponsibilities within the federal system;

12.5.3    explain why states have cons titutions, their purposes and the relationship of state constitutions to the f ederal constitution; and

12.5.8    define the concept of due proce ss of law and explain its im portance to individuals and society.

12.7    The learner will dem onstrate an understanding of the role of the citizen in American dem ocracy, including personal a nd civic rights, and responsibilities. The student should be able to:

12.7.3 identify the m ajor documentary sources of personal, political, and econom ic rights; and

12.7.4 evaluate and take and defend positio ns on issues involving p ersonal, political and econom ic rights.

## C.    SUGGESTED STUDENT ACTIVITIES

1.    Social Studies Standards:    5.5.5    8.7.4    12.4.10
                                                  8.7.5    12.4.11
                                                  8.8.7    12.7.4

Part A. Find some pictures of schools, both ru ral and city, that were built in your state more than 55 years ago.  Find out all you can about these schools.  W ere they seg regated?  Compare and contrast the schools with each other and with the school you attend.  Suggest reasons for th e differences in the schools.  Do you think the rea sons were justifiable?  Do any of your reasons have som ething to do with unfairness?  Discuss your answers.

Try to find a picture of an old (from before 1940) school bus if you can.  Do you think that every school had at least one school bus?   How do you think it was decided which students would  ride a school bus to get to  school in 1945?  Is bus transportation provided for som e students at your school?  If so, how is it decided which students ride the bus?

Part B. Learn about the Clarendon County quest for equality. What was the reason it was started? Which of the school pictures that you looked at probably is most similar to schools attended by African Americans in Clarendon County in 1945? Which school picture that you looke d at do you think is m ost similar to present-day Clarendon Count y schools attended by African Americans? Discuss the probable differences in Clarendon County schools in 1945 and now. W hich children in Clarendon County were provided with bus tr ansportation to school in 1945?

Part C. Explain how the U. S. Constitution wa s partly responsible for the change in the schools and the ways children get to school in Clarendon County.

2.      Social Studies Standards:      5.5            8.7            12.4

Part A. Interview a person who was born be fore 1945 and who attended school in the United States. D id s/he attend inte grated schools?   Ask what types of facilities were at the school (e.g., for drinki ng water, toilets, lunch, heating). How large were the classes? How far did the person live from the school? How did students travel to and from school? Were there teachers of different races in the school? How long was the sc hool year? How long was th e school day? W rite 2-4 paragraphs that summarize your interview.

Part B   After learning about the Clarendon County quest for equality, identify ways in which your school e xperience is different from that of the person you interviewed. W rite 1-2 paragraphs comparing your school experience to that of the person you interview ed.

3.      Social Studies Standards:      5.4            8.7            12.2
                                        5.5.1                         12.7

Part A. Read the Preamble to the United S tates Constitution. Explain in your own words what it means. Is there anything written in it about the treatm ent of different sexes ? Different races? Is there a statement that girls can participate equally in school sports? What does it say about voting rights? Is there anything that specifies freedom of speech? What does the word "preamble" m ean? Why is there a Preamble? If these guarantees are not in the Preamble, find and discuss the docum entation that does give us those rights.

Part B.   After learning about the Clar endon County quest for equality, demonstrate your understanding of the rule of law and minority rights. Describe the means by which Clarendon County bl acks influenced the politics and governm ent of South Carolina and of the nation.

From your knowledge of *Briggs et al. v. Elliott et al.*, explain why it is necessary to add amendments to the constitutio n. What is the Bill of Rights?

4.    Social Studies Standards:    5.5.2        8.7.7        12.2.5

Part A. With a group of your classmates, write and act out a skit that shows how a group of teenagers discriminates against a classmate who is somewhat different from them (for example, a student who has epilepsy or an unattractive student with a reading disability). Discuss the effects of the treatment on the person who is discriminated against. Suggest ways of addressing the situation. Discuss the challenges of solving the problem. Di scuss the relevance of the Fifth and Fourteenth Amendments to this situation.

Part B. After learning about the Clarendon County quest for equality, com pare the treatment of a "different" teenag er with the way that blacks were treated in Clarendon County. Evaluate how the quest for equality in Clarendon County affected the legal protection of the student s discussed above. W hat have been the benefits and challenges to m aking public schools more diverse?

5.    Social Studies Standards:                    8.7        12.4.10

Identify a news event from the last 12 months that demonstrates some kind of prejudice. Explain what you believe the prejudiced ac tion was. What is the difference between prejudice and discrim ination? Find a place in the U. S. Constitution that offers protection against the discrimination that results from this type of prejudice. Discuss whether there are possible resolutions for the prejudice. Identify and give exam ples of ways in which discrepancies between the reality and the ideals of American constitutional democracy can be reduced by individual action, social action and political action.

6.    Social Studies Standards:                                12.3

Write a proper business letter inviting a police officer, a lawyer or an elected official to your class to discuss a recen t case of discrimination. Make sure your letter explains what you w ould like the person to talk about. For example, you may want the official to talk about how the *Briggs v. Elliott* case violated the U. S. Constitution and to de fine how the laws of your state support (or contradict) the U. S. Constitution. Other questions you may want to ask are: (a) how your local laws are made and who m akes them, (b) what happens if most people disobey a law and (c) what happens if m ost people are unhappy with a law. Also, m ake sure to put details in your letter concerning when you want the person to speak to your class and where your school is locate d. (This is called "Answering W hat? Where? When? Why? and Who?"). Have your teacher approve the letter before you actually mail it.

7.      Social Studies Standards:                8.7             12.5

Read the 13<sup>th</sup> and Fourteenth Amendments.  Explain why Section 1 of the Fourteenth Amendment was necessary since the 13<sup>th</sup> Amendment had already been passed.

After learning about *Briggs v. Elliott*, describe one or more situations that can be interpreted as involuntary servitude.   Describe one or more than can be determined as interfering with pursuit of happiness?

Discuss the concept of states' rights.  Is there any provision in the Constitution that allows a state to apply special laws, or to have exceptions to laws, to a certain group of citizens?  Do you think this is right?  Defend your answer.

8.      Social Studies Standards:     5.4                         12.3

Identify the three branches of government as specified by the U. S. Constitution.  Discuss the functions of each.  In the Clarendon County Civil Rights effort, what role did each branch probably play at the local level?  At the state level? At the national level?

Discuss the process by which civil cases reach the U. S Supreme Court.


## D.  SUGGESTED TESTS OF KNOWLEDGE

5.4.1

How did the concept of majority rule and state sovereignty conflict with the rule of law and minority (in this case, African American) rights in *Briggs v. Elliott.*

5.5.2

Discuss the reasons given by the lawyers of the defense in *Briggs v. Elliott* for maintaining racially separate schools:
What, if any, were the benefits of separate schools?
What were the challenges presented by maintaining racially separate schools?

5.5.5

In the *Briggs v. Elliott* case, how were the principles of American democracy used to address the concerns of the African American parents?
How were support groups used to address these concerns?

8.7.2

In the *Briggs v. Elliott* case, were the plaintiffs' concerns mostly of a personal nature or were they political?  Justify your answer.

8.7.4

Describe how *Briggs v. Elliott* contributed to improving the practice of democracy in America.

8.7.5

List two ways in which the *Briggs v Elliott* (as part of *Brown et al. v. Board et al.*) decision has influenced South Ca rolina and national politics.

8.7.7

What kind of i mpact has the *Briggs v. Elliott (Brown v. Board)* decision had on ethnic enrollm ent in your school?
Has *Briggs v. Elliott* had an impact on girls' athletics in your school?  If so, explain how.
How have advocacy gro ups influenced na tional policies and practices reg arding special groups such as the handicapped?

12.2.5

Describe the im pact of the *Briggs v. Elliott (Brown v. Board)* decision on the struggle for racial and gender equality  as well as on civil liberties in your community.

12.3.3

Describe the role of the Fourteenth  Amendment (a "rule of law") in th e *Briggs v. Elliott (Brown v. Board)* decision.
Were the "rule of law" and the  "rule of man" in conflict in  *Briggs v. Elliott (Brown v. Board)*?  Defend your answer.

12.3.4

Explain how the United States Constituti on empowered the U. S. Supreme Court to overrule the South Caro lina Constitution in the *Briggs v. Elliott (Brown v. Board)* decision.
Of the five cases that were com bined by the Su preme Court as *Brown v. Board*, why was one ( *Bolling v. Sharpe* from Washington, D. C.) argued under the Fifth Amendment and the other four argued under the Fourteenth Am endment?

12.4.10

List three ways by which the U. S. Suprem e Court determined that the rights of some students were being violated as  a result of segregated schools.

12.4.11

Using your knowledge of hist ory, explain how you would a ddress a situation that you believe infringes on your  constitutional rights.

12.5.1

Evaluate the powers of the Suprem e Court and compare them with the powers and responsibilities of your state.

12.5.3

How was South Carolina's Constitution in conf lict with the Constitution of the United States in *Briggs v. Elliott*? Explain how you arrived at your answer.

12.5.8

As determ ined by the Suprem e Court, how was the state of South Carolina violating the due process guaranteed unde r the Fourteenth Amendm ent before *Briggs v. Elliott*?

12.7.3

Identify the docum entary source of the rights that the *Briggs v. Elliott* plaintiffs felt were being violated.
State the reason the defendants believed they had the authority to operate segregated schools

12.7.4

Discuss the ways in which your rights have been affected by the decision of *Briggs v. Elliott* (*Brown v. Board*).

## ACKNOWLEDGEMENTS:

It is impossible to m ention the na mes of ever yone who helped m ade this booklet possible. However, their help and cooperation is gr atefully acknowledged. Foremost am ong the people whose contributions m ust be individually acknowledged is Joseph A. DeLaine, Jr. His ideas and knowledge served as the inception for the booklet and his inform ation and resources drove it to completion. The work and assistance of the other people whose names follow were critical to the completion of the project. Suzanne DeLaine Carothers, Ph.D. and her colleague s in the Steinhart School of Education, New York University, reviewed an early draft and m ade many help ful suggestions. Barbara Jenkins, P h.D., retired lib rarian, South Carolina State Colleg e, meticulously reviewed and critiqued a later draft. Thomas Rivers, principal of C. A. Johnson Preparator y Academy, Columbia, S.C. (and formerly of the Departm ent of Instruction, South Carolina Department of Instruction), generously assist ed in regard to South Carolina Departm ent of Education's Social Studies Standards. Lauena Richardson Cochran, the child of a *Briggs v. Elliott* petitioner (now a retired South Carolina pu blic school teacher of social stu dies), developed m any questions for the Suggested Tests of Knowledge and assisted in developing the Suggested Student Activities. Marguirite L. DeLaine, retired S outh

Carolina Public Schools teacher o f English, also assisted in develo ping Suggested Student Activities and w as the primary editor for language and gramm ar. The handbook was compiled and written by Brumit B. DeLain e, retired North Carolina Public S chool Administrator, and Ophelia DeLaine Gona, Ph.D., Associate Professor of Surgery and Director of *The SMART Initiative*, UMDNJ-New Jersey Medical School. Funding for the project was generously donated by the South Carolina Humanities Council. The booklet was designed by Ophelia Gona, Ph.D.

The Humanities Council<sup>SC</sup>

*inspiring. engaging. enriching.*

# Chapter 5
# Bibliographies

**_Brown v. Board of Education_**
**Educational Resources**
Janet Sims-Wood

## Books:

General:

Atkinson, Pansye S. 1993. _Brown v. Topeka: An African American's View: Desegregation and Miseducation._ Chicago, IL: African American Images, 127 pp.

Armstrong, Julie Buckner, et. al. 2002. _Teaching the Civil Rights Movement: Freedom's Bittersweet Song._ New York: Routledge, 259 pp.

Bartley, Numan V. 1969. _The Rise of Massive Resistance: Race and Politics During the 1950s._ Baton Rouge: Louisiana State University Press, 390 pp.

Bell, Derrick, ed. 1980. _Shades of Brown: New Perspectives on School Desegregation._ New York: Teachers College Press, 150 pp.

Berman, Daniel M. 1966. _It Is So Ordered: The Supreme Court Rules on School Segregation._ New York: W. W. Norton, 161 pp.

Blaustein, Albert P., and Clarence Clyde Ferguson, Jr. 1957. _Desegregation and the Law: The Meaning and Effect of the School Segregation Cases._ New Brunswick, NJ: Rutgers University Press, 333 pp.

Boozer, Michael A., Alan B. Krueger, and Shari Wolkon. 1992. _Race and School Quality Since_ Brown v. Board of Education. Cambridge, MA: National Bureau of Economic Research, 27 pp.

Browning, R. Stephen, ed. 1975. _From_ Brown _to_ Bradley: _School Desegregation, 1954-1974._ Cincinnati, OH: Jefferson Law Book Company, 226 pp.

Burk, Robert Fredrick. 1984. _The Eisenhower Administration and Black Civil Rights._ Knoxville: University of Tennessee Press, 287 pp.

Chesler, Mark A., et al. 1988. _Social Science in Court: Mobilizing Experts in the School Desegregation Cases._ Madison: University of Wisconsin Press, 286 pp.

Cottrol, Robert J., Raymond T. Diamond, and Leland Ware. 2003. _Brown v. Board of Education: Caste, Culture and the Constitution._ Lawrence: University of Kansas Press.

Cray, Ed. 1997. _Chief Justice: A Biography of Earl Warren._ New York: Simon & Schuster, 603 pp.

Du Bose, Sonny, and Tom Poland (eds). 2002. *The Road to* Brown*: The Leadership of a Soldier of the Cross, Rev. J. A. De Laine: Recollections of Courage*. Orangeburg, SC: Williams Publishing, 174 pp.

Foster, Gerald Anthony, and Vonita White Foster. 1993. *Silent Trumpets of Justice: Integration's Failure in Prince Edward County*. Hampton, VA: U.B. & U. S. Communication System s, 107 pp.

Franklin Weekley, Rachel. 1999. *"A Strong Pull, A Long Pull, And a Pull Together": Topeka's Contribution to the Campaign for School Desegregation; Historic Resource Study*. Omaha, NE: National Park Service, Midwest Regional Office, 591 pp.

Friedman, Leon. 1969. *Argument, Argument: The Oral Argument Before the Supreme Court in* Brown v. Board of Education of Topeka *, 1952-55*. New York: Chelsea Hous e Publishers, 601 pp.

Greenberg, Jack. 1994. *Crusaders in the Courts: How a Dedicated Band of Lawyers Fought for the Civil Rights Revolution*. New York: Basic Books, 634 pp.

Hampton, Henry, and Steve Fayer. 1991. *Voices of Freedom: An Oral History of the Civil Rights Movement From the 1950s Through the 1980s*. New York: Bantam Books, 692 pp.

Hill, Herbert, and Jack Greenberg. 1955. *Citizen's Guide to De-Segregation: A Story of Social and Legal Change in America*. Boston, MA: Beacon Press, 185 pp.

Hill, Oliver W. 2000. *The Big Bang:* Brown v. Board of Education *and Beyond: The Autobiography of Oliver W. Hill, Sr*. Winter Park, FL: Four-G Publishers, 276 pp.

Hornsby, Benjamin F., Jr. 1992. *Stepping Stone to the Supreme Court: Clarendon County, South Carolina*. Columbia: South Carolina Department of Archives and History, Public Programs Division, 26 pp.

Howard, John R. 1999. *The Shifting Wind: The Supreme Court and Civil Rights from Reconstruction to* Brown. Albany: State University of New York Press, 393 pp.

Irons, Peter. 2002. *Jim Crow's Children: The Broken Promise of the* Brown *Decision*. New York: Viking Press, 376 pp.

Jackson, John P., Jr. 2001. *Social Scientists for Social Justice: Making the Case Against Segregation*. New York: New York University Press, 289 pp.

Jacobs, Gregory S. 1998. *Getting Around* Brown*: Desegregation, Development, and the Columbus Public Schools*. Columbus: Ohio State University Press, 291 pp.

Kalona, Howard I., and James J. Fishman, eds. 1978. *Limits of Justice: The Court's Role in School Desegregation.* Cambridge, MA: Balli nger Publishing, 655 pp.

Kluger, Richard. 1976. *Simple Justice: The History of* Brown v. Board of Education *and Black America's Struggle for Equality.* New York: Knopf, 823 pp.

Lageman, Ellen Condliffe, and LeMar P. Miller, eds. 1996. *Brown v. Board of Education: The Challenge for Today's Schools.* New York: Teachers College Press, 217 pp.

Lochbaum, Julie Magruder, and Ophelia Gona (eds). 1999. *The World Made Flesh: The Desegregation Leadership of the Rev. J. A. De Laine.* Pine Brook, NJ: Gona Press, 52 pp.

Lofgren, Charles A. 1987. *The* Plessy *Case: A Legal-Historical Interpretation.* New York: Oxford University Press, 269 pp.

Lomotey, Kofi, and Charles Teddlie. 1996. *Forty Years After the Brown Decision: Implications of School Desegregation for U. S. Education.* New York: AMS Press, 229 pp.

Martin, Jr., Waldo E. 1998. *Brown v. Board of Education: A Brief History with Documents.* Boston, MA: Bedford/St. Martin' s Press, 253 pp.

McNeil, Genna Rae. 1983. *Groundwork: Charles Hamilton Houston and the Struggle for Civil Rights.* Philadelphia: University of Pennsylvania press, 308 pp.

Motley, Constance Baker. 1998. *Equal Justice Under Law: An Autobiography.* New York: Farrar, Straus and Giroux, 282 pp.

Orfield, Gary, and Susan E. Eaton. 1996. *Dismantling Desegregation: The Quiet Reversal of* Brown v. Board of Education. New York: The New Press, 424 pp.

Patterson, James T. 2001. *Brown v. Board of Education: A Civil Rights Milestone and its Troubled Legacy.* New York: Oxford University Press, 285 pp.

Raskin, Jasmin. 2003. *We the Students: Supreme Court Cases For and About Students.* Washington, DC: Congressional Quarterly Press.

Reams, Bernard D., and Paul E. Wilson, eds. 1975. *Segregation and the Fourteenth Amendment in the States: A Survey of State Segregation Laws, 1865-1953: Prepared for U.S. Supreme Court in re* Brown v. Board of Education of T opeka. Buffalo, New York: W. S. Hein, 761 pp.

Sarat, Austin, ed. 1997. *Race, Law, and Culture: Reflections on* Brown v. Board of Education. New York: Oxford Uni versity Press, 238 pp.

Schwartz, Bernard. 1983. *Super Chief Earl Warren and His Supreme Court: A Judicial Biography.* New York: New York University Press, 853 pp.

Shujaa, Mwalimu J., ed. 1996. *Beyond Desegregation: The Politics of Quality in African American Schooling.* Thousand Oaks, CA: Corwin Press, 283 pp.

Smith, Bob. 1965. *They Closed Their Schools: Prince Edward County, Virginia, 1951-1964.* Chapel Hill: The University of North Carolina Press, 281 pp.

Speer, Hugh W. 1968. *The Case of the Century; A Historical and Social Perspective on* Brown v. Board of Education of Topeka *, With Present and Future Implications.* Kansas City, MO: University of Missouri, 281 pp.

Tushnet, Mark V. 1994. *Making Civil Rights Law: Thurgood Marshall and the Supreme Court, 1936-1961.* New York: Oxford University Press, 399 pp.

_____. 1987. *The NAACP's Legal Strategy Against Segregated Education, 1925-1950.* Chapel Hill: The University of North Carolina P ress, 222 pp.

_____, ed. 2001. *Thurgood Marshall: His Speeches, Writings, Arguments, Opinions, and Reminiscences.* Chicago, IL: Lawrence Hill, 548 pp.

U.S. Commission on Civil Rights. 1975. *Twenty Years After* Brown*: Equality of Educational Opportunity.* Washington, DC: U.S. Comm ission on Civil R ights, 94 pp.

The University of Notre Da me Center for Civil Rights. 1975. *Continuing Challenge: The Past and Future of* Brown v. Board of Education—*A Symposium.* Evanston, IL: Integrated E ducation Associates, 88 pp.

Wasby, Stephen L., Anthony A. D' Amato, and Rosemary Metrailer. 1977. *Desegregation from* Brown *to* Alexander*: An Exploration of Supreme Court Strategies.* Carbondale: Southern Illinois University Press, 489 pp.

Whitmark, Mark, ed. 1993. *Removing a Badge of Slavery: The Record of* Brown v. Board of Education. Princeton, NJ: Marcus W iener, 357 pp.

Wilkinson, J. Harvie, III. 1979. *From* Brown *to* Bakke*; The Supreme Court and School Integration, 1954-1978.* New York: Oxford Uni versity Press, 368 pp.

Williams, Juan. 1987. *Eyes on the Prize: America's Civil Rights Years, 1954-1965.* New York: Viking Press, 300 pp.

Wilson, Paul. 1995. *A Time to Lose: Representing Kansas in* Brown v. Boa rd of Education. Lawrence: Univer sity Press of Kansas, 252 pp.

Wolters, Raymond. 1984. *The Burden of* Brown*: Thirty Years of School Desegregation.* Knoxville, TN: The University of Tennessee Press , 346 pp.

Yarbrough, Tinsley E. 1987. *A Passion for Justice: J. Waites Waring and Civil Rights.* New York: Oxford Uni versity Press, 282 pp.

## Manuscript Resources:

General:

Earl Warren Papers
Library of Congress
Manuscript Division
Washington, D. C.

Over 250,000 items including personal files, file s from the U. S. Supreme Court, the lower courts, organizations, and his speeches and writings.

Kenneth B. Clark Papers
Library of Congress
Manuscript Division
Washington, DC

Includes family papers, professional file fr om 1897 to 1955. Clark did the doll study for the South Carolina case and testified on the psychological dam age of segregation.

NAACP Papers
Library of Congress
Manuscript Division
Washington, DC

Working files of the N AACP national office and the staff members, including Thurgood Marshall and Robert Carter. Very large co llection that also includes hundreds of photographs.

Thurgood Marshall Papers
Library of Congress
Manuscript Division
Washington, D. C.

Over 173,700 items including files of the U. S. Court of Appeals, the U. S. Solicitor General, and the U.S. Suprem e Court.
District of Columbia (*Bolling v. Sharpe*)

Consolidated Parents Group, Inc. Records, 1947-1954
Manuscript Division
Moorland-Spingarn Research Center
Howard University
Washington, DC

Washington, D. C.-based civic organization. Records consist of organizational m aterial, reports, minutes, information on community ac tivities, publicity materials, school data, court documents, manuscripts, photographs, and clippings. Reco rds relate to school desegregation in the Nation' s Capital. Correspondence with such people as George E . C. Hayes and the official comm unications primarily of the organizati on' s executive officers, Gardner L. Bishop and Bur ma Whitted.

George E. C. Hayes Papers 1922-1956 (1947-1956)
Historical Society of Washington, D .C.
Washington, DC

Includes m aterials Hayes accum ulated as the attorney for the Consolidated P arents Group, Inc. Also legal papers, news clippings, programs, reports, memorabilia, and photographs related to school desegregation, civil liberties , discrimination cases, and materials related to the *Bolling v. Sharpe* case.

Kansas (*Oliver Brown et. al. v. Board of Education*)

Attorney General' s Office, Papers
Center for Historical Res earch
Kansas State Historical Society
Topeka, KS

Includes state agency records on segregation and on the *Brown v. Board of Education of Topeka* case.

Brown Family Collec tion
Kansas Collection
Kenneth Spencer Research Library
University of Kansas Libraries
Lawrence, KS

Papers and materials of the Oliver Brow n family including infor mation on the case involving h is daughter, Linda, and other African American families in Topeka.

*Brown v. Board of Education*
Mabee Library Archives
Washburn University
Topeka, KS

Includes 30th anniversary commemoration, the sculpture "Common Justice," and newspaper clippings.

Charles Sheldon Scott Papers
Kansas Collection
Kenneth Spencer Research Library
University of Kansas Librarian
Lawrence, KS

Papers of one of the African American lawyers representing the *Brown v. Board of Education of Topeka* case.

Governor's Office Records – Gov. Edward F. Arm
Center for Historical Research
Kansas State Historical Society
Topeka, KA

State agency records of Governor Arm including general correspondence and information related to the *Brown v. Board of Education of Topeka* case.

Paul E. Wilson Papers
Manuscript Collections
Center for Historical Research
Kansas State Historical Society
Topeka, KS

Atty. Wilson represented Kansas in the historic *Brown v. Board of Education of Topeka* case.


South Carolina (*Briggs v. Elliott*)

Joseph A. De Laine, Sr., Papers
University of South Carolina
Carolina Library
Columbia, SC

Correspondence, speeches, booklets, FBI files, 80 photographs, and two volumes of newspaper clipping related to the *Briggs v. Elliott* case and other efforts to secure voting rights and educational opportunities. Correspondents include J. Waties Waring, John H. McCray, Harold R. Boulware, J. Edgar Hoover, and others.

Julius Waties Waring Papers
Moorland-Spingarn Research Center
Manuscript Division
Howard University
Washington, D. C.

Includes correspondence, legal case files, organizational materials, photos and 72 scrapbooks of clippings related to his civil rights cases in So uth Carolina and his cases as a federal judge.

Virginia (*Davis v. County School Board of Prince Edward County, Virginia*)

Archibald Gerard Robertson Document
Virginia Historical Society
Richmond, VA

Memoir of preparation of the case of *Davis v. County School Board of Prince Edward County* before the U.S. Supreme Court concerning school desegregation

Edward H. Peeples, Jr., Papers – 1946 – 1960' s
Special Collection s and Archives
James Branch Cabell Library
Virginia Common wealth University
Richmond, VA

Includes Dr. Peeples' research materials for his thesis on the Princ e Edward County, Virginia school segregation issue in the la te 1950s and early 1960s. Includes newspaper and journal articles and other pub lished materials on race relations and civil rights iss ues.

**Multimedia (Films, Video, Audio):**

*After Ten Years: The Court and the Schools.* 2002. Princeton, NJ: Films for the Humanities and Science s, 58 minutes.

*Brown v. Board of Education.* 1991. Northbrook, IL: Coronet/MTI Film & Video for Advanced Am erican Communications, Inc., 19 m inutes.

*A Case for Equality: Reading, Writing and Resistance.* 2002. Topeka, KS: Brown v. Board of Education National Historic Site, 12 m inutes.

*Fighting Back: 1957-1962.* 1999. Alexandria, VA; PBS Video, 60 m inutes.

*In Pursuit of Freedom and Equality: The Story of* Brown v. Board of Education of Topeka. 1996. Topeka, KS: Brown Foundation for Educational Excellence, Equity, and Research and the National Park Service, 27 minutes with teacher's guide.

*Race Against Time: School Desegregation Since 1954.* 1980. Washington, DC: National Public Radio, 4 sound cassettes.

*The Road to* Brown*: The Untold Story of "The Man Who Killed Jim Crow."* 1990. San Francisco: California Newsreel, 55 minutes.

*Saviors: In Search of the American Dream.* 1991. Princeton, NJ: Films for the Humanities and Science s.

*School, The Story of American Public Education—Episode 3, Equality, 1950-1980.* 2001. Chevy Chase, MD: Stone Latern Film s, 55 minutes.

*School Desegregation.* 1993. Topeka, KS: KTWU, 29 minutes.

*Separate but Equal.* 1971. Chicago, IL: Britannica Video Cassettes.

*A Separate Place (The Schools P. S. du Pont Built).* 2002. Wilmington, DE: Hagley Museum and Library, 55 minutes.

*Simple Justice.* 1993. Alexandria, VA: PBS Video.

*Supreme Court Decisions That Changed the Nation: Brown v. Board of Education.* 1986. Mount Kisco, New Yor k: Guidance Associates.

*Thurgood Marshall: Portrait of an American Hero.* 1991. Alexandria, VA: PBS Video, 28 minutes.

Wilson, Paul E. 1999. *Civil Rights and the Supreme Court: The African-American Journey.* West Lafayette, IN: Purdue University, Public Aff airs Video Archives , 91 minutes.


**Oral Histories:**

<u>Brown v. Topeka Board of Education</u>
Manuscript Collection #251
Oral History Collection
Library and Archives Division
Kansas State Historical Society
Topeka, KS

This collection provides a look at the backgr ound of the landm ark Supreme Court case, *Brown v. Board of Education of Topeka*, from those who, in one way or another, were involved with the cases before they reached the Supreme Court, or who were involv ed in or affected by the ruling in som e way (i.e., victims, plaintiffs, and beneficiaries). T hose interviewed include : former students, comm unity leaders and activists, attorneys, judges, and others affected by the outcom e of the case.

Ralph J. Bunche Oral History Collection
Moorland-Spingarn Research Center
Manuscript Division
Howard University
Washington, DC

This collection totals over 700 transcripts that provide valuable insight into the thoughts and actions of those who participated in and shaped the Civil Rights Movem ent. National and local leaders as well as community activ ists were interviewed.

**Special Journal Issues:**

"*Brown v. Board of Education* at 40: A Commemorative Issue Dedicated to the Late Thurgood Marshall." *Journal of Negro Education,* Vol. 63, Summer 1994.

"Desegregation." *OAH Magazine of History*, Vol. 15, No. 2, Winter 2001.

"Symposium on Commem orating the 25th Anniversary of *Brown v. Board of Education.*" *Howard Law Journal*, Vol. 23, No. 1, 1980.

"Symposium on Com pleting the Job of School Desegregation." *Howard Law Journal*, Vol. 19, No. 1, Winter 1975.

"25th Anniversary of the *Brown* Decision." *The Crisis,* Vol. 86, June/July 1979.

**Juvenile Literature, Books:**

Aldred, Lisa. 1990. *Thurgood Marshall: Supreme Court Justice.* New York: Chelsea House.

Dudley, Mark E. 1994. *Brown v. Board of Education (1954): School Desegregation.* New York: 21st Century Books, 96 pp.

Fauver, Bill, and Jim Ruderman. 1991. *Stride Toward Freedom: The Aftermath of* Brown v. Board of Education of Topeka— *A Unit of Study for Grades 9-12.* Los Angeles, CA: National Center for Hist ory in the Schools, Univers ity of California, 44 pp.

Harding, Vincent, Robin D. G. Kelley, and Earl Lewis. 1997. *We Changed the World: African Americans 1945-1970* (The Young Oxford History of African Americans, Vol. 9). New York: Oxford University Press, 190 pp.

Levine, Ellen. 1993. *Freedom's Children: Young Civil Rights Activists Tell Their Own Story.* New York: Putnam, 291 pp.

Rochelle, Belinda. 1993. *Witness to Freedom: Young People Who Fought For Civil Rights.* New York: Lodestar Books, 97 pp.

Ruderman, Jim, and Bill Fauver. 1991. *Keeping Them Apart:* Plessy v. Ferguson *and the Black Experience in Post-Reconstruction America—A Unit of Study For Grades 9-12.* Los Angeles: National Center for History in the Schools, University of California, 66 pp.

Stevenson, Janet. 1973. *The School Segregation Cases (*Brown v. Board of Education of Topeka *and others): The United States Supreme Court Rules on Racially Separate Public Education.* New York: Franklin Watts, 61 pp.

Tackach, James. 1998. *Brown v. Board of Education.* San Diego, CA: Lucent Books, 111 pp.

Turck, Mary C. 2000. *The Civil Rights Movement for Kids: A History with 21 Activities.* Chicago, IL: Chicago Review Press, 144 pp.

Ware, Leland. 1999. *Thurgood Marshall: Freedom Defender.* New York: Time-Life Books.

**Special Juvenile Periodical Issues:**

"NAACP." *Cobblestone,* February 2002

"Thurgood Marshall and Civil Rights," *Footsteps*, March/April 2003.

*The* Brown *Quarterly: Newsletter for Classroom Teachers,* 1996-2003

## Internet Resources on *Brown v. Board of Education*
Janet Sims-Wood

### *Roberts v. City of Boston*

Schwartz, Frederick. "The Time Machine—One Hundred and Fifty Years—Separate But Equal." *American Heritage*, Vol. 41, No. 2, April 2000.
*http://www.americanheritage.com/AMHER/2000/02/timemach.shtmlT*
The "Separate but Equal" section deals with the early desegregation case of *Roberts v. City of Boston.*

### *Plessy v. Ferguson*

"When the Future Was the Past: A Discussion on the Past—A Discussion Guide on the *Plessy* Decision and Its Aftermath." Southern Institute for Education and Research.
http://www.tulane.edu/~so-inst/Plindexhtm l
A study circle on the *Plessy v. Ferguson* case. Includes readings on Jim Crow, the fight to reverse *Plessy*, massive resistance, and affirmative action.

### *Brown v. Board of Education*

General:

"An Interactive Civil Rights Chronology: *Brown v. Board of Education*"
http://www.yale.edu/law web/jbalkin/brown/1502.htm l
A companion to Jack Balkin's book, What *Brown v. Board of Education* Should Have Said.

"And a Child Shall Lead Them"
http://www.stagestheatre.org/study_guides/
Written by Brian Grandison, this play, presented by the Stages Theater Company, tells the story of *Brown v. Board of Education*. The study guide was developed by Emilie Shields. Includes references and links to other sites.

"Brown@50: Fulfilling the Promise"
http://www.brownat50.org/
This is the Howard University Law School website on *Brown*. Lists a chronology of civil rights events, cases, and other laws, w ith general links and resources.

"*Brown v. Board of Education*"
http://artsci.wustl.edu/~rtvinson/388/BrownvBoa rd.ppt
This PowerPoint slide show documents the *Brown* case.

"*Brown v. Board of Education*"
http://www.nps.gov
The National Park Service site on *Brown* deals with the case, the site, activities, and a list of resources. (A cd of this website's information is also available.)

"*Brown v. Board of Education of Topeka*, 40 Years Later"
http://www.georgetown.edu/centers/woodstock/reports/r-fea34.htm
Site for the 1993 forum sponsored by the Woodstock Theological Center, which looked at the progress of African American education since *Brown*. Participants included Samuel Harvey, Jr.; Floretta Dukes McKenzie; and Roger Wilkins. Jim Vance moderated the forum.

"*Brown v. Board of Education*: 50 Years"
http://www.brownmatters.org/chrono.html
The NAACP Legal Defense and Educational Fund Inc., website lists activities of the group and a chronology of cases.

*Brown v. Board of Education* 50<sup>th</sup> Anniversary, May 1954-May 2004"
http://www.uky.edu/PCD/news/Brown%20resource%20page.php
This University of Kentucky website commemorates the 50<sup>th</sup> anniversary. Includes an annotated chronology of the case, resources and documents, organizations sponsoring activities on the campus, and a list of events taking place across the country.

"Cultural Frameworks for Civil Liberties"
http://www.uiowa.edu/~amstud/Events/BrownvBoard.htm
The University of Iowa American Studies Department will post a series of lectures on this topic from September 2003 thru April 2004 at this site.

Davis, Cheryl. "The Color of Justice"
http://artsedge.kennedy-center.org/cuesheet/pdf/justice.pdf
This site presents a cue-sheet for students of a production done by Theatreworks, USA, at the Kennedy Center. The play is based on the real-life events of the early 1950s in the lives of Linda Brown and Thurgood Marshall. Includes questions, vocabulary, activities for students to help them understand the time period, ideas for what to listen and look for before the performance, and a short list of resources.

"Friends of the Court Brief Submitted in *Brown v. Board of Education*"
http://archive.aclu.org/court/brown/html
This is the brief submitted on behalf of the American Civil Liberties Union, the American Jewish Committee, the Japanese American Citizens League, the American Ethical Union, the Unitarian Fellowship for Social Justice, and the Anti-Defamation League of B'Nai B'Rith, as *amice curiat*.

"Horizons of Opportunities: Celebrating 50 Years of *Brown v. Board of Education*"
http://www.nea.org/eve nts/brown/html
The National Education Association website contains historical inform ation, upcoming events, curriculum guides, and links to m any other sites.

"Landmark Documents"
http://www.factsonfile.co m
Lists most of the *Brown v. Board of Education* cases and the actual court decision for each case. Gives links to related do cuments such as the Fifth Am endment, the Fourteenth Amendment, and links to related im ages on Integration.

"Landmark Supreme Court Cases
http://www.landm arkcases.org/brown/hom e.html
Discusses the Suprem e Court cases. Includes teaching recommendations, background summary and questions, a diagram of how the case moved through the court system, biographies of Earl W arren and Thurgood Mars hall, classroom activities, and excerpts from *Brown I* and *Brown II.*

NAACP Legal Defense Fund Com pared Michigan Cases to *Brown v. Board*"
http://www.naacpldf.org /whatsnew/wn_doc/ldf_m ichigan_com pared.html
In an audio news conference, the NAACP Legal Defense Fund hailed the Michigan affirmative cases as a victory and compared it to the 1954 *Brown* decision.

"Opposing *Brown*"
http://azim uth.harcourtcollege.com /history/ayers/chapter 28/28.2module.htm l
Includes links to *The Rights of Interposition, 1955,* and the *Southern Manifesto, 1956. Brown* was met with opposition, especially in th e South. These two do cuments show the steps southern whites took to oppose integrating schools. This inform ation is highlighted in the book, *American Passages: A History of the United States.*

"Remembering Jim Crow"
http://www.am ericanradioworks.org/features/rem embering/
This American Public Radio site, a divisi on of Minnesota Public R adio, presents a documentary history on racial segregation. Includes several sections, with text, audio, and sideshow clips. (A cd and book are also available.)

Shaw, Theodore M. "Race Still Matters"
http://www.naacpldf.org /whatsnew/wn_doc_ldf_race_m atters.html
Published in the *Washington Post* on March 1, 2003, this article by Shaw discusses the *Bakke* case as he was heading back to court to fight for African Am erican and Latino undergraduate students who want ed to see affirm ative action continued at the University of Michigan.

"U.S. Supreme Court Multimedia"
http://oyez.org
This site provides a listing of m ost of the desegregation cases including *Brown I* and *Brown II* and *Bolling v. Sharpe*. Gives dates argued, reargued, and decided; facts of the case; questions presente d; and the conclusion.

"The Vinson Court – 1946-1953"
http://www.supremecourthistory.org/02_history/subs_history/02_c13.html
Brief history of the Chi ef Justice Fred M. Vinson. Judge Vinson died in June 1953 and President Eisenhower then nam ed Earl Warren as the new Chief Justice.

**Delaware: *Belton v. Gebhart (Bulah v. Gebhart)***

"About Louis L. Redding"
http://www.k12.de.us/redding/LLRedding.htm l
Short bio on Louis Redding suitable for elem entary school students.

Ambro, Thomas L. "Collins J. Seitz, 1914-1998." *INRE: Delaware State Bar Association*, Vol. 22, No. 4, November 1998.
http://www.dsba.org/novsto98.htm
A tribute to Judge Collin s Seitz, who ruled on the *Belton v. Gebhart* case in 1952.

Espinoza, Ricky. "Challenging a Nation: Teen Contends with Segregation."
http://fourthwrite.theranger.org/brown/
Article on E thel Belton and an interv iew with her daughter, A ndreia Brown.

Jurden, Jan R. "Perspective—L ouis L. Redding." *INRE: Delaware State Bar Association*, Vol. 22, No. 4, November 1998.
http://www.dsba.org/novper98.htm
A tribute to Louis L. Redding, the African Am erican lawyer who handled the Delaware cases for Belton and Bulah.

"Louis L. Redding."
http://www.hsd.org/DHE /DHE_who_redding.htm
A biography of Louis L. Redding suitable for elem entary/middle school students.

Morris, Irving. "Louis L. Redding, 1901-1998." *INRE: Delaware State Bar Association*, Vol. 22, No. 4, November 1998.
http://www.dsba.org/nov98.htm
A tribute to Louis Redding.

## Kansas: *Oliver Brown et al. v. Board of Education of Topeka*

"Brown Sisters Interview"
http://www.kawvalley.k12.ks.us/brown_v_board/interview_browns.htm
The Brown sisters (Linda and Cheryl) talk about the historic *Brown* case and the Topeka school system. Linda relates that when their parents tried to enroll them in the white school and they were denied, her mother told her it was because of the color of her skin. She did not comprehend what that meant.

"*Brown v. Board of Education*"
http://www.nps.gov
Profiles the National Historic Site with information on the four other cases that make up *Brown v. Board of Education*.

"*Brown v. Board of Education* Activity Booklet"
http://brownvboard.org/actvtybk/cover.htm
Includes fun activities, a court maze, a school maze, and word search on the *Brown* case.

"*Brown v. Board of Education:* In Pursuit of Freedom: Kansas and the African American Public School Experience, 1855-1955"
http://brownvboard.org/trvlexht/pn101.htm
Panels from a traveling exhibition on *Brown v. Board of Education.*

"*Brown v. Topeka Board of Education*"
http://www.kawvalley.k12.us/brown_v_board/
The Ross Valley Junior High School in Topeka website, with many narratives, graphics, and resource materials.

"Linda Brown Thompson"
http://www.pbs.org/kcet/publicschool/innovators/brown.html
Short biographical information on Linda Brown, who, as a third grader, was denied admission to a white school. This led to the historic *Brown* case.

## South Carolina: *Briggs v. Elliott*

"Practical Moral Philosophy for Lawyers: A Story About Community"
http://www.wvu.edu~lawfac/jelkins/tkam/community4.html
Looks at Judge J. Waties Waring and the *Briggs v. Elliott* case. Judge Waring so angered the southern white community with earlier rulings in favor of African Americans and in his dissent opinion in *Briggs v. Elliott*, he ended up leaving South Carolina. His body was returned to South Carolina after his death, but only a few whites attended his funeral while more than 200 African Americans attended. The NAACP conducted a memorial service for Judge Waring.

"The Status of African Americans in South Carolina: Fifty Years After *Brown v. Board of Education*"
http://ipspr.sc.edu/brown/research.asp
Details the project of the Institute for Public Service and Policy Research at the University of South Carolina to commemorate the *Briggs v. Elliott* part in the *Brown v. Board of Education* case. Lists faculty that specialize in civil rights.

"Will the Circle Be Unbroken?: A Personal History of the Civil Rights Movement in Five Southern Communities (Episode 3: "Under Color of Law—Columbia, South Carolina," by George King and Vertamae Grosvenor).
http://www.unbrokencircle.org/script03.htm
A production of the Southern Regional Council, this episode details the events of the *Briggs v. Elliott* case. Can listen to an audio clip of the script at this site.

**Virginia: *Davis et al. v. County School Board of Prince Edward County, Virginia***

"Argument of T. Justin Moore, Esq., on Behalf of Appellees, County School Board of Prince Edward County, Virginia, et. al."
http://www.soc.umn.edu/~samaha/cases/brown%20v%board%20of%20education%202moore.htm
In the *Brown II* case, Attorney T. Justin Moore argued on behalf of the county school board. His testimony was given on December 7, 1953.

"Civil Rights in U.S. and Virginia History" (HIST604)
http://www.vcdh.virginia.edu/reHIST604/
A course at the University of Virginia that traces the legal and social origins of segregation, especially the political organization of Harry F. Byrd and how he abetted segregation and massive resistance in Virginia to the *Brown* decision. Along with the assignments and course information, there are documents, images, interviews and resources. This was part of "The Ground Beneath Our Feet: Virginia's History Since the Civil War."

"Did Massive Resistance Work"
http://www.dailypress.com/extras/solutions/so/1050400.htm
Cartoon on the massive resistance effort in Virginia to keep from integrating.

"Eyewitness to Jim Crow: Joan Johns Cobb Remembers"
http://www.jimcrowhistory.org/resources/narratives/Joan_Johns_Cobb.htm
In this section of narratives as part of the "History of Jim Crow" series, Joan Johns Cobb relates how her sister, Barbara Rose Johns, led the students on a strike that led to the *Davis* case and then on to the historic *Brown v. Board of Education* cases.

Smith, J. Clay, Jr., "Oliver White Hill: Liberator of Virginia"
http://www.law.howard/edu/alum ni/legalgiants/huslgiantfeb2k.1.htm
This is the website of Howard Law School pr ofessor, J. Clay Smith. Jr.  He writes a
series entitled "In the Footsteps of Giants: The Roots and Wings of the Howard Lawyer."
This profile from February 2001 is on Oliver W. Hill, a 1933 graduate of the law school
and the lawyer who argued the Virginia cas e along with Spottsw ood W. Robinson, III.

"The Robert Russa Moton Museum"
http://www.moton.org
The Moton Museum is committed to the preser vation and positiv e interpretation of the
history of civil rights in e ducation, specifically as it rela ted to Prince E dward County,
Virginia.  Includes the history of the events that led up to the *Davis* case, news items of
recent activities at the Museum to comme morate the even t, a bibliography and relevant
Internet links.

## Washington, D.C.: *Bolling v. Sharpe*

"John Philip Sousa Junior High School"
http://www.cr.nps.gov/NR/travel/civlirights/dc4.htm
A National Historic Landm ark, the school is associated with the struggle to desegregate
schools in Washington, D.C.  In 1950, black children were refused adm ission to the
school.  This led to the *Bolling* case, which went on to becom e part of the *Brown* case.

"School Integration in Washington, D .C."
http://www.watson.org/~lisa/blackhi story/school-integration/washdc
Historical overview of educati on in Washington, D.C., and the *Bolling v. Sharpe* case.  In
the1950s the plaintiffs from Browne Junior High lost their class ac tion suit against the
schools. Spottswood Robinson and  James Nabrit, represented Spottswo od Bolling, Jr., a
student in the D. C. school system .

## Internet Lesson Plans and Classroom Activities:

Black, Chuck. "*Brown v. Board of Education of Topeka*"
http://www.iopa.sc.edu/grs/sccep /Lesson%20Plans/chuck_black1.htm
Deals with the issue of dese gregation, and especially look s at the role South Carolina
played in the landm ark decision.

Black, Mary. "From Desegreg ation to Resegregation"
http://www/edb.utexas.edu/facu lty/mblack/courses/deseg.htm
Graduate course in education, which explor es the desegregation history of Am erican
schools pre-1954 to the present, with particular emphasis on Texas.

Cartaina, John. "*Plessy v. Ferguson* and *Brown v. Board of Education*: Looking at Primary Source Documents"
http://www.jimcrowhistory.org/resources /lessonplans/hs_lp_sourcedocs.htm
Students compare and contrast two historic decisions within the cultural fabric of the times.

"Development of Federal Civil Rights Acts: 1950' s–Present"
http://filebox.vt.edu/users/ cecraig/portweb/timechan.htm
This lesson helps studen ts relate events that occurred over the past fifty years.  Students will also determine how the Civil Rights Movement reshaped the lives of citizens of the U.S.

"Documents Related to *Brown v. Board of Education*"
http://www.archives.gov/digital_classroom/lessons/brown_v_board_do.../teaching_activities.htm
This is a teaching-with- documents lesson in which students analyze primary documents from the National Archives.  Students will crea te a timeline, connect their research with poetry, write an editorial , and design a book jacket.

"The Freedom Rides: Movement, Place, and Region"
http://phschool.com /curriculum_support/black_history/student_activities /activity2a.html
After reading the essay and l ooking at the m ap showing the route taken by the freedom riders, students will answer questions about the freedom riders.  Links to the National Civil Rights Museum.

Hambouz, Annissa. "Action? Affirmative! Reviewing the June 2003 Suprem e Court Ruling on Affir mative Action"
http://www.nytimes.com/learning/teachers/lessons/20030625wednesday.html
In this lesson for grades 6- 12, students learn about and disc uss the implications of the June 23, 2003, Supreme Court rulings on affirm ative action.  They will research other cases, initiatives, propositions, and act s on the topic in order to prep are for a series of debates.

Hambouz, Annissa. "Marching On: Learning About the New Civil Rights Movem ent"
http://www.nytimes.com/learning/teachers/lessons/20030825monday.html
In this lesson, students in grades 6-12 lear n about the increasing ly diverse civil rights movem ent by researching and profiling its key issues, main organizations, and top lead ers.

"Jim Crow Lesson Plans"
http://www.jimcrowhistory.org/resources/lessonplans.htm
One of the teach er resources on "The History of Jim Crow" website.  Has over 25 lessons, from history to literature.

Klein, Rachel, and Javaid Khan. "The Race to Learn: Exploring the Historical Role of Race in Education"
http://www.nytimes.com/learning/teachers/lessons/20030117friday.html
For grades 6-12, students will learn about the hist ory of education and race in the U. S. by researching Suprem e Court cases.

Koren, Michael. "Reconstruction to *Plessy v. Ferguson*: A 'Newscast' Activity"
http://www.jimcrowhistory.org/resources/lessonplans/hs_lp_newscast.htm
Designed for students with varying abilities, examines the changes that took place between the Reconstruction period and the *Plessy* decision.

McIntosh, Kristine A. "Civil Rights Movement, 1954-1968"
http://www.askeric.org/Virtual/Lessons/Social_Studies/US_History/USH0045.html
Students will examine the various political and social changes during the 1950's and 1960's. Students will create a visual/photographic timeline.

"New Kent School and the George W. Watkins School: From Freedom of Choice to Integration"
http://www.cr.nps.gov/nr/twhp/wwwlps/lessons/104newkent/104newkent.htm
A "Teaching with Historic Places" lesson plan dealing with the New Kent School and the George W. Watkins School, located in New Kent County, Virginia. These schools achieved token desegregation after the *Brown* decision.

"Parallel and Crossover Lives: Texas Before and After Desegregation"
http://www.public-humanities.org/crossoversite/pclclassroomactivities.html
In this classroom extension activity, students will create a synchronistical desegregation timeline. Students will then add significant events from each time period.

Rhodes, Henry A. "The *Brown* Decision: Fact or Myth in Connecticut?"
http://www.yale.edu/ynhti/curriculum/units/1992/1/92.01.09.x.html
Middle school-level lesson, which explores the history of segregation in the U.S. Students will then study why many of the schools in Connecticut are still predominantly segregated.

Rognas, Liza R. "The *Brown v. Board of Education* Cases: An Education Unit on the Cases Comprising the Landmark 1954 School Desegregation Decision"
http://jimcrowhistory.org/resources/lessonplans/hs_lp_brownunit.htm
Lessons for high school and college students. Looks at each case and the reaction to the cases.

"Schools of Thought on Segregation: Exploring Differing Viewpoints on the Battle to Integrate America's Public Schools"
http://www.nytimes.com/learning/teachers/lessons/20000403monday.html
For grades 6-12, students will analyze how education in America affects its youth and the nation by looking at how the courts and communities are dealing with the end to "separate-but-equal' education.

"Teacher Talk: Lesson Plan on School Desegregation Before *Brown*"
http://brownvboard.org/brwnqurt/04-2/02-2g.htm
Students will take a U.S. map and do a state-by-state analysis of school desegregation.

"Thurgood Marshall and Civil Rights"
http://www.geocites.com/CollegePark/Field/6064/lesson.html
Lesson focuses on the protection of Civil Rights and the impact of the enforcement of the Fourteenth Amendment in the case of *Murray v. the University of Maryland Law School*.

"U.S. Civil Rights Movement #2: *Brown v. Board of Education II*: All Deliberate Speed?"
http://www.africana.com/blackboard/bb_his_000141.htm
For high school students, this lesson follows the progress of desegregation from the *Brown II* decision through today. Students examine primary and secondary sources.

Wolff, Karen. "From *Plessy v. Ferguson* to *Brown v. Board of Education*: The Supreme Court Rules on School Desegregation"
http://www.yale.edu/ynhti/curriculum/units/1982/3/82.03.06.x.html
High school-level lesson plans on the Fourteenth Amendment, *Plessy v. Ferguson* and Justice Harlan, Richard Wright Remembers Jim Crow, etc. At the end of the lesson, students must take a position on a topic and present their argument in class

Zimbalist, Alison. "Revisiting 'Separate but Equal': Examining School Segregation 45 Years After *Brown v. Board of Education*"
http://www.nytimes.com/learning/teachers/lessons/19990614monday.html
For grades 6-12. Students examine the struggle for desegregation during the Civil Rights Movement.

(Editor's note: This is just a sampling of the many Internet sites dealing with the *Brown* cases. For more sites, you may also do subject searches on the Internet. Possible topics include: each case name, names of individual people involved in the cases, Southern Manifesto, bussing, affirmative action, etc. Teachers can use each lesson plan as is or adapt them to suit their own specific teaching objectives.)